METHODS OF RESEARCH
IN
PHYSICAL EDUCATION

METHODS OF RESEARCH IN PHYSICAL EDUCATION

By

JO ANNE L. THORPE, Ph.D.

Professor of Physical Education
Southern Illinois University
Carbondale, Illinois

CHARLES C THOMAS • PUBLISHER
Springfield • Illinois • U.S.A.

Published and Distributed Throughout the World by

CHARLES C THOMAS • PUBLISHER

2600 South First Street

Springfield, Illinois 62717

© *1986 by* CHARLES C THOMAS • PUBLISHER

ISBN 0-398-05174-7

Library of Congress Catalog Card Number: 85-14841

Printed in the United States of America

Q-R-3

Library of Congress Cataloging in Publication Data

Thorpe, Jo Anne.
  Methods of research in physical education.

  Bibliography: p.
  Includes indexes.
  1. Physical education and training--Research. 2. Report writing.
I. Title.
GV361.T48 1985   613.7'072   85-14841
ISBN 0-398-05174-7

THIS TEXT is dedicated to the three persons who created and instilled in me a love for teaching the methodology of research. If this book is worth anything, it is because of you:

Gail Hennis, University of North Carolina
   at Greensboro
Gladys Scott, University of Iowa
Claudine Sherrill, Texas Woman's University

ACKNOWLEDGMENTS

Grateful thanks are extended to:

    my students who made me learn as they learned,

    my mother who was patient with me as I was doing the writing,

    my friends who supported me,

    Elizabeth Eames for proofing the copy, and for contributing to the section on Philosophical Methods,

    Ron Hickman for contributing the section on the Use of Computers in Research,

    Jeff Motluck who did the figures, and

    Joyce Tally, my word processor, who was so fastidious throughout it all.

The support of all of these persons can never be properly estimated.

CONTENTS

LIST OF FIGURES

LIST OF TABLES

METHODS OF RESEARCH
IN
PHYSICAL EDUCATION

Chapter I

INTRODUCTION

IT IS ESSENTIAL to understand where we were, where we are, and
how we arrived where we are as a possible aid to understanding our future in research. Without belaboring the history it is probably still necessary to say that physical education is a part of the historical development
of the scientific approach to understanding. This chapter is devoted to
this very basic concept of research.

ORIGIN AND GROWTH OF RESEARCH
IN PHYSICAL EDUCATION

It is not clearly documented that scientific inquiry began at a certain
date; and we have to believe, therefore, that whenever it began, physical
educators (or whatever they were then called and wherever they were
then situated) were keeping up with the times and delving into a scientific
approach to explaining and understanding their discipline. Our earliest
records in a formal publication of the profession occur in the first *Research
Quarterly* of March, 1930.[1] We know, however, that research in our area
was occurring long before that because our first presidents of our physical
education association were organizing themselves for several reasons, but
at least one reason was to discuss their research. William G. Anderson,
Edward Hitchcock, and Dudley Sargent are notably associated with the
forming of the National Association for Physical Education, out of an interest in discussing their research, which at that time was predominantly
anthropometric measurement.

The scientific method as a way of approaching, organizing, and dealing with data was appropriate for the research of physical education; and
so the work of the earlier developing disciplines which has utilized the scientific method provided quite appropriate models (with some exceptions)

for the research of physical education. Our colleagues in psychology, sociology, history, anthropology, zoology, biology, and chemistry, for example, have been helpful in the design and conduct of many of our studies. Just as they, we have some uniqueness, however, which is a major motivation for this text.

DEFINITION AND IMPORTANCE OF RESEARCH

Research is defined by persons in many different ways but the essential elements include, at least, a search which is organized, unbiased, and representative of an important problem to be solved. The importance of research is varied, and the importance of specific problems are varied but would include the following:

1. The necessity to interpret our discipline to others
2. The need to upgrade teaching
3. The need to contrast graduate study with undergraduate study
4. The obligation for the preparation of doctoral students for teaching in a university
5. The need for verification of professional credentials for purposes of promotion, salary increments, and/or tenure
6. The necessity to have in our discipline professionals who can read professional literature intelligently
7. The need to prepare Master's candidates for Ph.D. level work.

TERMS ASSOCIATED WITH RESEARCH

Many terms are associated with the academic jargon of the discipline of research methodology, and it is essential that all researchers, beginning or otherwise, understand this language:

1. *Pure or Basic Research*: That which is devoted simply to finding the facts and developing theories
2. *Applied Research*: That which is designed to modify or improve practice and is based upon the facts and theories developed in basic research
3. *Method*: A general approach to a problem
4. *Technique*: A specific tool or device used for gathering data
5. *Philosopher*: Someone concerned with judgments and problems of values

6. *Scientist*: Someone concerned with explaining, predicting, and controlling conditions and events
7. *Researcher*: Someone who should be both a philosopher and a scientist
8. *Research Hypothesis*: One's best guess about the outcome of the data
9. *Statistical Hypothesis*: The null-hypothesis of "No difference"
10. *External Criticism*: In historical research testing the genuineness of the document itself; whether it really is what it purports to be. Judging the form and appearance of a document rather than the meaning of its content
11. *Internal Criticism*: In historical research examining the accuracy, intelligence, and good faith of the author and the validity or truth of the statements made
12. *External Validity*: In experimental research the extent to which the findings can be generalized to other populations, settings, and other treatment variables
13. *Internal Validity*: In experimental research the extent to which the study has been designed and conducted properly so that the researcher can correctly attribute any treatment effect(s) to the experimental variable(s)
14. *Extrapolation*: Going beyond the obtained statistical data to infer what some score might be (also going beyond the conclusions)
15. *Interpolation*: Predicting a score within the range of scores obtained
16. *Significance*: Meaningfulness, importance
17. *Statistical Significance*: Sureness or level of meaningfulness (Significance at the .01 level means that the statistic of the size obtained would only be attributable to sampling error or chance in one out of one hundred cases)
18. *Type I Error*: Rejecting a null-hypothesis which is true, or accepting a difference, for example, when there really is no difference
19. *Type II Error*: Accepting a null-hypothesis which is false, or accepting no difference when there really is a difference (The .01 level results in more Type II and fewer Type I errors whereas the .10 level results in more Type I and fewer Type II errors.)
20. *Dependent Variable*: The score(s) analyzed
21. *Independent Variable*: The classification(s) by which statistical data are categorized or grouped
22. *Placebo Effect*: A neutral or inactive medicine or other stimulus resulting in an experimental effect

23. *Hawthorne Effect*: An experimental effect or an increase in work productivity under the experimental conditions of the research project, regardless of efforts to increase and decrease efficiency
24. *Self-fulfilling Prophecy*: Seeing what one expects to see or overly motivating the experimental group (Eliminating the experimenter as a primary participant helps to avoid this problem)
25. *Post Hoc Error*: After this, therefore, because of this or attributing a cause and effect to descriptive designs (Concluding, for example, that in a relationship study *x* causes *y*.)
26. *Documentary Analysis*: An analysis which includes an inspection of the authenticity and accuracy of the documents utilized
27. *Content Analysis*: A philosophical analysis of the meaning of an article with the principles of logic applied

CHARACTERISTICS OF A GOOD RESEARCHER

The researcher is encumbered with the tremendous responsibility for the perpetuation of all kinds of knowledge in her/his field. The following are characteristics which seem to be universally accepted as necessary for becoming a good researcher:

1. Knowledge of the field
2. Knowledge of the techniques
3. Access to proper equipment
4. Access to subjects needed
5. Appropriate mental attitudes
6. Flexibility and open-mindedness
7. Ability to avoid drawing conclusions prematurely
8. Ability to sort out irrelevant material.

SELECTION OF A PROBLEM

The problem selected must be of vital interest to the investigator but also there must be many additional considerations in the choice of the problem. Some of these considerations include the following questions:

1. Is the study duplicating another study?
2. Is the study characterized by some originality?
3. Are the data available?

4. Does the investigator have the skill to utilize the method involved?
5. Is the required equipment available?
6. Does the investigator have an interested sponsor?
7. Has the administrator who has jurisdiction over the situation given permission for the study to be conducted?
8. Have the subjects agreed to participate?
9. Will the conclusions contribute important and useful information to the field of study?

Among the many sources for problems some may seem more useful than others, but since persons tend to work in different ways the following suggestions may include an acceptable approach for at least a beginning in the search:

1. Analyze what you know about the discipline. Do you know these things because they have been learned through conclusive research or because they have been handed down from one generation to the next and along the way have been accepted as fact? Would these theories be testable through research?
2. Analyze some of your beliefs that you have strong convictions about but know are not based upon pure fact. Decide if these beliefs could be tested.
3. Study some popular movement or approach to Physical Education. Either substantiate or challenge the soundness of the activity associated with the movement.
4. Become associated with persons who are engaged in research. It may be possible to engage in some small facet of a larger project.
5. Read bibliographies and suggestions for further research. Almost every thesis or dissertation includes at least three researchable topics suggested at the end of the study.
6. Discuss your ideas with your classmates and your professors, also look to your course work for topics of interest.
7. Finally, read critically and analytically all that you read, and do not try to get too specific in the first stages.

Problems are everywhere, since your profession is relatively young in comparison with some other academic disciplines; and much of our efforts have been devoted to many hours of teaching and service sometimes at the expense of research. We, nevertheless, have a large amount of very sophisticated research being conducted; however, there will always be new and significant problems to be solved in a field so diverse as ours.

DELINEATION OF THE PROBLEM

The initial step in identifying a problem usually results in a broad concept of what is to be done. Beginning researchers should normally choose to research a problematic area rather than a specific problem. This approach is appropriate and productive because all facets of the more general problem area may be considered; however, at some point delimitation of the problem must occur.

Drew[2] referred to the stage of finally identifying the problem as "problem distillation" and suggested that identification and distillation are a continuous process. Distillation is often (usually) difficult for the younger researcher who is imbued with enthusiasm for conquering on all fronts. Some aids to delineation are further reading and study of existing research and determination of the experimental variables (independent and dependent). The temptation to over-collect and over-analyze may result in the need to delineate further even after data are collected. Usually, this problem can be offset by prudent advice and thought in the planning stages.

COMMON ERRORS IN SELECTING
AND FORMULATING A PROBLEM

Isaac and Michael stated the following common errors in formulating a research study:[3]

1. Selecting the problem after course work is finished
2. Prematurely accepting the first idea that is thought of or suggested
3. Selecting a problem that is too broad in scope
4. Developing vague or untestable hypotheses
5. Failing to consider methods and analyses in the planning stages.

AREAS FOR RESEARCH IN PHYSICAL EDUCATION

In the discipline of physical education various subdisciplines have been identified. The identification has not come through a unified effort from the total association (The Alliance for Health, Physical Education, Recreation, and Dance), but rather from an emergence of certain scholars who have held professional associations with allied disciplines. For example, Thomas Cureton, Bryant Cratty, and Charles Cowell had a significant impact on the recognition of physiology, psychology, and sociology as subdisciplinary areas of physical education in general.

In the absence of a formalized recognition of subdisciplinary areas, the *Research Quarterly for Exercise and Sport* (the only journal published by the Alliance which is devoted totally to research) offers some identification of areas in which research articles are being reviewed. These areas are the following:[4]

1. Activities for Special Populations
2. Biomechanics
3. Growth and Development
4. Health Behavior
5. History and Philosophy
6. Measurement and Evaluation
7. Motor Control and Learning
8. Pedagogy
9. Physiology
10. Psychology
11. Sociology and Cultural Anthropology

Section editors exist for all of the categories and subcategories, and readers are identified in each area. A notable absence in the list is the area of administration. This exclusion has the general effect of overlooking the work of Zeigler and his associates in the rapidly developing theory of administrative sciences.[5]

Baker and Collins reviewed research in physical education which was directly related to the administration of physical education and athletics. They utilized as their source *Completed Research in Health, Physical Education, and Recreation (CHPER)* and reviewed 7,855 thesis and dissertation abstracts. Of the 7,855, 758 were classified as being in the area of administration. This was 9.6 percent of all theses and dissertations reported in *CHPER* during the years 1971-1981.[6] It is obvious that administration as a subdiscipline must be recogized as a legitimate area for research and graduate study.

LAGNIAPPE

In the fiftieth anniversary issue of the *Research Quarterly*, March 1980, Dotson reminded the profession of Physical Education that their research was of questionable density.[7] In this article Dotson was making a plea for physical educators to begin to use models for discovering facts which could be used to develop general theories rather than conducting studies which were concerned with one factor at a time. He cautioned researchers about a prejudice for rejection of the null-hypothesis and urged the readers to strive to increase statistical power. His lagniappe (tip) was that "the 'integration' of the past work with current thought is needed if we wish to advance exercise and sports models to a state of high logical density."[8]

An example of the modeling suggested by Dotson is the classic international study by Kenyon, in which he collaborated with researchers from four countries to ascertain demographic and motivational characteristics for participation in physical activity.[9] Professors and graduate students may wish to consider the advantages of this kind of modeling which may result in greater theoretical discoveries than the piecemeal master's or doctoral theses normally produced. Fractional, rather than analytical and synthesizing, approaches have at this point in our development as a profession outlived their usefulness.

SUMMARY

Our research interests in physical education date from the late eighteen hundreds, and our first official publication was the *Research Quarterly* in March, 1930. The scientific method was appropriate for the research of physical education, and our colleagues in the allied disciplines have been supportive. Research involves an organized, unbiased search of an important problem. Certain terms are associated with research, and their meanings are necessary for understanding the language of researchers. Certain qualities differentiate researchers from just good professionals. The potential researcher, in contemplating the undertaking of a research topic, should subject the topic to the test of the nine questions presented in this chaper. Many sources for problems exist, and once a problem is identified, it is essential to delineate, to the finest degree possible, that problem. Errors in selecting problems, as mentioned by Isaac and Michael, should be avoided.

Legitimate areas for research in physical education are stated in the *Research Quarterly for Exercise and Sports (RQES)* where the section editors are listed. Administration has been overlooked.

"Modeling" has not been prominent in the researcher reported in *RQES*. It is, however, recommended for moving our studies from research characterized as "one factor at a time" into sophisticated and comprehensive designs which permit the emergence of general theories as opposed to isolated, unrelated facts.

SUGGESTED PROJECTS

1. Read biographical entries for Anderson, Hitchcock, and Sargent, *Journal of AAHPER*, Volume 31, No. 4, April, 1960, pp. 34, 126; 35, 122; 36, 106.
2. Propose a topic for research. Then, subject that topic to the nine questions for judging the appropriations of the topic as presented in this chapter.
3. Suggest a study in which modeling would be appropriate. Describe the modeling and suggest a theory which might emerge.

REFERENCE NOTES FOR CHAPTER I

[1] *Research Quarterly*, March, 1930.
[2] Clifford J. Drew, *Introduction to Designing Research and Evaluation* (St. Louis: The C. V. Mosby Company, 1976), pp. 8-9.
[3] Stephen Isaac and William B. Michael, *Handbook in Research and Evaluation* (San Diego, CA: Edits Publishers, 1981), p. 35.
[4] *Research Quarterly*, September, 1984.
[5] Earle F. Zeigler and Marcia J. Spaeth, *Administrative Theory and Practice in Physical Education and Athletics* (Englewood Cliffs, NJ: Prentice-Hall, Inc., 1975).
[6] John A. W. Baker and Mary S. Collins, *Research on Administration of Physical Education and Athletics 1971-1982: A Retrieval System* (Reseda, CA: Mojave Books, 1983), p. xiv.
[7] Charles O. Dotson, "Logic of Questionable Density," *Research Quarterly*, 51 (March 1980), pp. 23-36.
[8] Dotson, p. 35.
[9] Gerald S. Kenyon, "Values Held for Physical Activity by Selected Urban Secondary Students in Canada, Australia, England, and the United States," (Washington, D.C.: The United States Office of Education, 1968).

Chapter II

WRITING THE REPORT

INTRODUCTION

RESEARCH is not complete, regardless of time spent, until the effort is reported, usually in writing. For the student in a course in the methodology of research or for the master's or doctoral candidate, the writing of the report can be the most tedious aspect of the entire venture of obtaining a degree.

Most courses in research methodology have a synthesizing experience of the preparation of a prospectus, or mini-thesis; and most advanced degree programs require a thesis, dissertation, or paper which would qualify as a thesis if expanded. The word "thesis" encompasses all of these discourses on a particular subject.[1]

Because there are apparently quite mixed guidelines for writing research reports and because writing appears to be problematic for many people, this chapter is devoted to clarifying the matters of preference, style, grammar, and the contents of specific parts of the paper. This chapter is elaborated in greater detail than in most texts because of the extreme importance of communicating clearly the work of the researcher whether it be that of the student, the professor, or others conducting serious investigations through research techniques.

CONTENTS OF THE CHAPTERS

The contents of the chapters, and even the titles of the chapters, are a matter of preference. A review of fifteen sources revealed that there was limited agreement; and associations with colleagues from various orientations confirm this fact. Professor "A" strongly argues for an expanded Statement of the Problem which resembles a review of literature. Professor "B" states profoundly in favor of conciseness. The student is trapped.

The matters of preference are usually influenced by many things, but particularly by the adviser, the rules of the university, the method of research being employed, and the academic discipline involved. These factors render it impossible to state one approach. The "Contents of the Chapters of the Report" in Chapter III of this text represent an attempt to consider the most typical divisions of a paper. As long as the necessary parts are somewhere, preference and common sense may dictate where exactly they appear.

STYLE

Styles of writing also have considerable influence on the writing of the report. For example, the strict requirements for formal writing (such as for a research report) vary greatly from almost no requirements for informal writing to very strict requirements for formal writing. Spoken and written English also vary greatly whether it be formal or informal. In formal writing one must use the third person (he, she, they, the investigator, the researcher, etc.), and never the use the first person (I, we, you, etc.). In their public addresses, although formal, it was perfectly acceptable for Martin Luther King to say "I had a dream," and for JFK to say "Ask not what your country can do for you." The rules of grammar should prevail, without exception, in the written report.

GRAMMAR

A complete presentation of grammatical rules is beyond the scope of this text; however, some common mistakes are given here. The reader may note some contradictions which in the following example are corrected.

1. No antecedent
    Example: Grading in co-educational situations is complicated by the absence of ability grouping. *This* makes more work for the teacher.
    Correction: This absence, therefore, causes more work for the teacher.
2. Information expressions
    Example: The absence of ability grouping, therefore, is *bound to cause more work* for the teacher.
    Correction: The absence of ability grouping, therefore, results in

increased deliberations for the teacher.

3. Comparatives

Example: The absence of ability grouping results in *greater deliberations* for the teacher.

Correction: The absence of ability grouping results in greater deliberations *than* otherwise for the teacher.

4. Editorializing

Example: *It is obvious that* the absence of ability grouping results in problems for the teacher.

Correction: Eliminate the opinion, "It is obvious that . . ."

5. Intent to prove

Example: The purpose of this study is *to prove* that the absence of ability grouping presents complications for the teacher.

Correction: Substitute the words, *to investigate whether* for *to prove*.

6. Use of present tense

Example: The purpose of this study *is* to investigate whether . . .

Correction: Substitute *was* for *is*.

7. Weak beginnings

Example: *There are* problems in grading without ability grouping.

Correction: Without ability grouping, problems *are created*.

8. Passive voice

Example: Problems *are created*.

Correction: Problems *exist*.

9. Circumlocution

Example: *It may well be that* problems exist . . .

Correction: *Perhaps* problems exist . . .

10. Short sentences

Example: Some teachers do not utilize ability grouping. Problems may exist.

Correction: When teachers do not utilize ability grouping, problems may exist.

11. Inanimate subject with animate verb

Example: *Ability grouping resolves* many problems in the teaching situation.

Correction: Many problems in the teaching situation *may be solved* through ability grouping.

12. Noun used as adjective

Example: *Ability* grouping . . .

Correction: Grouping by ability . . .

Note: This fault may be overcome in some instances by hyphenating and using the two words as one, i.e., ability-grouping.

13. Split infinitives
    Example: Grouping by ability may be used *to effectively reduce* problems in grading.
    Correction: Grouping by ability may be used effectively *to reduce* problems in grading.

The foregoing examples are representative of some of the most typical of errors in grammar that the beginning researcher is apt to make. Faults in logic and errors in grammar, if prominent, should be studied under the tutelage of a professor of philosophy and/or English. Physical educators cannot necessarily be masters of all disciplines. This is what a University is about — a collection of scholars with whom we should communicate.

OTHER MATTERS OF PREFERENCE

Not all matters of preference can be addressed but some of the predominant of these choices must be mentioned.,

Summaries

Some disagreement exists as to whether summaries should be included in each chapter or at the end of the entire study. It is typical to do both. It is a matter of tradition in formal writing to have both an introduction and a summary for any complex presentation of material. It is wise to say: (1) Here is what I want to say; (2) Here is what I am saying; and (3) Here is what I said; whether it be a theme, paper, a chapter, an article, or an oral address.

Completeness

Considerable support exists for having each chapter stand alone so that a person interested in any part of the study would know what the entire study was about by reading any chapter. In order to do this some redundancy is necessary, but for the reader this redundancy is quite helpful.

Discussions

Discussions are normally included in conjunction with the analysis of data; however, a discussion of the entire study should occur somewhere; and it is most logical to place this discussion in the last chapter. Therefore a discussion of specific findings might occur in the chapter devoted to the analysis of data, but a discussion of the entire study might be placed in the section just prior to the conclusions. The specifics of these discussions are presented later in this chapter.

Style Manuals

Several style manuals are currently available. The preferred manual is somewhat influenced by the discipline, the university, and the adviser. Consistency is almost always acceptable, but the primary goal of the writer should be to provide maximum information for the reader in the most concise and accurate fashion. Two of the most predominant style manuals utilized in physical education are the *Publication Manual of the American Psychological Association*[2] and the *Turabian Manual for Writers*.[3] Each has some advantages over the other. The particular study may dictate which manual has the greatest advantages. The Turabian manual is much more explicit than the APA style, but students find the APA style easier to utilize with respect to referencing. An experienced typist can deal with either with equal facility. Consideration for the reader, rather than for the writer or the typist, should be foremost in the decision of the manual to be followed; and consistency is an absolute requisite.

OUTLINES AND HEADINGS

Outlines and headings are necessary and are directly related since the outline will determine the hierarchy of headings. It is, therefore, essential that an outline be developed for any complex section.

Outlines

Several principles of outlining should be followed in order to develop a logical and clear presentation. These principles include the following:[4]

1. Do not make coordinate any matter that is logically subordinate, and do not make subordinate any matter that is logically coordinate. In other words, determine the importance of topics and let those topics have the place of same importance in the outline.
2. Remember that subdivision requires division into at least two parts. Otherwise incorporate the idea into the main division.
3. Paralellism should be utilized in all divisions and subdivisions of the same level.

The scheme for numbering and lettering in outlining and their indentations are the following:[5]

I.
  A.
    1.
      a.
        (1)
        (2)
      b.
    2.
  B.
II.

Principle number 2, stated previously, simply means that if one determines a need for an "A," there must also be a "B"; otherwise "A" should be incorporated into the Roman heading.

In outlining it is not necessary to have parallelism throughout the entire outline. It is, however, necessary that all topics at each level be parallel in construction. For example, all Roman numerals should be parallel, and all capital letters should be parallel, but that parallelism may differ between any two categories.

Headings

The system for assigning headings differs in the various style manuals. For example, both the Turabian Manual[6] and the APA Manual[7] list five standard levels.

The Turabian levels are the following:

1st: Center heading, underlined
2nd: Center heading, not underlined
3rd: Side heading, underlined
4th: Side heading, not underlined
5th: Heading indented as a paragraph is and underlined as the beginning of the paragraph

The APA levels are the following:

1st: Center heading, uppercase
2nd: Center heading, not underlined, upper and lower case
3rd: Center heading, underlined, upper and lower case
4th: Side heading, underlined, upper and lower case
5th: Indented, underlined, lower case paragraph, with a period.

For information concerning capitalization see the style manual.

In the Turabian system one may eliminate certain levels if five are not needed, but the hierarchy must prevail. In other words, the writer could move from center headings underlined to side headings underlined, thus eliminating the center heading not underlined; however, the order of importance would remain.

The outline and the hierarchy of the headings have a direct relationship, and that relationship typically in the Turabian format is as follows:

Outline	*Heading*
I.	Center, underlined
A.	Center, not underlined
1.	Side, underlined
a.	Side, not underlined
(1)	Paragraph, underlined

The APA is as follows:

Outline	*Heading*
I.	Center, uppercase
A.	Center, not underlined, upper and lower case
1.	Center, underlined, upper and lower case
a.	Side, underlined, upper and lower case
(1)	Indented, underlined, lower case paragraph, with period

The option in APA if four levels are required is to begin with a center heading all in capital letters.

SUMMARY

The contents of the chapters vary according to preference. Styles of writing, rules of grammar, and other matters of preference such as summaries, completeness, discussions, and the style manual utilized influence the format of the report.

Outlines and headings are necessary and are directly related. The various levels in an outline must be parallel in construction, and at least two subdivisions must be utilized if one divides a major topic. The use of I., A., 1., a., and (1) indicates the hierarchy of the symbols in the outline. The use of headings varies according to the style manual being employed.

Suggested Projects

1. Use the thirteen grammatical rules enumerated in this chapter and furnish examples other than those given for seven of the thirteen.
2. Take a textbook that is currently one which you are using and analyze the accuracy of its headings.

REFERENCE NOTES FOR CHAPTER II

[1] A. Merriam-Webster, *Webster's New Collegiate Dictionary*, 9th ed. (Springfield, Mass.: G. & C. Merriam Co., 1983), p. 1225.

[2] American Psychological Association, *Publication Manual*, 3rd ed. (Washington, D.C.: American Psychological Association, 1983).

[3] Kate L. Turabian, *A Manual for Writers*, 4th ed. (Chicago: The University of Chicago Press, 1973).

[4] Norman Foerster and J. M. Steadman, Jr., *Writing and Thinking* (Cambridge: The Riverside Press, 1941), pp. 243-244.

[5] Floyd C. Watkins and Edwin T. Martin, *Practical English Handbook* (Boston: Houghton Mifflin, 1961), p. 313.

[6] Turabian, p. 7.

[7] American Psychological Association, p. 66.

Chapter III

CONTENTS OF THE CHAPTERS OF THE REPORT

THIS CHAPTER is organized under the following general headings: the introductory chapter, the review of related literature, the procedures, the analysis of data, the final chapter, and other parts of the report.

THE INTRODUCTORY CHAPTER

The titles and contents of the introductory chapter vary greatly among the writers of books on methods of research. A review of seven texts which are in considerable usage will confirm this fact.

Titles and Contents

Best[1] did not state a title for the chapter but alluded to the contents as comprising the following: an introduction, a clear statement of the problem, questions or hypotheses, significance, purposes, assumptions, limitations, and delimitations.

Clarke and Clarke[2] labeled Chapter I "The Statement of the Problem" and stated that it should contain an orientation to the importance and need for the study. Definitions of terms were also recommended for inclusion in Chapter 1.

Only a general reference to the introductory chapter was suggested by Good.[3] He recommended that one or more chapters be devoted to an analysis of the problem, limits, and scope. No particular format was recommended.

Isaac and Michael[4] suggested a checklist of items for possible inclusion:

Introduction

Background of the problem
Statement of the problem
Purpose of the study
Questions to be answered
Assumptions
Rationale and theoretical framework
Delineation
Hypotheses
Importance
Definitions
Scope and delimitations

They did not recommend that all of these topics were essential to include. Some, in fact, may overlap.

Kerlinger[5] stated that the first section of the report should contain theory, hypotheses, and definitions. He agreed that the first chapter differs greatly in various reports.

Only a brief discussion of Chapter I was presented by Kidder.[6] She labeled the chapter "Introduction" and suggested that the chapter should contain the background and nature of the problem.

Travers[7] stated that the introductory chapter should have a clear and concise statement of the purposes, the background of the problem, and the theory on which it is based. He suggested that this approach might serve as the basis for an article.

The foregoing review will verify the absence of mandate with respect to format and inclusions in the introductory chapter. The writer must, therefore, be guided predominantly by matters of preference whether it be her or his own, a collaborator's, or that of the adviser.

Specifics of the Contents

The following section will be devoted to consideration of the details which normally appear somewhere in an introductory chapter. Two of the texts reviewed listed the review of literature as a part of the introductory chapter; however, the review of literature will be treated separately in this section.

Introductory Statements

Introductory sentences should be used to interest the reader in the topic. These sentences are usually very general and sometimes quite lofty, sweeping, and even poetic.

Need for the Study

The need for the study should be convincing. Some references are necessary to show briefly that what is known about the topic contains important voids, and therefore the investigation intends to supply that important information. Avoid the temptation to be dogmatic, in other words, saying "This study needs to be done because it is important." The "need" must not be just an utterance not substantiated by fact. A beginning researcher may assume that everyone shares her/his enthusiasm and is equally convinced of the importance. The writer must not assume but must *convince* in this section. Opinions differ with respect to the length of the need for the study; and those authors who suggested that the review of literature be placed in Chapter I were obviously in favor of a lengthy "need." The "need" must be clearly stated and should be so labeled by a heading. Headings assist the reader in the same way that road signs assist the driver.

Statement of the Problem

Statements of the problem vary considerably. A concise version may contain as few as four sentences. Longer versions may resemble a review of literature. Two examples of short versions follow:

EXAMPLE 1: STATEMENT OF THE PROBLEM

The purpose of this study was to describe selected measures of batting ability using both the standard and the angular bats. The subjects in the study were 75 students enrolled in two general studies softball classes at Southern Illinois University at Carbondale. Data were collected through the observation technique with the aid of a mechanical speedgun for measuring velocity. Data were analyzed by *t* tests for correlated samples, correlation coefficients, percentages, and frequencies.[8]

EXAMPLE 2: STATEMENT OF THE PROBLEM

The purpose of this study was to determine if a variation of Russian Downhill Training affected the one-hundred-yard dash times of selected college students. The subjects included twenty-four students enrolled in a general studies track and field class and twenty-seven students enrolled in a Physical Education major track and field class at Southern Illinois University during the spring semester of 1979. Data were collected from the results of tests of one-hundred-yard-dash times conducted at zero, two, four, and six weeks during the study. Data were analyzed by correlation coefficients, analysis of variance, regression analysis, and percentages.[9]

The short version contains four parts: (1) the general purpose, (2) who the subjects were, (3) how the data were collected, and (4) how the data were analyzed.

Purposes

Purposes may be stated in at least three forms: (1) objectives (infinitives), (2) questions, or (3) hypotheses. The form is a matter of preference. Examples of these approaches follow:

Objectives

EXAMPLE 1: PURPOSES OF THE STUDY

The general purpose of the study was to examine sex-role orientation and attitude toward physical activity of selected college age students.[10]
Specific purposes were:

1. To identify intercorrelations of the variables of the ATPA, for males, females, and the total group
2. To determine if differences exist among the means for the seven variables of ATPA for the categories of sex-role orientation based upon Bem's medians
3. To determine if differences exist among the means for the seven variables of the ATPA for the categories of sex-role orientation based upon Mize's medians
4. To compare scores made by males and females on the seven variables of the ATPA
5. To analyze the interaction effects associated with sex and sex-role orientation for the dependent variables of the ATPA based upon the Bem medians
6. To analyze the interaction effects associated with sex and sex-role orientation for the dependent variables of the ATPA based upon the Mize medians
7. To examine the effects of utilizing the Bem medians and/or the Mize medians for males, females, and the total group.

Questions

EXAMPLE 1: PURPOSES OF THE STUDY

The general purpose of the study was to determine whether there were differences in grades received by male and female students for general studies service courses in physical education in a private church-related liberal arts college. Dependent variables were Knowledge Grades, Skill Grades, and Final Grades. Specific purposes for the study were to answer the following questions: [11]

1. Do differences exist in grades received by students for the following independent variables?
    A. Teachers
    B. Activities
    C. Sex of Student
    D. Sex of Teacher
    E. Same or Separate Grading Scales for the Sexes
2. Is there an interaction between the independent variables?
    A. Sex of Student and Teacher
    B. Sex of Student and Activity
    C. Sex of Student and Sex of Teacher
    D. Sex of Student and Same or Separate Grading Scales for Skill for the Sexes
    E. Sex of Teacher and Same or Separate Grading Scales for Skill for the Sexes

Hypotheses

EXAMPLE: PURPOSES OF THE STUDY

The following hypotheses were proposed in order to fulfill the purposes of the study: [12]

HYPOTHESIS I

The measures utilized in computing velocity, vertical angle of projection, and lateral angle of projection can be made objectively for each of the selected sports skills. More specifically, the hypothesis was:
    A. In obtaining performance measures, a nonsignificant amount of variance can be attributed to timer disagreement in measuring time
    B. In obtaining performance measures, a nonsignificant amount of variance can be attributed to reader disagreement in measuring actual distance and perpendicular distance to the intended line of flight
    C. In obtaining performance measures, a non-significant amount of variance can be attributed to scorer disagreement in estimating actual distance and perpendicular distance to the intended line of flight
    D. In obtaining performance measures, a non-significant amount of variance can be attributed to scorer disagreement in estimating lateral angle of projection

HYPOTHESIS II

Individual measures of performance are reliable for each of the selected sports skills. More specifically, the hypothesis was:

A. Measures of velocity are reliable estimates of performance
B. Measures of vertical angle of projection are reliable estimates of performance
C. Measures of lateral angle of projection are reliable estimates of performance
D. Measures of the difference between actual and ideal velocity are reliable estimates of performance
E. Measures of the difference between the actual and the ideal vertical angle of projection are reliable estimates of performance.

HYPOTHESIS III

Measures of velocity, vertical angle of projection, and lateral angle of projection are related in each of the selected skills.

HYPOTHESIS IV

Measures of actual and ideal velocity are related in each of the selected skills.

HYPOTHESIS V

Measures of actual and ideal vertical angle of projection are related in each of the selected skills.

Research Hypotheses

It is conceivable that the researcher might want to use combinations of the three approaches because when one states a purpose as an objective, no point of view as to outcome (hypothesis) is proposed. It would be perfectly acceptable, therefore, to state objectives and hypotheses, or questions and hypotheses. If hypotheses are stated, research hypotheses are more appropriate than statistical hypotheses.

Research hypotheses are normally stated positively and represent the writer's "best guess" about the outcomes of the study. Statistical hypotheses are always stated in the null or negative form. The following examples will illustrate the point:

A. Research hypothesis: Certain demographic characteristics predict a successful student teaching experience
B. Statistical hypothesis: Demographic characteristics have no relationship to a successful student teaching experience. More typically this hypothesis is stated, "There is no relationship between demographic characteristics and a successful student teaching experience."

It is reasonable that the researcher has undertaken the foregoing study because he/she believes that demographic characteristics may be associated with success; therefore it makes no sense to state the hypothesis, which generically means "a tentative theory or supposition," in the null. The null is, of course, required for statistical computations.

Whereas research hypotheses should be stated in a positive way, they may have negative meanings. The following illustrates this point:

A. Stated positively with negative meaning:

In obtaining performance measures, a non-significant amount of variance can be attributed to timer disagreement in measuring time.

B. Stated negatively the hypothesis would be:

In obtaining performance measures, variance is not attributable to timer disagreement.

Purposes should be stated in a chronological and logical order so that when procedures, results, and conclusions are reported they parallel the same order. This procedure makes for good organization on both the writer's and the reader's part.

Definitions

The choice of which terms to define should be guided primarily by whether the term has a universally understood meaning. In some instances words, although having common understanding, may need defining with respect to some particular use in the study. For example, the term "response accuracy" is comprised of two words, both of which are commonly understood, but when used together need definition. Walters defined this term for her study as follows: "The ability to conceptualize external stimuli in a game or practice situation and move correctly in response to those stimuli."[13]

Ferrer studied errors which terminate play in volleyball. While the term "error" is generally understood, errors in his study had to be defined specifically as follows. "Errors in the present study were only those resulting in an immediate termination of play."[14] This definition then gave a quite specific meaning to a quite general term.

Although the term "athletes" has clear meaning, Kildea found it necessary to define athletes in a particular way for her study:

"A female student involved in one or more competitive sports offered by the Women's Intercollegiate Athletic program at Southern Illinois University, Carbondale, during the 1978-79 academic year."[15]

Trying out an introductory chapter on an intelligent, but unknowledgeable, person can aid in identifying terms that may need definition. If in doubt, it is better to over-define than to under-define.

If a definition of terms section tends to become too lengthy, a glossary of terms placed in the appendix should be considered. In highly technical studies, this approach may offer the most practical solution.

The placement in the chapter of the definitions depends largely upon the clarity in reading the opening statements, the need for the study, and the purposes. Many times it is necessary to define terms before the reader embarks upon understanding these sections. In a highly technical study this may well be the case. In Anthony's[16] paper entitled, "Running Death," it was necessary to define the term in the introductory paragraph since this is the topic of the entire paper and a very unusual expression.

Delimitations

Delimitations are those boundaries or conditions of the study which are set by the investigator. Some typical delimitations are the following:

EXAMPLE: DELIMITATIONS

The writer controlled the following factors in the study:
1. All subjects were participants in racquetball tournaments
2. Subjects used regulation racquets of their choice
3. The racquetballs which were used for each match were new; the brand was selected by the tournament sponsors or hosts
4. Data were collected only during tournament play
5. Both female and male subjects of varying levels of skill were observed
6. Only singles matches were observed
7. Both left and right-handed players were observed.[17]

The researcher has control at the outset of the study over delimitations. He/she has no control over limitations.

Limitations

Once the delimitations are decided upon, certain limitations are encumbered. The limitations accompanying the preceding delimitations are the following:

EXAMPLE: LIMITATIONS

The writer had no control over the following factors in the study:
1. Previous racquetball experience was not the same for all subjects at

any level of skill

2. The subjects were observed at various racquetball facilities, which had various court surfaces and possibly different lighting
3. Coaching by outsiders could not be controlled
4. There was only one observer, the writer
5. Different types of racquetballs and racquets were used from tournament to tournament
6. The observer's viewing position varied from observation to observation, although in each situation there was a clear vantage point.[18]

Often a delimitation results in a limitation; however, there may well be limitations imposed simply by the decision to deal with human subjects. An example is: no control over their health habits, going and coming, exercise, times of day, preferences, weather effects, etc. The writer should consider whether a delimitation poses a limitation. If a delimitation does result in a limitation, a proper way to state such a delimitation and corresponding limitation would be the following:

Delimitation: Twenty-four subjects were utilized in the study.

Limitation: Twenty-four subjects may not have constituted an adequate sample.

In deciding upon the limitations one may ask the question, "What that I did, or did not do, might have turned out differently had I done otherwise?" Some limitations also may surface at the defense of the paper or at an oral presentation where questions and answers are a part of the format.

Often it is appropriate to qualify a limitation in the following way:

The results of the study cannot be generalized to other junior high schools within the city; *however*, the investigator has no reason to believe that this sample would not be typical of all other junior high schools in the city.

Still no attempt is made to generalize, but the reader may have a more positive feeling about the credibility of the results than he/she would have without the qualification.

Summary of Chapter I

Whether to include a summary of Chapter I depends upon the format selected. If the chapter has been developed to encompass the review of literature, a summary would be essential. If the chapter is organized into distinctly different sections such as Need, Statement of the Problem, Purposes, Definitions, Delimitations, and Limitations, a Summary is not necessary.

Transition to Chapter II

The transition from Chapter I to Chapter II should take the form of telling the reader what is to follow, such as: "In the following chapter the investigator will present a review of related literature which will serve to strengthen the need for the study and to contrast the present study with those of similar design." The matter of transition is a requirement of both formal writing and formal speaking.

Summary

The titles and contents of the introductory chapter vary greatly. The specific contents generally include introductory statements, a need for the study, a statement of the problem, purposes, definitions, delimitations, and limitations. Because of the variety of topics usually considered in the introductory chapter, a transition to the next chapter may be more logical than a summary of the first chapter.

THE REVIEW OF RELATED LITERATURE

The Review of Related Literature is often the longest and most complex of chapters to write since the contents vary greatly from study to study and the material must be so specifically related to the study in question. Length may be difficult to control in both extremes of little published on the topic to volumes of both published and unpublished information available. The task of the writer is in either case to provide readers with a comprehensive, but concise, review of technical information and related studies. It is to provide for the reader a clear understanding that the study has importance, does not merely duplicate another study, and needs to be done. The review of literature focuses on background, contrasts, and voids.

Determining Relatedness

Few, if any, guidelines exist for determining the topics in an outline (which is essential) for the review of literature. Of the seven texts reviewed for determining the contents of introductory chapters none addressed the topic of relatedness. An example of an outline in its original and revised form may illustrate the point of determining relatedness.

EXAMPLE: A FILM ANALYSIS OF THE SPIKE IN VOLLEYBALL

Original Chapter II Outline

I. Introduction
II. Motor Learning
III. Execution of the Spike
    A. Process
    B. Product
IV. Cinematographical Procedures
    A. Marking
    B. Filming
    C. Reading
    D. Taking Measurements
V. Film Analyses of the Volleyball Spike
VI. Film Analyses of Other Volleyball Skills
VII. Film Analyses of Other Related Skills
VIII. Summary

Revised Chapter II Outline

I. Introduction
II. Execution of the Spike
    A. Process
    B. Product
III. Cinematographical Procedures
    A. Marking
    B. Filming
    C. Reading
    D. Taking Measurements
IV. Film Analyses of the Volleyball Spike
V. Film Analyses of Similar Overarm Patterns
VI. Summary

"Motor learning" has been omitted because this would lead the writer to become inundated. The topic is, first of all, too broad for even a thesis title much less a subheading in a chapter. Without doubt motor learning is related to performing the spike in volleyball. It is related to every physical performance, so while it is related it is too broad and general rather than specifically related.

Also notice that the original VI and VII have been combined under the topic, "Film Analyses of Other Similar Overarm Patterns." A film analysis of a forearm pass or an underarm serve which employ an underarm pattern would not be expected to have much implication for the spike, which employs an overarm pattern. However, the tennis serve, softball throw, and a volleyball serve may well be worth comparison.

For some studies many other very similar studies may have been completed. For others there may be very few. If a great deal has been done on the topic, it is possible that a comprehensive review exists. For example, the *Encyclopedia of Educational Research*[19] and *Review of Educational Research*[20] contain such reviews. If a review is available, use the review as a source rather than reading all of the articles reviewed. Our own *Research Quarterly for Exercise and Sport*[21] periodically contains reviews.[22,23,24]

Choice of Words

Words should be varied. Overuse of the same words is monotonous to the reader and is indicative of a limited vocabulary and a poor style on the writer's part. A standard dictionary (the larger the better) and a comprehensive thesaurus are essential.

When writing and the temptation to use the same word twice within one sentence arises, look for a synonym. When a word does not seem quite right, consult the thesaurus. Words have shades of meaning that do not necessarily cause one word to be right or wrong, but do cause one to be preferred and more precise.

Developing an Outline

Prior to developing an outline, some initial reading and browsing will probably be necessary, unless there is considerable familiarity on the writer's part with the subject involved. As the reading continues subtopics and a feeling for relative importance should emerge. The topics that others have used in the articles read and tables of contents are useful in the attempt to develop the outline. (See the earlier chapter in this book for mechanics of outlining and the relationship of headings to outlining.) The outline developed at this stage may later be revised as reading continues and a grasp for the subject increases.

Developing a Working Bibliography

Reference materials such as the *Education Index*, the *Encyclopedia of Educational Research*, the *Review of Educational Research*, the indexes of the *Research Quarterly*, and other bibliographical indexes will provide the sources for developing the working bibliography. A good approach is that of making a list of all articles to be read. It is economical to do this on paper, rather than cards, at this stage. A notation by the reference as to where in the outline the article would appear is helpful in determining whether the working bibliography is complete.

The indexes mentioned previously are excellent for developing the working bibliography; however, a great deal of time and effort may be saved by utilizing an ERIC search. The cost is nominal for the services provided. While only a list of related articles, etc. is provided, actual reprints may be obtained. If the library with which you are associated does not have information on ERIC it would be worthwhile to write for the manual entitled, *How to Use ERIC*. ERIC are initials for the Educational Resources Information Center. The manual is available from the U.S. Government Printing Office, Washington, D.C. 20402. The central office for ERIC is at the National Institute of Education, Washington, D.C. 20208. Information can also always be obtained from the Department of Health, Education, and Welfare, Washington, D.C. 20208.[25]

Researching Related Materials

The matter of researching the chosen materials is integrally related to notetaking. At this point, it is advisable to take notes on cards. A 5 inch by 7 inch card provides ample space for most note entries. Another sized card may be used for the bibliographical reference. A 4 inch by 6 inch is usually adequate.

Using cards or sheets of paper for notetaking is actually a matter of preference. If paper is preferred, then the sheets should be treated in the same way that cards are as discussed in this section. The back of the sheet should not be used so that the sheets could be cut for reorganization or for the addition of afterthoughts.

Referencing

The researcher should attempt to work through the bibliography by reading each article or passage and making a reference card for each entry that is read. If after reading the entry the investigator finds that the material is really not as pertinent as he/she earlier thought, the reference card should, nevertheless, be retained; and a note to that effect should be made. A procedure such as this will prevent retracing steps and will save considerable time as memories of the early stages of the research fade.

A sample of the foregoing suggestion for a reference card (3 inches by 5 inches) in Turabian style follows:

Note that in the upper right-hand corner the numbers "I.A.2" appear to cue into the place that this reference would have occurred in the out-

```
┌─────────────────────────────────────────────────────────────┐
│                                                               │
│   Chapter II                                        I.A.2     │
│                                                               │
│                                                               │
│        Mushi, Lee T.   "On Procuring."   Dog World 50         │
│             (January 1984):   1-25.                           │
│                                                               │
│                                                               │
│                                                               │
│                                                               │
│        [NOT APPROPRIATE FOR HUMANS.]                          │
│                                                               │
└─────────────────────────────────────────────────────────────┘
```

line, had it been appropriate. In the upper left the chapter identification is noted. The four corners could be used if other categories would facilitate the organization of the paper.

Eventually all cards upon which the references have been entered and used may be given to the typist. The cards can be shuffled in order to alphabetize them, and no additional copying or typing is necessary.

Note-taking

Let us say that the reference by Mushi had been pertinent, and notes were taken. A sample of that note card (5 inches by 7 inches) appears as follows:

```
┌─────────────────────────────────────────────────────────────┐
│                                                               │
│   Chapter II                                      I. A. 2.    │
│                                                               │
│      Lee T. Mushi, "On Procuring," Dog World 50 (January 1984):│
│      2-4.                                                      │
│                                                               │
│   p. 2     Bandy Lee T. does relatively nothing because her   │
│            father is a procurer.                              │
│                                                               │
│   p. 3     Procurer has many meanings.  Some are not so       │
│            flattering.  For example:  obtaining by any means  │
│            to acquire or get, to contrive for a favor.  In    │
│            the case of Bandy's father he is just an attentive │
│            dog, who is really                                 │
│   p. 4     probably looking out for himself when he           │
│            successfully secures treats, walks, rides in the   │
│            car, and the daily meal.                           │
│                                                               │
│                                               Card 1          │
│                                                               │
└─────────────────────────────────────────────────────────────┘
```

Notice that a third corner has been used to indicate that this is card 1 of a series for this entry. The exact page reference is placed in the left margin. A line indicates when the reference shifts from page 3 to 4.

When notes for the same entry are made on second and third or more cards, the author's last name is all that is needed on the card unless there is more than one reference by that same author. In that instance the date could be used after the same, or a shortened title could identify the specific reference.

All of the notes are paraphrased. Otherwise exact quotes would be shown by quotation marks. Paraphrasing is preferable to quoting unless some unusual material would lose impact or dignity by paraphrasing. Quoting usually takes more time, and paraphrasing presents the opportunity for synthesis.

Criticizing the Source Materials

One purpose of the review of literature is to demonstrate that you, as the writer, are familiar and well-read on the topic. The kinds of sources reported become very important in reaching this position of being maximally informed.

Some criteria for judging completeness and appropriateness are the following:

1. Predominantly research-oriented
2. A good distribution among books, periodicals, microfilms, theses, dissertations, other unpublished materials, etc.
3. Predominantly primary sources, rather than abstracts or other secondary accounts of primary sources
4. Relatively few popular magazines and non-technical journals
5. Human sources with high credibility (big game).

Writing the Review

If the cards, or sheets, are prepared carefully and the material has been paraphrased, it is sometimes possible to type the first draft directly from the notes. Triple spacing makes editing easy; however, double spacing sometimes saves retyping pages that have few errors since final copy will be double-spaced.

Refer to the earlier section on grammar for guidance in the actual writing of the chapter on the related literature. Adherence to the outline, use of the past tense, and contrast of the present study with others are essential. The reader of the review should be thoroughly convinced that the present study adds to the body of knowledge and is important. The review of literature should be more than just a report. It should also have an element of critique.

Summary

The review of literature is complex and usually lengthy. It, therefore, requires good organization. That organization is predominantly a matter of preference. Relatedness of the topics must be carefully considered in order not to become buried in extraneous material.

Initial reading of a browsing nature is necessary prior to developing the outline. As reading continues a working bibliography should be developed from many indexes which are available in all academically-oriented libraries. An ERIC search should be considered for its thoroughness and economy.

The manner of note-taking is extremely important and will determine how much retracing of steps is required. Cards or sheets may be used and should be referenced accurately and be correlated to the outline. Pages should be carefully noted on the cards or sheets. Paraphrasing is more practical than quoting except for exceptional passages which might lose their impact if summarized or reworded.

A final step in writing the review of literature should be to criticize the completeness of the source materials. Good distribution of types of sources is essential.

For many writers this is the most difficult chapter to write. It need not be, with good organization and systematic research techniques.

THE PROCEDURES

A detailed and accurate account of all procedures employed is an extremely important part of any research report. Some researchers prefer to label this chapter, or section, "Methodology." The words are synonymous, so the choice is preferential.

In most instances a chronological approach to the chapter on procedures is advisable. Dated accounts are helpful in recalling the chronology and in formulating an outline which is essential for this chapter.

Contents of the Chapter

Just as the review of literature varies greatly from study to study, the procedures chapter is developed on an individual basis. No one format fits every study, but some similarities do exist. They are the following:

1. Design of the study
2. Reviewing related literature
3. Conduct of a pilot study, or preliminary procedures
4. Selection of subjects
5. Selection of sites or testing areas
6. Selection of judges, observers, scorers, etc.
7. Selection of tests, instruments, measures, equipment, etc.
8. Training of scorers, judges, observers, etc.
9. Collection of data
10. Preparation of data for submission to the computer (if appropriate)
11. Analysis of data.

The foregoing list of some typical procedures are not necessarily appropriate for historical, philosophical, or creative research. Procedures for these methods will be discussed in the chapter devoted to "Methods of Research." The list presented is most often appropriate for descriptive and experimental approaches.

In some studies the preliminary procedures are lengthy and involved, and those procedures may well deserve a major heading and section in the chapter. In other studies preliminary work may be minimal, and there may be no need to differentiate the preliminary procedures from the actual procedures. A good test for the completeness of the procedures chapter is to ask an intelligent person who is reasonably knowledgeable, but not expert, if he/she could duplicate the study given the procedures as presented in the first draft. Asking colleagues to read one's work is perfectly legitimate and is, in fact, a quite advisable procedure. The writer, and even the adviser, is often too familiar with the study to identify omissions.

Summary

A chronological, dated account of all procedures may be used to formulate the outline for the chapter. The contents vary and are a matter to be dealt with individually. Most studies have preliminary and actual procedures. Asking a colleague to react to the completeness of the procedures stated, with a view toward duplication, is recommended.

THE ANALYSIS OF DATA

The Analysis of Data is sometimes called the findings, especially in articles appearing in journals. The analysis is the essence of the work and must, therefore, be organized, precise, and clear. An outline is essential. The writer has some preference in the manner in which the data are presented, but some convention does exist particularly for presenting statistical data, which will be discussed here.

Presentation of Statistical Data

When statistical data are to be discussed they are usually presented in tabular form. The writer should:

1. Announce the coming of the table
2. Have the table appear as soon as feasible in order to present it in its entirety
3. Tell the reader what is important in the table
4. Discuss the table.

Two actual examples of utilizing this approach follow: [26,27]

Example 1

In addition to the previously discussed family characteristics, parental occupation was also examined. Because of the wide variety of occupations obtained, four vocational categories were utilized in summarizing the data. These four vocational categories included (1) professional, (2) merchant, (3) trade/labor, and (4) clerical. Data related to parental occupation appear in Table 3-1.

A majority of the fathers of the subjects were involved in trade or labor occupations. Forty percent of the mothers were involved in trade or labor occupations. An additional 40 percent of the mothers were involved in clerical occupations. These data seemed to suggest that parental occupation may influence the success of the subjects. Parents involved in trade/labor and clerical occupations may influence their children toward more prestigious vocations than their own. Parents may view the teaching profession as being prestigious.

Example 2

Pearson's *r* was computed for the studies of objectivity. The correlation coefficients appear in Table 3-2.

TABLE 3-1

PARENTAL OCCUPATION

| | Father | | Mother | |
	f	%	f	%
Professional	6	20.7	5	16.7
Merchant	4	13.8	1	3.3
Trade/Labor	19	65.5	12	40.0
Clerical	0	0.0	12	40.0
Total	29[a]	100.0	30[b]	100.0

[a] Deceased/Unable to Work = 3
[b] Deceased = 1, No Response = 1

TABLE 3-2

CORRELATION COEFFICIENTS FOR THE STUDIES OF OBJECTIVITY

Two Judges	*r Obtained*	*Number of Trials*
1. Timers	.94[a]	23
2. Distance recorders	.96	25
3. Height of contact and landing recorders	.92	25
4. Effectiveness recorders	.97	35

[a] The number of observations was 50.

The correlation coefficients revealed that very high levels of objectivity existed between each of the different types of recorders. Since all of the relationships were extremely high, objectivity existed between any of the four types of recorders.

Presentation of Nonstatistical Data

Historical, philosophical, and creative studies normally do not have statistical data. These types of studies will be discussed later when those specific methods are discussed. In the meantime certain data, even in statistically-oriented studies, are nonstatistical and are presented in figures. Most often these are in the form of graphs. The following figures illustrate the point:[28,29]

Summarization of Statistical Data

When statistical data are summarized, summary tables often provide a clear way of synthesizing detailed and complicated findings. Some examples follow:[30,31,32]

Example 1

Although her study was not totally statistical, Kildea used a tabular format for describing the variables used in the study. The example follows:[33]

Summary tables, like figures and graphs, can often elucidate for the reader large quantities of data and give a quick feel for what really happened without going through a long written summary. Summary tables are often appropriate even in the review of literature. For example, if a study requires reviewing a number of tests or instruments, a summary table of the reviews might clarify similarities and differences, thus identifying the reason for the choice of a certain test or instrument.

Appropriate tables for reporting various specific statistical results will be presented in the chapter on statistical techniques.

Summary

Some convention exists for reporting statistical data. Tables are used normally and are introduced, follow as soon as possible, and are then discussed. Some nonstatistical data also may be presented in tables or figures. Figures are handled in the same way as tables. Summary tables offer a concise way of synthesizing large amounts of data or material of a nonstatistical nature.

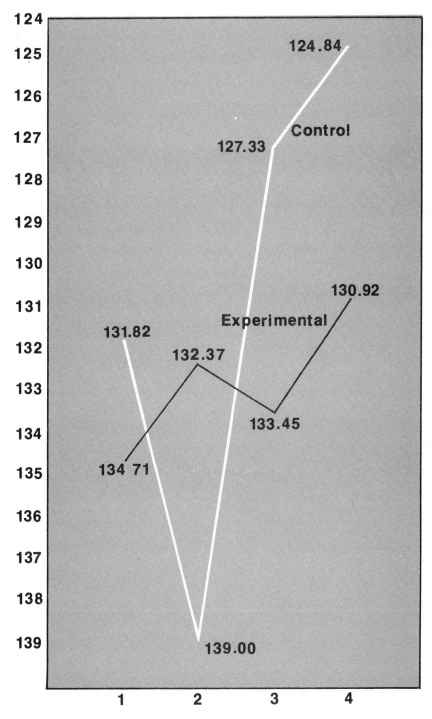

Figure 3-1. Interaction for repeated measures — four tests — average of trials one and two for control and experimental methods.

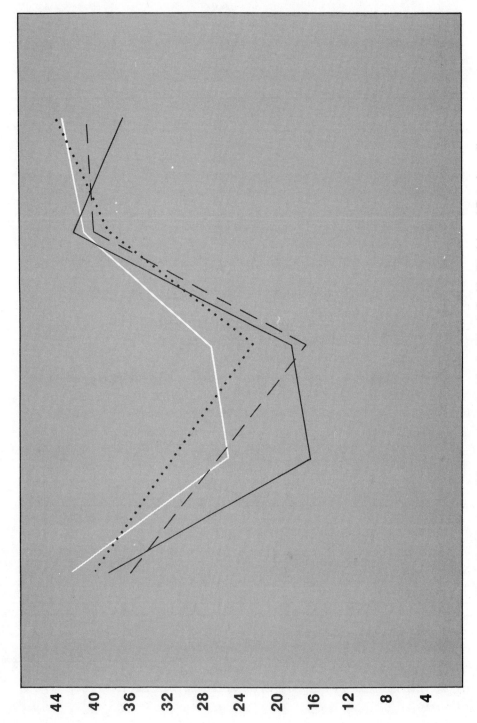

Figure 3-2. Average of the means reported in the Wood, Smith, Daniel, and Francis studies.

TABLE 3-3

SUMMARY OF SIGNIFICANT FINDINGS

Dependent Variable	Direction	Statistic	Prob.[b]
MEANINGFULNESS IN LIFE			
Athlete — Nonathlete	Ath. > N-Ath.	$F = 11.67$	.0008
Athlete Differences	Lo > Med > Hi	$F = 19.41$	.0001
LC Levels	A > M, F & U	$F = 6.33$	.0007
SRO Categories	M > F & U		
Nonathlete Differences			
LC Levels	Lo & Med > Hi	$F = 4.95$	.0090
SRO Categories	M > F & U	$F = 2.35$	.0730
LOCUS OF CONTROL			
Athlete Differences			
MIL Levels	Hi > Med > Lo	$F = 11.94$	.0001
SRO Categories	U, F & A > M	$F = 3.56$	.0173
Nonathlete Differences			
MIL Levels	Hi & Med > Lo	$F = 14.96$	.0001
SEX-ROLE ORIENTATION			
Athlete — Nonathlete	Ath > A & M	$X^2 = 23.24$	.0001

THE FINAL CHAPTER

Of the seven references consulted, all agreed that the final chapter should consist of a summary, conclusions, and recommendations for further research. The additional sections of a final chapter seem to be a matter of preference. For example, one author suggested placing limitations and weaknesses here.[34] Others stated that a discussion of the study in relationship to other similar studies should be placed here. The following sections will address the typical parts of a final chapter, with the obvious recognition that these sections may vary from writer to writer and/or from setting to setting.

TABLE 3-4

SUMMARY TABLE OF SIGNIFICANCE

Variable Scale	Social Experience (SE) Health and Fitness (HF) Vertigo (V)	Aesthetic (Ae) Cathartic (Ca) Ascetic (As) Chance (Ch)
Intercorrelations	1) Male subjects: significant correlations existed among all variables except chance with health and fitness, aesthetic, and cathartic. 2) Female subjects: significant correlations existed among all variables except chance with social experience, chance with aesthetic, cathartic with vertigo, ascetic with aesthetic, and aesthetic with vertigo. 3) Total sample: significant differences in sex-role orientation existed on ATPA on the vertigo variable only (Mize medians).	
Duncan's Multiple Range Test	1 = Androgynous 2 = Masculine 3 = Feminine 4 = Undifferentiated	
	Bem medians: 1 > 4 on SE, 2 > 4 on SE, 1 > 4 on HF, 2 > 4 on V, 2 > 3 on V, 2 > 1 on V, 3 > 4 on Ae, 1 > 4 on Ca, 2 > 4 on Ca, 2 > 3 on As, 2 > 1 on As	
	Mize medians: 2 > 4 on V, 2 > 3 on V, and 2 > 1 on V.	
t-Test	Significant differences existed between male and female subjects on vertigo.	
Interaction	No significant interactions between sex and sex-role orientation resulted in the two-way analyses of variance.	

TABLE 3-4 (Continued)

Chi-Square	The contingency coefficient was .83 for males and .82 for females which indicated a high relationship between both methods of categorizing subjects regardless of sex.
	2) The contingency coefficient indicated a high relationship between the categorical data from the two sets of medians. A total of only 30 subjects (11 percent) were classified differently by using the Mize medians in contrast to the Bem medians.

TABLE 3-5

SUMMARY OF SIGNIFICANT FINDINGS
ANOVA

Skill	Situation	Comparison	Direction of the Difference
Set	Receiving the Serve	Games Won and Games Lost	Lost > Won
Block	Receiving the Serve	Games Won and Games Lost	Los > Won
Spike	Serving	Place in Tournament	1st > 4th = 2nd = 8th
Block	Serving	Place in Tournament	2nd > 1st = 8th = 4th
Set	Receiving the Serve	Place in Tournament	2nd > 8th > 1st = 4th
Total	Receiving the Serve	Place in Tournament	2nd > 8th = 1st > 4th

Summary

The length of the summary may depend upon the amount of summarizing which the writer has done in previous chapters. However, some summaries, even if short, should be provided for the reader who really may be interested in judging whether or not to use the thesis or article (if long) as a reference. Readers should be able to read the first and last chapters or sections and judge relevance on that basis.

Summaries should be substantive rather than procedural. An example of this point follows:

Procedural Statement:	The investigator reviewed in this chapter all of the published tests for the volleyball serve and chose the test for this study.

TABLE 3-6

DESCRIPTION OF THE VARIABLES UTILIZED IN THE STUDY

Variable	Measurement scale	Possible limits of scores from lowest to highest values	Mode of reporting measurement of variable	Possible range of scores
Meaningful- ness in life	Interval (Dependent Variable)	40-low MIL 140 = high MIL	Continuous: double or triple digit score	101
	Ordinal (Independent Variable)	40-107 = low 108-118-medium 119-140 = high	Discrete: double or triple digit score	
Locus of Control	Interval (Dependent Variable)	0 = Internality 40 = Externality	Continuous: double or single digit score	41
	Ordinal (Independent Variable)	0-6 = low 7-9 = medium 10-above = high	Discrete: single or double digit score	
Sex-role Orientation	Nominal	*Medians*: $M = 4.95^{a}$ $F = 5.15^{a}$ Therefore: -above M and above $F =$ -above M and below $F =$ -above F and below $M =$ -above M and below $F =$	Discrete: Androgynous Masculine Feminine Undifferentiated	121 121 121
Kind of participant	Nominal	Group membership	Athlete/non- athlete	1 or 2

[a]Medians of the present study

Substantive Statement: After a careful review of all of the published
                           tests for the volleyball serve, the investigator
                           chose the Thorpe-West Accuracy and Veloc-
                           ity Test for Beginners.

The first statement simply says something was done. The reader
knows nothing about what was concluded. The second statement tells the
reader that the test chosen appeared to be superior after a careful review.

Discussion

Whether or not there is a discussion is a preference which may depend
somewhat upon the amount of discussion which has occurred in previous
chapters. The discussion referred to here is a discussion of the entire
study, rather than one of findings, literature, or procedures. This discussion would be one of a reflective nature.

Some questions that might be addressed are the following:

1. What have I learned?
2. What is the most important finding?
3. What practical application can be made of this study?
4. What would I do differently if I were just beginning the study?
5. Why did I obtain the results I did?
6. Do my results compare favorably with similar studies?
7. What is the next step?

The discussion is one part of the study where the writer can editorial-
ize, fail to use referencing if he/she wishes, and philosophize. He or she,
however, while being somewhat informal must, nevertheless, still use formal English.

Conclusions

Conclusions differ from findings in at least four ways which are the
following:

1. Conclusions are very general.
2. Conclusions are stated as absolutes.
3. Numbers and statistics, if appropriate, are normally omitted in conclusions.
4. Whereas the point of view for findings is the past tense, the present
   tense is used for conclusions.

Examples of a comparative nature follow:

The Study	Finding	Conclusion
1. Errors in Women's Volleyball[35]	The greatest number of errors occurred for the "dig" 41%).	The most frequent errors are for the "dig."
2. Development of A Player-Coach-Interaction Inventory[36]	The reliability for the total score on the inventory for two days was $r = .87$.	The inventory has good test-retest reliability.
3. Impact of Title IX on Athletic Administrative Structure[37]	The most frequent response, when subjects were asked what kind of impact Title IX was making, was that mergers or combined programs were resulting (47%).	While Title IX does not address administrative structure, there is evidence that Title IX is having an impact in the form of the merging of men's and women's programs.

The third example contains a lengthier approach than the first two examples, especially with respect to the conclusion. Either approach is acceptable.

Recommendations

Everything on a particular subject cannot be accomplished in one study; therefore, recommendations for further study should be noted for other researchers. These recommendations should be reasonable and substantiated by some rationale. At this point in the study the student is in the throes of completion of the paper and is apt to list anything, whether the suggestion is reasonable or not.

A. Example of a poor recommendation: Repeat the study.

B. Improvement: Repeat the study after establishing the number of trials which will yield reliable performances on the batting test.

The improved statement has the rationale as to why the study should be repeated. In some cases, replications of studies are perfectly reasonable, but even then some reason to replicate exists; and this should be explained.

Summary

The final chapter should consist of a summary of the study, conclusions, and recommendations for further study. Some precedent exists also for including a discussion of the entire study in this final chapter.

OTHER PARTS OF THE REPORT
AND SUGGESTIONS

Other parts of the report include the front matter and the appendix(es). The suggestions offered in this section may save the investigator time and grief in completing the study.

Other Parts

If the report is for a thesis or dissertation it will include the following front matter:

Title Page
Approval Sheet
Dedication (optional)
Acknowledgments
Table of Contents
List of Tables (if appropriate)
List of Figures (if appropriate)

This suggested order may vary from one university to another, and certain other inclusions such as an abstract or a vita in the front or end matter might be required.

After the final chapter, certain additional sections are reasonably standard. The bibliography or reference list should follow the final chapter. If using APA style the reference notes should follow the final chapter, and the reference list would follow the reference notes. The writer must refer to the particular style manual in use for details on these sections.

The appendixes follow next and may be organized separately, thus using A, B, C, etc. to differentiate one from the other, or all of the material may be placed in one appendix. The decision to have more than one appendix is determined partially by length and similarity of materials. If the appendix has a considerable number of entries, and some categories of materials can be identified, it is probably best to separate the appendixes. If the writer has only two or three items, it would be unnecessary to separate them even though they be of a different nature.

Some typical types of material that appear in the appendix are the following:

Raw data
Statistical formulas
Sample problems
Computer programs
Computer outputs
Questionnaires
Tests or other written instruments
Score sheets
Floor diagrams
Pictures
Graphs
Directions
Letters
Interviews
Records

Whether to place an item in the body of the text or in the appendix is a matter of choice which should be guided by ease of understanding on the reader's part. A statistical formula in common usage, for example, would not add anything to reading the analysis of data in most cases. If the study, however, were focused on a discussion of alternate formulas for the same statistic, the formulas would best be placed in the body of the text within the discussion.

Suggestions

1. Keep all old copy until everything is approved or accepted.
2. Keep an extra copy of everything.
3. Send copies through the mail return-receipt-requested (certified mail).
4. Date all copies and revisions.
5. Number all pages whether a rough draft or a final draft.
6. Ask for a sample of a typist's work before making a contract.
7. Clarify agreements about payment, corrections, etc. before employing the typist.
8. Read the first chapter as soon as it is typed in order the judge the number of errors and quality of the work before proceeding further.
9. Have a substitute typist in place if deadlines could become a problem.
10. Reduce long tables through a copy machine that has that function.

11. The student researcher should submit the outline for the chapter along with the draft. If it is a second draft, the first draft bearing the adviser's corrections should be resubmitted for the adviser's convenience in determining how the student has dealt with the corrections. This procedure tends to ensure consistency in corrections required and causes fewer changes. It is also time saving for an adviser to see what he/she recommended in the last reading.

12. Prepare time tables for completing the report.

13. If data get old, the point of view for the analysis and conclusions will have to be changed. For example, a qualifying clause such as the following may be necessary: "At the time of the collection of the data . . . ." Conclusions should still be stated in the present tense, but the writer and the reader must understand that the state of affairs now may well be different from what it would have been when the data were collected. It is difficult to deal with a change in point of view. It is best to write the paper in as close proximity in time to the collection and analysis of data as is possible.

Summary

The titles and contents of the introductory chapter vary greatly. The specific contents generally include introductory statements, a need for the study, a statement of the problem, purposes, definitions, delimitations, and limitations.

The review of literature is complex and usually lengthy. It, therefore, requires good organization. That organization is predominantly a matter of preference. Relatedness of the topics must be carefully considered in order not to become buried in extraneous material.

Initial reading of a browsing nature is necessary prior to developing the outline. As reading continues a working bibliography should be developed from many indexes which are available in all academically-oriented libraries. An ERIC search should be considered for its thoroughness and economy.

The manner of note-taking is extremely important and will determine how much retracing of steps is required. Cards or sheets may be used and should be referenced accurately and be correlated to the outline. Pages should be carefully noted on the cards or sheets. Paraphrasing is more practical than quoting except for exceptional passages which might lose their impact if summarized or reworded.

A final step in writing the review of literature should be to criticize the completeness of the source materials. Good distribution of types of sources is essential.

For many writers this is the most difficult chapter to write. It need not be with good organization and systematic research techniques.

A chronological, dated account of all procedures may be used to formulate the outline for the chapter. The contents vary and are a matter to be dealt with individually. Most studies have preliminary and actual procedures. Asking a colleague to react to the completeness of the procedures stated, with a view toward duplication, is recommended.

Some convention exists for reporting statistical data. Tables are used normally and are introduced, follow as soon as possible, and are then discussed. Some nonstatistical data also may be presented in tables or figures. Figures are handled in the same way as tables. Summary tables offer a concise way of synthesizing large amounts of data or even material of a nonstatistical nature.

The final chapter should consist of a summary of the study, conclusions, and recommendations for further study. Some precedent exists also for including a discussion of the entire study in this final chapter.

Other parts of the report include the front matter, the bibliography or reference list, and the appendix(es). Suggestions for expediting the work with one's adviser and typist were enumerated in the preceding section. In general they urged caution in disposing of material, meticulousness in making and keeping agreements, and an encouragement to move quickly to finish the work before the data might get old.

SUGGESTED PROJECTS

1. Locate in the library the *Encyclopedia of Educational Research*. Cite one entry on a topic of interest. Make a note card and a bibliographical reference card according to the style manual of your choice.
2. Locate the periodical *Completed Research in Health, Physical Education and Recreation*. Do the same as for Number 1.
3. Write a statement of a problem.
4. Make an outline for a Need for the Study. Designate headings.
5. Write the Need for the Study.
6. State purposes for a study in the form of objectives, questions, and hypotheses.
7. State delimitations and limitations for a study.
8. Make an outline for a Review of Literature. Designate headings.

9. Write a skeletal review of literature and demonstrate use of appropriate authoritative sources.
10. Make a list of procedures in chronological order.
11. Make a list of hypothesized outcomes.
12. Have a colleague check your review of literature for style and grammar.

REFERENCE NOTES FOR CHAPTER III

[1] John W. Best, *Research in Education*, 4th ed. (Englewood Cliffs, NJ: Prentice-Hall, Inc., 1981), p. 376.

[2] David H. Clarke and H. Harrison Clarke, *Research Processes in Physical Education, Recreation and Health* (Englewood Cliffs, NJ: Prentice-Hall, Inc., 1970), p. 435.

[3] Carter V. Good, *Essentials of Educational Research*, 2nd ed. (New York: Meredith Corporation, 1972), p. 433.

[4] Stephen Isaac and William B. Michael, *Handbook in Research and Evaluation*, 2nd ed. (San Diego, CA: Ed ITS Publishers, 1981), p. 221.

[5] Fred N. Kerlinger, *Foundations of Behavioral Research*, 2nd ed. (New York: Holt, Rinehart and Winston, Inc., 1973), pp. 694-5.

[6] Louise H. Kidder, *Research Methods in Social Relations*, 4th ed. (New York: Holt, Rinehart and Winston), pp. 344-347.

[7] Robert M. W. Travers, *An Introduction to Educational Research*, 3rd ed. (New York: The MacMillan Co., 1969), p. 376.

[8] Deborah L. O'Hare, "Batting Performance With a Standard and an Angular Bat" (Master's thesis, Southern Illinois University at Carbondale, 1982), p. 3.

[9] Jeanne Marie Suellentrop, "A Variation of Russian Downhill Sprint Training for Selected College Students" (Master's thesis, Southern Illinois University at Carbondale, 1979), pp. 3-4.

[10] Monica Mize, "Attitude Toward Physical Activity as a Function of Sex-Role Orientation" (Ph.D. dissertation, Southern Illinois University at Carbondale, 1979), pp. 5-6.

[11] Michael J. Kovalchik, "Grades Received by Males and Females in General Activity Classes of Physical Education" (Ph.D. dissertation, Southern Illinois University at Carbondale, 1981), pp. 4-5.

[12] Charlotte West, "Estimates of Reliability and Interrelationships Among Components of Selected Projectile Skills" (Ph.D. dissertation, University of Wisconsin, Madison, 1969), pp. 7-9.

[13] Betty L. Walters, "Response Accuracy of Female Collegiate Basketball Players in Complex Situations" (Master's thesis, Southern Illinois University at Carbondale, 1978), p. 5.

[14] Jose R. Ferrer, "Errors Which Terminate Play in Women's Competitive Volleyball" (Master's thesis, Southern Illinois University at Carbondale, 1981), p. 6.

[15] Alice E. Kildea, "Meaningfulness in Life, Locus of Control, and Sex-Role Orientation of Selected Female Athletes and Non-Athletes" (Ph.D. dissertation, Southern

Illinois University at Carbondale, 1979), p. 16.

[16] Robert P. Anthony, "Running Death," paper prepared for PE 530, Southern Illinois University at Carbondale, Spring, 1982.

[17] Suzan Kinn McDonald, "The Frequency of Occurrence and Effectiveness of Serves in Racquetball" (Master's thesis, Southern Illinois University at Carbondale, 1979), p. 6.

[18] McDonald, pp. 6-7.

[19] *Encyclopedia of Educational Research* (New York: American Educational Research Association, MacMillan Co., 1939 to date).

[20] *Review of Educational Research* (Washington, D.C.: American Educational Research Association, 1931 to date).

[21] American Alliance for Health, Physical Education, and Recreation, *Research Quarterly* (Reston, VA: AAHPERD, 1930 to date).

[22] Research Council of AAHPER, "The Contributions of Physical Activity to Human Well-being," *Research Quarterly*, 31 (May, 1960).

[23] Research Council of AAHPER, "Skill Learning and Performance," *Research Quarterly*, 43 (October, 1972).

[24] American Alliance for Health, Physical Education, Recreation, and Dance, "Fiftieth Anniversary Issue," *Research Quarterly for Exercise and Sport*, 51 (March, 1980).

[25] Dept. of Health, Education and Welfare and National Institute of Education, *ERIC Manual* (Washington, D.C.: National Institute of Education).

[26] Leesa Jan Barnard, "Demographic Characteristics of Successful Student Teachers in Physical Education" (Master's thesis, Southern Illinois University at Carbondale, 1981), pp. 60-61.

[27] Jose Acero, "Relationship Between Ball Velocity and Effectiveness of the Serve in Volleyball" (Master's thesis, Southern Illinois University at Carbondale, 1983), pp. 40-41.

[28] Suellentrop, p. 58.

[29] Beth A. Wood, "Job Satisfaction in the Departments of Physical Education, Art, Health Education, and Zoology" (Master's thesis, Southern Illinois University at Carbondale, 1983), p. 75.

[30] Kildea, p. 127.

[31] Mize, pp. 96-97.

[32] Ferrer, p. 56.

[33] Kildea, p. 105.

[34] Kerlinger, p. 697.

[35] Ferrer, pp. 68, 78.

[36] Pamela R. Medford, "The Construction of an Inventory for Measuring Player-Coach Interaction" (Master's thesis, Southern Illinois University at Carbondale, 1980), pp. 67, 78.

[37] Barbara Derouin, "Administrative Structure of Athletic Departments and the Impact of Title IX" (Master's thesis, Southern Illinois University at Carbondale, 1981), pp. 67, 82.

Chapter IV

BASIC STATISTICS

INTRODUCTION

STATISTICAL procedures are concerned with the collection, classification, description, and interpretation of data through numerical properties of samples and/or populations. Glass and Stanley[1] referred to the popular attitude toward statistics and described it as a mixture of "awe, cynicism, suspicion, and contempt." They also suggested that persons beginning the study of statistics should realize that nonsense can be expressed as readily verbally as quantitatively. Correcting a negative attitude about statistics is best accomplished through understanding basic statistics and their practical applications in giving meaning to numerical data.

This chapter is devoted to the practical use of basic and widely used statistics which are well within the grasp of all researchers, whether they be undergraduate students or senior professors. The chapter contains definitions, sampling procedures, descriptive techniques and applications, inferential statistics and applications, and a summary.

DEFINITIONS

1. *Population*: An aggregate of subjects or units (finite and infinite)

2. *Samples*: A subgroup drawn by some specific method from the population

3. *Estimate*: A property of a sample drawn from a population (Estimates in statistics are indicated by Roman letters.)

4. *Parameter*: A property descriptive of the population (Greek letters are indicative of parameters.)

55

5. *Variable*:   A property such as sex, intelligence, skill, fitness, age, etc.

6. *Continuous Variable*:   A variable with an infinite series of values which are capable of any degree of subdivision, such as height, weight, times, etc.

7. *Discrete Variable*:   A variable which is not continuous and may have specific values only, for example the number of children in a family, numbers on dice, etc.

8. *Nominal Variable*:   A property used for placing objects or members of a group into classes

9. *Ordinal Variable*:   A property which permits rank ordering of the objects or members of the group.

SAMPLING PROCEDURES

Widely used sampling procedures include the simple random, stratified random, proportional stratified, and cluster samples.

Simple Random

A simple random sample is accomplished by drawing names or numbers from the population so that being included in the sample is by pure chance. Other methods include using an alphabetized list and selecting, for example, every *n*th subject or using a table of random numbers (Table 4-1, Appendix A.[2] When using the table of random numbers, for example, to select a sample of 5 from a population of 20, read 2-digit numbers from 01 to 20. One may enter the table at any point. In this example, however, let us enter at the first number in the upper left corner. The first number is 03; therefore, subject number 3 is selected. The next 2-digit number which is 20 or under, reading horizontally, is 11, then 04, 08, 17 (line 3). Notice 08 appeared twice in line 2 but had already been drawn so was passed over. Reading line 1 again, if we had been looking for 5 subjects out of a list of 200, we would have read 3-digit numbers. In this case we disregard the spaces between the columns and read the first number as 039, the next numbers as 911, 046, 193, 176, etc. Numbers 39 and 46 would be chosen and so on until 5 numbers of size 200 or smaller had been selected. The use of a table of random numbers gives the best assurance of independence and lack of bias.

Stratified Random

The stratified random sample involves protecting some characteristic or property in the sample. If it is important to have both sexes, for example, represented equally in a sample, we could order the population by sex, drawing first one sex, then the other. If an equal number of males and females existed in the population, no further calculations would be necessary. If, however, there was a disproportionate number of one sex, we would want to protect that proportion in the sample so that the sample accurately resembled the population.

Proportional Stratified

Let us say that from a population of 20 (8 females and 12 males) we wish to draw a sample of 6. We would use the following problem in proportions to calculate the correct number for each sex:

Female = 8
Male   = 12

$$\frac{F}{6} = \frac{8}{20} \qquad\qquad \frac{x}{6} = \frac{8}{20} \text{ (cross multiply)}$$

$$20x = 48 \qquad\qquad\qquad 6.0 \text{ Total}$$
$$x = 2.4 \text{ Females} \qquad\qquad \underline{-\ 2.4 \text{ Females}}$$
$$3.6 \text{ Males}$$

Since we cannot have part of a person, we would round and choose 2 females and 4 males. The proportion is not exact because in the population females constitute 8/20 or 40 percent, whereas in the sample they constitute 1/3 or 33.3 percent. The situation is unavoidable. Stratifying has this associated problem and also at least one other. When stratifying for one variable, assumptions of random appearance of other variables or properties may be violated. If we were interested in the sexes and wanted to study differences in motor ability, for example, stratifying by sex may destroy the assumption that motor ability is randomly distributed between the sexes; therefore, the null-hypothesis of no difference would be biased.

Cluster

When random sampling is impractical, researchers may resort to the use of cluster sampling. This technique may introduce a serious limitation on the inferences which can be made about the population. For example, if we wished to study the motor ability of the school children in Illinois, it would be impractical to test all of the children. It would, likewise, be impractical to go to every school; so we may decide to select schools (clusters) randomly for inclusion. The problem with this procedure is the risk of geographic influence and socioeconomic status on motor ability. Failure to consider these two factors, and possibly many others, can lead to false conclusions.

For additional information on stratification and sampling, in general, see Ferguson.[3] Problems increase when other than random sampling is used. Some problems can be overcome by increasing the sample size. See Isaac and Michael[4] for a comprehensive, but concise, discussion of estimating the sample size required for various magnitudes of population proportions.

SAMPLING ERROR

Sampling error is the difference between the population value and the sample value for the same variable using the same statistic. The population value is usually not known in practical situations, and so is estimated from the sample value. The following explanation may serve to clarify sampling error.

Let us suppose that we have a population of 12 children and wish to demonstrate the concept of sampling error with scores that they have made on some skill test. Obviously with only 12 cases, sampling would not normally be necessary, but we can illustrate the point here in a practical way (Table 4-2).

TABLE 4-2

SCORES FOR THE POPULATION OF 12 CASES

2	3	5	6	7	8	9	10
		5	6		8		
			6				

If we use a drawing procedure and then number the subjects according to their being drawn to form four groups, or samples, from four draws, we would have a facsimile of the following: (Table 4-3).

TABLE 4-3

SCORES AND MEANS BY GROUP AFTER RANDOM DRAWING

Ss. No.	Scores Group 1	Ss. No.	Scores Group 2	Ss. No.	Scores Group 3	Ss. No.	Scores Group 4
1	6	4	6	7	2	10	5
2	9	5	8	8	8	11	3
3	5	6	10	9	7	12	6
	20/3 = 6.67		24/3 = 8.00		17/3 = 5.67		14/3 = 4.67

Grand Mean = 20 + 24 + 17 + 14 = 75
75/12 = 6.25

In Table 4-3, notice that the group means of 6.67, 8.00, 5.67, and 4.67 only approximate the grand or total mean of 6.25. If we drew again, the groupings would be different again. The probability, then, that the sample mean will be identical to the population mean is remote, but one can readily see by this example that increasing our sample size from three to six would also increase our chances that six people represent 12 better than three.

The standard error is a statistic for estimating error attributable to sampling as opposed to measuring the entire population, and it can be calculated mathematically. Prior to introducing that formula, we should consider two other related concepts, those of the standard deviation and the variance.

Standard Deviation

The standard deviation is a statistic which expresses variability about the mean, or average score. It relates to the normal curve and is a way of interpreting one's position in a group. For all practical purposes, three standard deviation units above the mean and three below the mean will encompass all of the scores made in a distribution.

The normal curve and the corresponding standard deviation units are shown in Figure 4.1.

The interpretation of the standard deviation is quite simply to add to or subtract from the mean whatever score unit is reported to be the standard deviation (*s*). Thus, with a mean of 20 and a standard deviation of 2, the score which is located at an *s* of +1.0 would be 22. The score of 18 would be at the −1.0 *s*. See Figure 4-1 for additional score units.

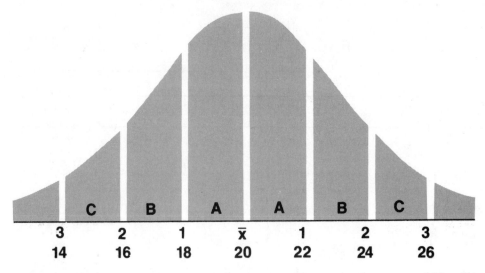

C	B	A	A	B	C	
3	**2**	**1**	**x̄**	**1**	**2**	**3**
14	**16**	**18**	**20**	**22**	**24**	**26**

Figure 4-1. Normal curve, standard deviation units, and percentages for a mean of 20 and a standard deviation of 2.

Percentage of Scores for Each Area	*Percentage of Scores for Each Area* × 2
A = 34.13%	A = 68.26%
B = 13.59%	B = 27.18%
C = 2.14%	C = 4.28%
	99.72%

The range of scores is the highest score minus the lowest score plus one. If the range divided by the standard deviation is less than 2.5 or greater than 5.5, it is probable that a computational error has been made.[5]

The standard deviation may be 2 passes, 6 inches, 3 baskets, 10 pins, or any number in any score unit. Logic should be applied, however, to the answer. The foregoing rule for dividing the range by the standard deviation is a mathematical approach. Some logic would indicate that if a group had a mean score of 4 baskets and a standard deviation of 2 and the Range was observed to be 3, something would definitely be wrong. The following figure illustrates how that curve would be impossible (Figure 4-2 on following page). The range would have to be 13 for the mean and standard deviation to have been correct; and if negative scoring was indicated on the curve but negative scoring was not possible on the test, then some error would have to exist in the computation(s).

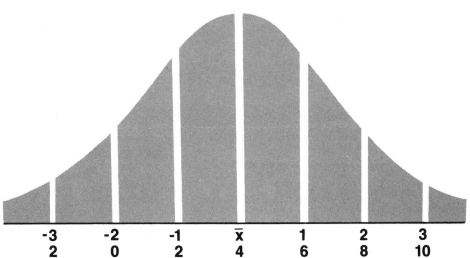

-3	-2	-1	x̄	1	2	3
2	0	2	4	6	8	10

Figure 4-2. Normal curve and standard deviation units for a mean of 4 and a standard deviation of 2.

A computationally simple formula for deriving the standard deviation is the following:[6]

$$s = \sqrt{\frac{N\Sigma X^2 - (\Sigma X)^2}{N(N-1)}}$$

Let us use group 1 from Table 4-3 to illustrate the computation of the standard deviation with this formula:

	X Scores	*X²* Squared Scores	
Ss 1	6	36	
Ss 2	9	81	$n = 3$
Ss 3	5	25	$n - 1 = 2$
	20	142	
	Sum of Scores	Sum of Scores Squared	
	ΣX	ΣX^2	

Substitution is as follows:

$$s = \sqrt{\frac{3(142)-(20)^2}{3(2)}}$$

$$s = \sqrt{\frac{426 - 400}{6}} = \sqrt{\frac{26}{6}} = \sqrt{4.33} = 2.08$$

A rough check on the $\dfrac{\text{Range}}{s}$ **is:** $\dfrac{\text{Range}}{s} = \dfrac{5}{2.08} = 2.40$

The previous calculation plotted on the normal curve would be as follows (Figure 4-3).

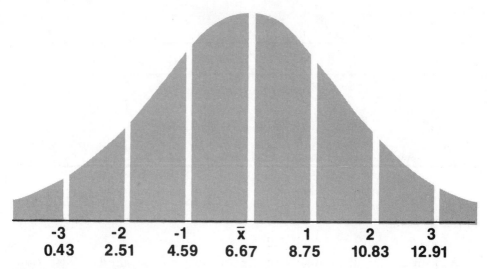

	-3	-2	-1	x̄	1	2	3
	0.43	**2.51**	**4.59**	**6.67**	**8.75**	**10.83**	**12.91**

Figure 4-3. Normal curve and standard deviation units for a mean of 6.67 and a standard deviation of 2.08.

Variance

Like the standard deviation, the variance is an expression of deviations from the mean; however, the variance is calculated by adding together the squares of the score deviations from the mean. The variance is the square of the standard deviation. Refer to the sample problem for the standard deviation and note that at the point where we have $\sqrt{4.33}$ we actually have the variance. When we extract the square root, we have the standard deviation. Both the standard deviation and the variance are very useful measures of variation in further computations.

STANDARD ERROR

With an understanding of the standard deviation and variance, it is now possible to return to the discussion of sampling error and the statistic for its calculation. Recall Table 4-3. Four samples of the finite population of 12 subjects yielded four sample means. If we simply consider these four means as we would consider any other set of four scores and calculate their standard deviation, we have the standard error. It can be shown (but will not be done here) that the standard deviation of the sample distribution in the example of the four groups is given by:

$$s_{\bar{x}} = \frac{s}{\sqrt{N}}$$

where s = standard deviation in the sample,

N = the size of the sample, and s_x is the symbol for the standard error of the means.

It can be seen that the standard error of the mean is directly related to the standard deviation of the population and is inversely related to the size of the sample. As the size of the sample increases, the standard error decreases.

The following example will clarify the relationship between the sample standard deviations, size of N, the population standard deviation, and, therefore, the standard error resulting.

The standard deviation for group 1 in Table 4-3 has already been calculated to be 2.08. Using the same procedures, the standard deviations for groups 2, 3, and 4 are 2, 3.2, and 2.3, respectively. The population standard deviation is 2.34 and corresponds reasonably well except for group 3. In most situations, we never know the population standard deviation, since if we did, there would be no need to sample.

Using the sample standard deviations and N's to estimate the standard deviation of the sample means (standard error), we obtain:

Formula: $\dfrac{s}{\sqrt{N}}$

Group 1 $\quad \dfrac{2.08}{\sqrt{3}} = \dfrac{2.08}{1.73} = 1.20$

Group 2 $\quad \dfrac{2.00}{\sqrt{3}} = \dfrac{2.00}{1.73} = 1.16$

Group 3 $\quad \dfrac{3.21}{\sqrt{3}} = \dfrac{3.21}{1.73} = 1.86$

Group 4 $\quad \dfrac{2.33}{\sqrt{3}} = \dfrac{2.33}{1.73} = 1.35$

If we were to increase the sample size to six with the same sample standard deviations, we would reduce the standard error in the following way:

Group 1 $\quad \dfrac{2.08}{\sqrt{6}} = \dfrac{2.08}{2.45} = 0.85$

Group 2 $\quad \dfrac{2.00}{\sqrt{6}} = \dfrac{2.00}{2.45} = 0.82$

Group 3 $\dfrac{3.21}{\sqrt{6}} = \dfrac{3.21}{2.45} = 1.31$

Group 4 $\dfrac{2.33}{\sqrt{6}} = \dfrac{2.33}{2.45} = 0.95$

To summarize the discussion of the standard error, the reader is reminded that an inspection of the means in Table 4-3 would indicate that group 2 was quite disparate from the population, whereas consideration of the variances places group 3 in the same circumstance. It is, therefore, obvious that both means and variances must be considered simultaneously in order to predict the statistics of the population.

The rest of this chapter is devoted to a discussion of the most basic and widely used descriptive and inferential statistics that are within the grasp of a beginning researcher. For the more sophisticated statistical tools the researcher should consult a knowledgeable person in that area and a complete book on statistics.

DESCRIPTIVE STATISTICS

Included in descriptive statistics are the use of averages, graphs, scattergrams, percentages, percentiles, standard deviations, standard scores, and other nonparametric procedures. In this section only standard scores and the correlation coefficient will be considered in detail.

Standard Scores

Standard scores provide a means of interpreting unlike scales on the same scale. For example, when tests are measured in unlike units, such as "feet" on one test and "time" on another, or even when two tests are measured in the same way but have different standard deviations, standard scales serve as a common denominator. The most basic of standard scores is the Z score, upon which all other standard scores are based.

Z Score

The Z score is a transformation of a raw score and is an interpretation of that score in standard deviation units. In other words, a Z score of $+1.0$ means that the raw score was located at the $+1.0$ standard deviation. A Z of -2.0, likewise, would mean that the raw score was 2 standard deviations below the mean.

Once the mean and standard deviation of a distribution are known, the computation of a Z score is quite simple. The following sample problem will illustrate this point:

If the mean is 5 and the standard deviation is 4, Z scores would be the following for raw scores of 9 and 3.

$$Z = \frac{X - \bar{X}}{s}$$ where $X =$ any score, $\bar{X} =$ the mean, and $s =$ the standard deviation

For the score of 9: $Z = \dfrac{9 - 5}{4} = \dfrac{4}{4} = 1.0$ and

For the score of 3: $Z = \dfrac{3 - 5}{4} = \dfrac{-2}{4} = -0.5$

Since Z scores may involve negative numbers, many test users prefer T-scores which are always positive.

T-Score

The T-score has a practical range of from 20-80 and is computed from the following formula:

$$T = 10Z + 50$$

or to utilize the complete formula, it would be:

$$T = 10 \times \left(\frac{X - \bar{X}}{s}\right) + 50$$

For the raw scores of 9 and 3, then T would be the following:

$$T = 10 \times \left(\frac{9 - 5}{4}\right) + 50$$
$$T = 10 \times \ (1) + 50$$
$$T = 60$$

and

$$T = 10 \times \left(\frac{3 - 5}{4}\right) + 50$$
$$T = 10 \times \left(\frac{-2}{4}\right) + 50$$
$$T = 10 \times \ (-0.5) + 50$$
$$T = 45$$

Relationship of Z to T

Plotting Z and T scores on the same scale offers a clear presentation of their relationship. See Figure 4-4.

The Z and T scores are exactly comparable, but some researchers find T scores more practical because they are always positive, whereas Z scores involve negative numbers. The T score has a mean of 50 and an s of 10, whereas the Z score has a mean of 0 and an s of $+1.0$.

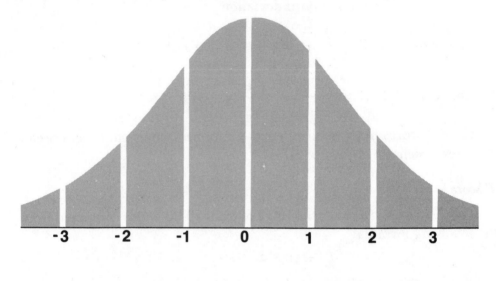

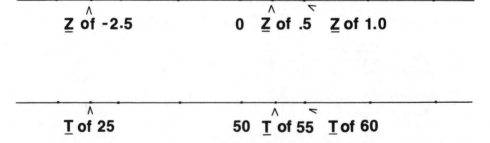

Figure 4-4. Plotting of Z and T on the same scale with the standard deviation units.

The Correlation Coefficient

The correlation coefficient is a statistic which is used to express the relationship between two variables or observations. The symbol r is used for the coefficient and ranges from $+1.0$ (a perfect relationship) to -1.0 (also perfect, but inverse).

If, for example, two persons scored at a basketball game and never disagreed on the points made, the *r* would be + 1.0. If they sometimes disagreed, the + 1.0 would change in the direction of zero. A zero correlation would indicate that they rarely agreed.

If four people took a a basketball shooting test twice and perfectly reversed their performance from one test to the next, the *r* would be − 1.0 (still perfect). The scores might look like this:

Test 1	Score	Test 2	Score
Ss1	10	Ss1	1
2	8	2	5
3	5	3	8
4	1	4	10

It is rare in most situations to obtain a coefficient of + 1.0 or − 1.0 and never possible to obtain an *r* of greater than + 1.0 or − 1.0. When this occurs, there is an error in the computation.

Expectancy for r's

Certain events are more repeatable than others; and when this is the situation, we expect high relationships. For example, the following variables would normally yield high *r*'s:

1. Two persons independently scoring the number of baskets made
2. Two persons independently grading a true-false test
3. Two persons independently scoring a game of bowling
4. Two persons independently scoring an end in archery
5. I.Q. score on two successive days

Variables which would be quite less repeatable than the foregoing examples are the following:

1. Two persons independently scoring an essay exam
2. Two judges independently judging the same dive
3. Two judges independently rating a person's golf swing
4. One's putting performance on two successive days

The two variables are usually referred to as *x* and *y*; and when *x* and *y* correspond very closely, a high *r* is the result. When the association appears random and unpredictable, there is usually a very low *r*.

Standards for Size and Direction of r

Safrit[7] suggested that in the interpretation of the correlation coefficient there should be concern for two aspects—the size and the sign. The size indicates the degree of relationship, and the sign indicates the type of relationship (+ or −). Safrit also gave some suggestion for the classification of r's as to high, moderate, and low. They are the following:

$r = +1.00$	perfect positive relationship
$r = +0.82$	high positive relationship
$r = +0.23$	low positive relationship
$r = 0$	no relationship
$r = -0.43$	moderate inverse relationship
$r = -0.90$	high inverse relationship
$r = -1.00$	perfect negative relationship

Barrow and McGee[8] also suggested standards for interpretation as follow:

Coefficients	Validity	Reliability and Objectivity
.95 to .99	excellent	excellent
.90 to .94	excellent	very good
.85 to .89	excellent	acceptable
.80 to .84	very good	acceptable
.75 to .79	acceptable	poor
.70 to .74	acceptable	poor
.65 to .69	questionable (except for very complex tests)	questionable (except for groups)
.60 to .64	questionable	questionable (except for groups)

In some cases the direction of r is predictable; in others it is not. For example, when two variables are measured in the same units, we expect a positive correlation. When they are measured in different units, we sometimes expect a negative r. The following examples will illustrate the point:

Variables	Expectancy (+ or −)
1. Time and distance	−
2. Rank in tournament and test performance when high score is desirable	−
3. Day 1 with Day 2 test scores	+
4. Day 1 odd scores with Day 1 even scores	+
5. Time in a dash with rank in the finish	+

Notice that when the preferred scores are the following, the expectancies for r are:

Preferred Scores	Expectancy (+ or −)
high score with high score	+
high score with low score	−
low score with high score	−
low score with low score	+

Uses of the Correlation Coefficient

From these examples several uses of the correlation coefficient are apparent: for estimating the objectivity of scoring, judging, rating, etc.; for estimating the reliability of measures; for estimating statistical validity; for prediction; and for the study of relationships which might later lead to prediction. Consult a measurement text for more detailed discussions of these measurement concepts.

Pearson's r

Karl Pearson developed the method of correlation most widely used today—the Pearson product-moment method. This method utilizes raw scores which include two observations per subject usually referred to as *x* and *y* observations. A sample computation follows in the next section.

SAMPLE COMPUTATION (PEARSON'S R)

$$\text{Formula: } r = \frac{N\Sigma XY - [(\Sigma X)(\Sigma Y)]}{\sqrt{[N\Sigma X^2 - (\Sigma X)^2][N\Sigma Y^2 - (\Sigma Y)^2]}}$$

X	Y	X²	Y²	XY
5	1	25	1	5
10	6	100	36	60
5	2	25	4	10
20	9	150	41	75
ΣX	XY	ΣX²	ΣY²	ΣXY

$$r = \frac{3(75) - [(20)(9)]}{\sqrt{[3(150) - (20)^2][3(41) - (9)^2]}}$$

$$r = \frac{225 - 180}{\sqrt{[450 - 400][123 - 81]}}$$

$$r = \frac{45}{\sqrt{[50][42]}} = \frac{45}{\sqrt{2100}} = \frac{45}{45.8} = .98$$

Extraction by Hand for Square Root

$$\begin{array}{r}
4\;5.\;8 \\
\sqrt{2100.00} \\
16 \\
\end{array}$$

$$85 \mid \begin{array}{l} 500 \\ 425 \end{array}$$

$$908 \mid \begin{array}{l} 7500 \\ 7264 \\ \hline 236 \end{array}$$

Degrees of Freedom $(df) = n - 2$

Pictorial Representation of r

The values of x and y can be plotted, and the strength of the relationship can be judged from the plots (scattergram). When the relationship is perfect, all plots fall on a straight line. The diagrams which follow illustrate both the perfect positive and perfect negative plotted coefficients.

PERFECT r's AS PLOTTED BY SAFRIT

Individuals	One-handed Push Shot	Two-handed Push Shot
A	12	10
B	10	8
C	8	6
D	6	4
E	4	2

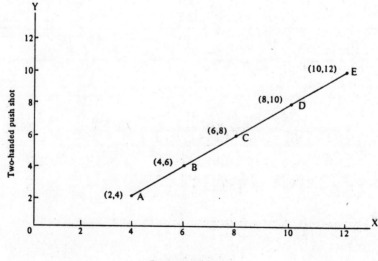

One-handed push shot

r = +1.00

PERFECT r's AS PLOTTED BY SAFRIT

Individuals	One-handed Push Shot	Two-handed Push Shot
A	12	2
B	10	4
C	8	6
D	6	8
E	4	10

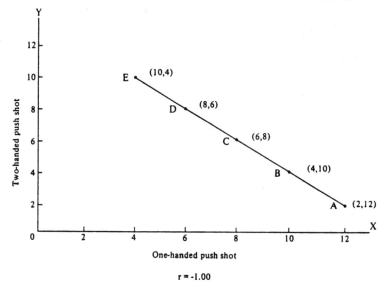

r = -1.00

As the relationship becomes less than perfect and moves toward zero, the plots begin to appear to move from the imaginary straight line that would exist if the relationship were perfect; and finally at an *r* of zero there is no pattern, and the plots appear to be randomly scattered. See the preceding diagrams and Figure 4-5 from Safrit.[9]

It can be noted that while the plots are represented by different scores on *x* and *y*, the relationship is still perfect because the absolute and relative changes are the same. The scores in column form are the following:

	r = + 1.00		*r* = − 1.00	
	x	*y*	*x*	*y*
Ss 1	12	10	12	2
2	10	8	10	4
3	8	6	8	6
4	6	4	6	8
5	4	2	4	10

The absolute change for each subject was uniform, and each person retained her or his relative position in the group. In other words, the same change existed between the observations and among the subjects.

Figure 4-5 illustrates the usefulness of pictorial representations in estimating quickly the strength of a relationship by merely plotting the scores when *n* is small. Another approach to the quick estimation of *r* is the use of Spearman's Rho.

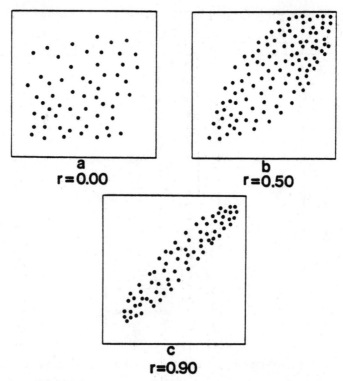

Figure 4-5. *r*'s of zero, .50, and .90 as plotted by Safrit.

Spearman's Rho

The symbol for Spearman's Rho is *ρ*, and Rho utilizes ranked data. Whereas dealing with raw scores and the use of Pearson's *r* is more precise than transforming raw scores to ranked data, occasionally there is no satisfactory continuous measure for some trait such as merit performance, but persons could be put in rank order with respect to their relative position in the group. Rho assumes equal distance between the ranks, but in actual practice this is seldom the true state of affairs. For example, when the following scores on a basketball test are changed to ranked data, notice the difference between subjects on raw scores and the difference between them on the ranked scores:

	Raw Scores	*Ranked Scores*
Ss 1	25	1
2	23	2
3	18	3
4	17	4

The rank differences are each 1, but the raw score differences are 2, 5, and 1, meaning that there is actually more variation in the performances than the ranked data show.

In ranking data, it is not always possible to give a clear rank. Two or more subjects might be tied in score. In that case tied ranks may be used. The following example will illustrate the point:

	Raw Scores	Ranked Scores
Ss 1	25	1
2	22	2.5
3	22	2.5
4	20	4
5	18	5

The correct procedure for determining the tied ranks is to add the two ranks (in this case 2 and 3) and divide the summed ranks by the number of persons tied. This example results in ranks of $2 + 3 = 5/2 = 2.5$.

SAMPLE COMPUTATION (SPEARMAN'S RHO)

The formula for Rho is the following:

$$\rho = 1 - \frac{6\Sigma d^2}{N(N^2 - 1)}$$

	Ranked Scores	Ranked Scores	Deviation d	d^2
	x	y		
Ss 1	5	4	1	1
2	2	1	1	1
3	3	3	0	0
4	1	2	− 1	1
5	4	5	− 1	1
				$\Sigma d^2 = 4$

$$\rho = 1 - \frac{6\,(4)}{5\,(25\text{-}1)}$$

$$\rho = 1 - \frac{24}{5\,(24)}$$

$$\rho = 1 - \frac{24}{120}$$

$$\rho = 1 - .20$$

$$\rho = 0.80$$

The ρ in this case is positive, but Rho, like Pearson's r, has a range of from $+1.0$ to -1.0 and is interpreted in the same way.

Significance of the Correlation Coefficient

Prior to judging the size of the coefficient, and therefore the strength of the relationship, whether or not the coefficient is significantly different from zero must be determined. Once it is established that a relationship exists, comment upon its appropriateness can be considered. Otherwise, no interpretation, other than there is no relationship, can be made. Because the size of n is integrally related to the statistical significance of r and ρ, large sample sizes enhance one's chance of observing significant relationships. Separate tables are used for determining the significance of r and Rho. The degrees of freedom (df) for $r = n - 2$. The table for interpreting Rho utilizes the number of subjects (n). Consult a textbook on statistics for these tables.

Summary — Descriptive Statistics

Widely used descriptive statistics in research include Z and T scores and the correlation coefficient. Z scores range from -3.0 to $+3.0$ and are expressed in standard deviation units. T scores are Z scores transformed to have a mean of 50, an s of 10, and a practical range of 20-80.

Pearson's r is used to express the relationship between two variables, x and y. The range for r is -1.0 through zero to $+1.0$. Standards for interpreting the strength of the relationship must be considered in relation to the kind of variables under study. Certain r's are expected to be higher than others. The direction of r is also important when judging an r. Certain r's are expected to be positive, while others should be negative.

The correlation coefficient is used for estimating objectivity, reliability, and validity. It is also used for prediction and the study of relationships in general.

Two approaches to computation are Pearson's r and Spearman's Rho. Pearson's r uses computation from raw data, while Rho is used with ranked data. Both are interpreted in the same way, but r is more accurate than Rho. Rho is, however, more computationally simple. Pictorial representations provide ease of judging the strength of relationships for both r and ρ.

Prior to placing judgment on any r or ρ, statistical significance should be determined. If the coefficient is not significant, no further statements can be made, except that there is no relationship.

INFERENTIAL STATISTICS

Included among the more widely used inferential statistics are Chi Square (X^2), the *t*-tests, the Analysis of Variance (ANOVA), multivariate analysis of variance (MANOVA), and regression analysis. This section will be limited to discussion of those techniques.

Chi Square

Chi square (X^2) is a statistic which is utilized to determine whether or not frequencies of occurrences are greater or less than would be the result of chance or sampling error. It is a test of differences between observed and expected frequencies.

If we were to flip a coin 12 times, the expected frequencies for heads and tails would be 50-50 or six heads and six tails. If we roll dice, each of the six numbers should appear (under probability theory) an equal number of times. When large departures from these expected frequencies occur we may wish to use Chi Square to test whether or not the disproportion(s) are statistically significant.

Sample Computation 1 with Known Expectancy

The following sample computation is for tossing a coin 12 times to observe the occurrence of heads and tails.

Toss a coin 12 times

	O	E	$O - E$	$(O - E)^2$	$\dfrac{(O - E)^2}{E}$
Heads	10	6	4	16	$16/6 = 2.67$
Tails	2	6	-4	16	$16/6 = 2.67$
					$\Sigma = 5.34 = X^2$

O = observed frequencies
E = expected frequencies X^2 = chi square

The determination of whether or not X^2 is significant in this problem will be discussed later in this section.

Sample Computation 2 Without Known Expectancy

When expectancy is not known because the literature offers no information on the subject, and clear cases such as with coins or dice do not exist, the expected frequencies may be calculated. The following example might be an attempt to answer the following research question:

Do a proportionate number of basketball, volleyball, and softball participants place in high, medium, and low motor ability groups? The example is for 34 basketball participants, 32 volleyball participants, and 22 softball participants.

The table of frequencies for X^2 is as follows:

Numbers in the lower right are expected f's.

	High		Medium		Low		Totals
B.B.	6		10		18		34
		11.6		9.3		13.1	
V.B.	20		8		4		32
		10.9		8.7		12.4	
S.B.	4		6		12		22
		7.5		6.0		8.5	
Totals	30		24		34		88

Grand Total

The marginal totals are used to determine the expected frequencies. For example, the number of basketball participants in the high group should be:

$$\frac{34 \times 30}{88} = 11.6$$

The number of basketball participants in the medium group should be:

$$\frac{34 \times 24}{88} = 9.3$$

From these f's X^2 is computed as follows:

		O	E	O – E	$(O – E)^2$	$(O + E)^2$
B.B.	H	6	11.6	– 5.6	31.36	2.70
	M	10	9.3	+ .7	.49	.05
	L	18	13.1	+ 4.9	24.01	1.83
V.B.	H	20	10.9	+ 9.1	82.81	7.60
	M	8	8.7	– .7	.49	.06
	L	4	12.4	– 8.4	70.56	5.69
S.B.	H	4	7.5	– 3.5	12.25	1.63
	M	6	6.0	0.0	0.00	.00
	L	12	8.5	+ 3.5	12.25	1.44

$$\Sigma = 21.00 = X^2$$

$$df = \text{N categories } - 1 \text{ or } 9 - 1 = 8$$

Determination of Significance

Sample Computation 1 — In order to determine whether 5.34 is significantly different from what was expected we must consult a table for the critical values of chi square. Table 4-4 (Appendix A). The table is read by determining the degrees of freedom (df) and reading across until the predetermined alpha level (level for rejection of the null-hypothesis) is found. The number at the point of intersection of the df and the alpha level is the figure required for X^2 to be significant. In the foregoing example the following numbers would be required:

With a df of 1 which is determined by the number of categories minus 1 ($2 - 1 = 1$) and alpha levels of .10, .05, .02, and .01, X^2 would have to equal or exceed 2.71 (.10), 3.84 (.05), 5.41 (.02), and 6.64 (.01) in order to be significant. Since a X^2 of 5.34 was obtained we could only claim significance at the .05 level. If the .05 level had been the *a priori* decision for alpha, we would then go back to the table of frequencies to attempt to determine where the disproportions existed.

If the .02 or .01 level had been selected, and X^2 was found to be nonsignificant, further discussion of differences among the frequencies would be inappropriate since numerical differences are somewhat meaningless once statistical nonsignificance has been established.

Sample Computation 2—In the second example with degrees of freedom equal to N – 1 or 9 – 1 = 8, X^2 would have to equal or exceed the following numbers for the .10, .05, .02, and .01 levels: 13.36, 15.51, 18.17, and 20.09; so X^2 is significant.

While it is tempting to look at the results and then establish the alpha level, this is an erroneous procedure. The decision with respect to alpha should be based upon the seriousness of the consequences of a Type 1 error. For example, if dosages of potentially lethal drugs are being studied and five of 100 subjects die, the researcher should not be comfortable with rejection of the hypothesis that the drug is not lethal because 95 subjects lived. A much smaller alpha should have been used. If, on the other hand, two classes learn to bowl by different teaching techniques and one is shown to be superior, the risk does not seem as great. It would be important in the latter case, however, to know that while one method was superior, both groups learned to bowl.

The discussion of beta levels is beyond the scope of this text. The interested reader is referred to texts dealing solely with statistics for additional material on this topic.

t Tests

Among the *t* tests, the *t* test for independent samples and the *t* test for correlated samples are probably the most widely used. These are presented in the following section.

t Test for Independent Samples

The *t* test for independent samples is a technique used to compare the means of two samples. The numbers of subjects in the two groups need not be equal. Let us say, for example, that from a population of 20 professional golfers we wish to compare the number of putts over par in a single round for players who have had more than 10 years in playing the circuit with those who have had fewer than 10 years. In a group of 20 players and with easy access to the data it would be unnecessary to sample, but for purposes of this example we will draw two samples (five from each group) and assume that through some unforeseen occurrence one player from Group A (under 10 years) withdraws from the tournament. We then have four in Group A and five in Group B.

Sample Calculation

Group A (fewer than 10 years)			Group B (10 or more years)	
x	x^2		x	x^2
			3	9
9	81		1	1
4	16		5	25
5	25		1	1
2	4		4	16
$\Sigma = 20$	$\Sigma X^2 = 126$		$\Sigma = 14$	$\Sigma X^2 = 52$

Variance is calculated by formula introduced earlier in this chapter:

$$s^2 = \frac{N\Sigma X^2 - (\Sigma X)^2}{N(N-1)}$$

Utilizing the preceding data we obtain the following variances for Groups A and B:

Group A

$$s^2 = \frac{4(126) - (20)^2}{4(3)}$$

$$s^2 = \frac{504 - 400}{12}$$

$$s^2 = \frac{104}{12} = 8.7$$

Group B

$$s^2 = \frac{5(52) - (14)^2}{5(4)}$$

$$s^2 = \frac{260 - 196}{20}$$

$$s^2 = \frac{64}{20} = 3.2$$

The t formula can now be utilized. It is:

$$t_i = \frac{\text{mean A minus mean B}}{\sqrt{\begin{array}{l}\text{The estimate of the}\\\text{standard error for}\\\text{both groups combined}\end{array}}}$$

OR

$$t_i = \frac{\bar{X}_A - \bar{X}_B}{\sqrt{\dfrac{s_A}{N_A} + \dfrac{s_B}{N_B}}}$$

OR

$$t_i = \frac{5 - 2.8}{\sqrt{\dfrac{8.7}{4} + \dfrac{3.2}{5}}} = \frac{2.2}{\sqrt{2.2 + 64}}$$

$$t_i = \frac{2.2}{\sqrt{2.84}} = \frac{2.2}{1.7} = 1.29$$

INTERPRETATION OF SIGNIFICANCE

The degrees of freedom are N-2 and we must use this df to determine if the t of 1.29 is significant statistically. The df's are $4+5=9-2=7$. See Table 4-5, Appendix A.

For 7 df t's of 1.90, 2.37, and 3.50 would be required for the .10, .05, and .01 levels respectively. We must, therefore, accept the null-hypothesis of "no difference" and refrain from any temptation to talk about 5 being greater than 2.8. Notice in Table 4-5 that if we had had an infinite number of subjects, we still could not have claimed a difference at the .10, .05, or .01 level. In this case the differences between the means in relation to the estimate of the standard errors of the samples was not great enough to warrant rejection of the null-hypothesis. The t ratio obtained must be larger as alpha becomes smaller (reading the table from left to right) and may be smaller as n increases (reading the table from top to bottom) in order to observe statistically significant differences.

The beginning researcher is cautioned not to become disappointed when the null-hypothesis is accepted. It is just as important to know that there is no difference as it is to know that there is a difference. We may naturally experience some disappointment when our research hypotheses are not true because they were our best guesses about the data, and we were wrong (at least at a certain level of probability). There is always the chance that we really were right since our results could have been in that

10, 5, or 1 time in 100 as a result of sampling error or chance. The assurance of internal validity is our best protection in finding our research hypotheses to be true and the desired outcome for our statistical hypotheses becoming reality.

t Test for Correlated Samples

When a single group is tested twice, the *t* test for correlated samples is utilized to determine any significance in differences between the means of the two observations. This statistic is designed primarily for looking at change between two sets of scores.

SAMPLE CALCULATION

Ss	Pretest	Posttest	Difference (D)	D²
1	7	10	− 3	9
2	9	8	+ 1	1
3	4	6	− 2	4
4	6	7	− 1	1
	26	31	Σ = − 5	Σ = 15

The formula for the *t* test for correlated samples is the following:

$$t_c = \frac{\Sigma D}{\sqrt{\dfrac{[N\Sigma D^2 - (\Sigma D)^2]}{N-1}}}$$

OR

$$t_c = \frac{-5}{\sqrt{\dfrac{[4 \times 15 - (-5)^2]}{3}}}$$

OR

$$t_c = \frac{-5}{\sqrt{60-25}} = \frac{-5}{\sqrt{11.67}} = \frac{-5}{3.41}$$

$$t_c = -1.47 \quad \text{with } df = N-1 \text{ or } 3$$

Using the same table (Table 4-5, Appendix A) for interpreting t_c as that for interpreting t_i but using $df = N - 1$ rather than N − 2 we read that the values of 2.35, 3.18, and 5.84 are required for significance at the .10, .05, and .01 levels respectively. With the t_c of − 1.47 we conclude that no significant change occurred between the two observations.

Because t_c is nonsignificant the negative sign has no meaning. Had t_c been significant, we would have concluded that at the chosen alpha level the subjects improved on the second test. A negative sum of D means higher scores on test 2 than on test 1 for the group.

Analysis of Variance

The analysis of variance is a technique for identifying the sources of variance in experimental data. In its simplest form which is referred to as the one-way classification, the two sources of variance considered are the "between group" and the "within group" variances. These factors are used to form an F ratio which is a simple proportion between the two factors. The F ratio is then tested for significance by use of a table for certain probability levels.

One-Way ANOVA

The one-way classification indicates that the subjects are categorized by only one independent variable. For example, we may wish to know the answer to the following research question: "Do basketball, volleyball, and softball participants score equally well on a certain motor ability test?" Since we have more than two groups the t test is not applicable so we use analysis of variance (ANOVA) to test the differences among the means of three sport groups. Sport is the independent variable of classification.

A sample calculation for this problem follows:

SAMPLE CALCULATION[10]

	Basketball	Volleyball	Softball
Ss 1	4	10	20
2	6	12	20
	Σ = 10	Σ = 22	Σ = 40
	X = 10/2 = 5	X 22/2 = 11	X 40/2 = 10

The mean for the entire group (Grand Mean or M) = $4 + 6 + 10 + 12 + 20 + 20 = 72/6 = 12$.

The F ratio in this model is comprised of the following:

$$F = \frac{\text{Between group variance estimate}}{\text{Within group variance estimate}}$$

We must now calculate these variance estimates as follows:

Calculation of Between-group Variance Estimate

Treatment	Ss	Treatment Mean	Grand Mean	$\bar{x} - M$	$(\bar{x} - M)^2$
A	1	5	12	−7	49
	2	5	12	−7	49
B	3	11	12	−1	1
	4	11	12	−1	1
C	5	20	12	+8	64
	6	20	12	+8	64

$$\Sigma = 228$$
(Sum of Squares Between Groups)

Calculation of Within-group Variance Estimate

Treatment	Ss	x	$(x - \bar{x})$	$(x - \bar{x})$	$(x - \bar{x})^2$
A	1	4	4 − 5	+1	1
	2	6	6 − 5	+1	1
B	3	10	10 − 11	−1	1
	4	12	12 − 11	+1	1
C	5	20	20 − 20	0	0
	6	20	20 − 20	0	0

$$\Sigma = 4$$
(Sum of Squares Within Groups)

The final step is to formulate our variance table:

Source	Sum of Squares	df	Variance Estimates	F
Between	228	2	114.00	85.7
Within	4	3	1.33	
Total	232	5		

```
                    85.7
          1.33 | 114.00 0
                 1064
                 ----
                  760
                  665
                 ----
                  950
                  931
                 ----
```

df Between = N groups − 1
df Within = NSs − N groups

INTERPRETATION OF SIGNIFICANCE

The F table (Table 4-6, Appendix A) is organized for utilizing two kinds of degrees of freedom rather than one as was used for chi square and the t tests. The numerator (between) in the foregoing problem has 2 df and the denominator (within) has 3. The total df is N – 1 or 5. To read the ANOVA table (Appendix A), read from left to right and find the df for the numerator. Then read down to find the df for the denominator. At the intersection of these two points, the lower number of the two in each set will be the F required for significance at the .01 level. The upper number represents the F required for the .05 level. Complete tables are available but are not necessary for this discussion.

In the sample problem for $df_n = 2$ and $df_d = 3$ with an F ratio of 85.7 we conclude that there is a difference among the means of the three sport groups since F's of 9.55 (.05 level) and 30.81 (.01 level) were required; and the F obtained is quite in excess of those required.

Now we know that there is significance, but actually we know only that the highest mean differs from the lowest mean. In the sample problem we know only that 20 differs from 5. We now need to apply one of the post hoc tests for "multiple comparisons" in order to determine which other means may differ. In other words, we must determine whether 20 differs from 11, and 11 differs from 5.

A number of methods exist for making these multiple comparisons. See Edwards[11] for information concerning the use of these procedures. Regardless of which technique is preferred, all were developed for avoiding the problems created by using a series of t tests to test two means at a time since this procedure introduces the probability of increasing Type I errors. Computer packages such as the Statistical Analysis System (SAS)[12] and others contain subroutines for multiple comparisons.

From a practical point of view, a significant F tells us that the samples, whereas hypothesized to be from the same population, were not; and that something about one or more samples is different from another (always at a certain level of probability, of course). The expectancy of F is 1.0, and when F becomes significantly greater than 1.0, we become suspect (maybe even hopeful) that some experimental variable is affecting the size of the F ratio. If the beween group variance were equal to the within group variance we would obtain $F = 1.0$. When the between group variance is greater than the within group we obtain an F of greater than 1.0, and when this difference increases dramatically, we observe statistical significance.

Two-Way ANOVA

As more complex research questions are asked, the statistics for answering those questions must also become more complex. Such is the case with the analysis of variance involving two independent variables rather than one. Using the same example of the six basketball, volleyball, and softball participants let us suppose that we wished to know if sex had any effect on how the participants scored on the motor ability test. We are now asking two questions: (1) Do the means of the three sport groups vary? and (2) Do the sexes differ in motor ability within these three sports?

The two questions are called the main effects questions. A diagram for this model is as follows:

	Basketball	*Volleyball*	*Softball*
Male	Motor Ability Scores	Motor Ability Scores	Motor Ability Scores
Female	Motor Ability Scores	Motor Ability Scores	Motor Ability Scores

With only six subjects in the original one-way example, it would not be possible to use only six subjects in this two-way example. Some cells might have no subjects, or some might have one; and neither zero nor one subject per cell allows the calculation of variance; so we must increase the sample. The calculation of complex models is beyond the scope of this text, but a discussion of the theory follows.

MAIN EFFECTS AND INTERACTION EFFECTS

In the foregoing pictorial representation of the two-way model the main effects are sport and sex. Since there are two sexes and three sports, we refer to this as a 2×3 model, and to the interaction effect as sex by sport. The research questions are the following:

Main Effects:
1. Do the means of the motor ability scores differ for the three sports groups?
2. Do the means for the sexes differ in motor ability?

Interaction Effect: Are any differences which might exist between the means of the main effects of the same or similar magnitude for both factors?

When the main effect of sex is tested, sport is disregarded; and when the main effect of sport is tested, sex is disregarded so that only the means in question are compared. These comparisons could be accomplished for sex through a t test for independent samples, since there are only two groups for sex. With three groups for Sport, the t test is inappropriate. Even if the model were a 2×2 (two levels of sex and two levels of sport), more information can be gained by using the ANOVA because the interaction effect cannot be tested by t_i.

The test for interaction is a test to determine whether the lines connecting the plotted means are parallel. In their most dramatic lack of parallelism the lines usually cross; however, the reader is cautioned to remember that interaction may be quite significant without the lines crossing.

For purposes of illustrating the point consider the following example:

	Basketball	Volleyball	Softball
Female	$\bar{X} = 12$	$\bar{X} = 16$	$\bar{X} = 8$
Male	$\bar{X} = 14$	$\bar{X} = 18$	$\bar{X} = 10$

See Figure 4-6 in this chapter for a plot of these means and their connecting lines. The figure illustrates parallelism and no interaction.

Now consider the plots and connecting lines for the following means:

	Basketball	Volleyball	Softball
Female	$\bar{X} = 18$	$\bar{X} = 4$	$\bar{X} = 8$
Male	$\bar{X} = 2$	$\bar{X} = 20$	$\bar{X} = 10$

See Figure 4-7 in this chapter for these illustrations.

In the example of no interaction (Figure 4-6) which follows, notice that females are always lower than males, whereas in interaction examples A and B in Figure 4-7 of this chapter, females are higher in basketball while males are higher in volleyball and softball. When the interaction effect is significant, reversals such as these are typical. In example C (Figure 4-7) the lines are not parallel but also do not cross. The test for interaction is not only for parallel lines but also is one for determining if differences in the main effects are of the same magnitude at all levels of the other factors. If the differences are uniform, the lines cannot interact. When the differences are disproportionate but the lines do not interact such as in example C, significant interaction, nevertheless, results. The implication is that with additional sampling at a point in time, lines may interact.

Because significant interaction must be interpreted in relation to the main effects, many statisticians suggest that the test for interaction be considered first. Others recommend that the main effects be tested first but be reconsidered if the interaction is significant. Either approach may be used, but both effects must be considered in the relationship of one to the other.

N-Way ANOVA

When the researcher is interested in more than two independent variables, models of higher order in the analysis of variance may be devised. Using the example of motor ability as the dependent variable and sports and sex as the independent variables we could add any number of additional independent variables, but let us just add one (I.Q.) for purposes of illustration:

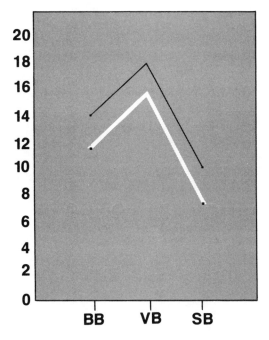

Figure 4-6. Plotting of means—no interaction.

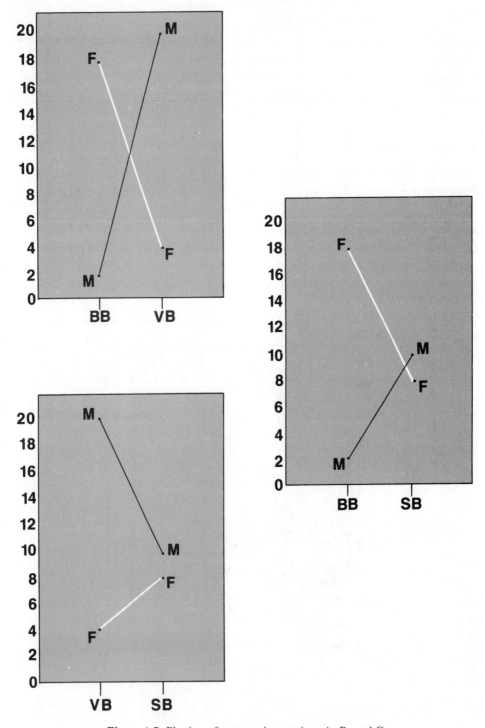

Figure 4-7. Plotting of means—interactions A, B, and C.

		Basketball	Volleyball	Softball
High I.Q.	Female	Motor Ability Scores	Motor Ability Scores	Motor Ability Scores
	Male	Motor Ability Scores	Motor Ability Scores	Motor Ability Scores
Low I.Q.	Female	Motor Ability Scores	Motor Ability Scores	Motor Ability Scores
	Male	Motor Ability Scores	Motor Ability Scores	Motor Ability Scores

The research questions have now been expanded to include whether or not I.Q. has any effect on any of the other factors. This is a $2 \times 2 \times 3$ model, and will involve both first order (2-way) and second order (3-way) interactions.

Be aware of the necessity for increasing the sample size to avoid small n's in the cells in these n-way models. The discussion of higher order interaction is beyond the scope of this text, although it is not beyond the grasp of beginning researchers with a basic knowledge of statistics.

Multivariate ANOVA

Multivariate ANOVA (MANOVA) is a technique which permits the same analyses already described for ANOVA but involves the utilization of more than one dependent variable simultaneously. It is obvious that MANOVA and higher order ANOVA are techniques which are impractical through hand calculations. The use of computers in research will be discussed later in a separate section in Appendix G. In our foregoing example of the motor ability scores for sport, sex, and I.Q. groups we might hypothetically expand the ANOVA model to a MANOVA model as follows:

		Basketball	Volleyball	Softball
High I.Q.	Female	Motor Ability Scores + Motor Educability Score	Motor Ability Scores + Motor Educability Score	Motor Ability Scores + Motor Educability Score
	Male	Motor Ability Scores + Motor Educability Score	Motor Ability Scores + Motor Educability Score	Motor Ability Scores + Motor Educability Score
Low I.Q.	Female	Motor Ability Scores + Motor Educability Score	Motor Ability Scores + Motor Educability Score	Motor Ability Scores + Motor Educability Score
	Male	Motor Ability Scores + Motor Educability Score	Motor Ability Scores + Motor Educability Score	Motor Ability Scores + Motor Educability Score

Regression Analysis

Regression analysis is a technique which utilizes vector algebra and is the generalized case of the analysis of variance. Since vector computations are beyond the scope of this text, only the general theory of the regression approach will be presented here. For details concerning computational procedures see Kelly, Beggs, and McNeil.[13]

Full and Restricted Models Approach

Regression analysis is concerned with using predictor variables to explain variation in some criterion variable. The criterion variable is expressed as $\tilde{Y}^2$, and we will use P to refer to the predictor(s). An underlying assumption is that the criterion variable is in the form of continuous data, and that the predictors may be continuous or discrete. To illustrate the point let us return to our example of three groups of sport participants and their motor ability scores. The motor ability score is the criterion variable, and the sport groups are the predictors. The full model might be represented as follows:

Motor Ability Score	=	Basketball Participants (P_1)	+	Volleyball Participants (P_2)	+	Softball Participants (P_3)	+	Error (E)
$\tilde{Y}^2$	=	(P_1)	+	(P_2)	+	(P_3)	+	(E)

We then set about placing restrictions on the full model by eliminating first one group and then another. If by eliminating the softball group we find a serious reduction in explaining the total variance in the motor ability scores overall, then we conclude (at a certain probability level, of course) that softball participants accounted for a great amount of variance and might therefore be different from the other groups. If, however, the amount of variance in the criterion was not significantly reduced by removing the softball group, then we would conclude that they did not add much and that they were like everyone else.

To test the difference which might be attributable to volleyball people we would place the softball people back in, along with the basketball people and eliminate only the volleyball group. We would then do the same for basketball.

R^2 is a symbol used to refer to a percentage of variance accounted for in the criterion variable by the predictor variable(s). Let us assume that the following example is a true representation of the percentages of variance accounted for:

Motor Ability

Score (Criterion) 100%	=	Group I Basketball 5%	+	Group 2 Volleyball 10%	+	Group 3 Softball 20%	+	Error 65%

By leaving out the softball group we would have the following:

Criterion 100%	=	Basketball 5%	+	Volleyball 10%	+	Error 85%

We would probably find that the 20 percent contributed by softball was a significant amount. Notice that "Error" must increase when one predictor is eliminated in order to balance the equation.

The example so far has dealt with the sport groups in discrete categories only. The model would be the same, and the approach would be the same if we had continuous data, such as some average experience score for each of the three groups.

In the earlier example, the research question being answered was: Does knowledge of group membership significantly explain variance in the criterion variable of their motor ability scores?

In the latter example, the research question is the following: Does knowledge of a person's experience score in basketball, volleyball, and softball significantly explain variance in the criterion variable of their motor ability scores? Another way of stating this question might be: Does experience in basketball, volleyball, and softball significantly predict a person's motor ability score?

In the traditional analysis of variance approach the independent variables are the predictor variables of the regression approach. The dependent variable in ANOVA is the criterion variable in regression analysis.

Regression significance is interpreted by an F ratio through the same procedures explained earlier for ANOVA. Whereas ANOVA focuses on differences among means, regression analysis is concerned with differences in percentages of variance in the criterion accounted for by the predictors.

Step-Wise Approach

The step-wise approach involves identification of the greatest predictor first, the next greatest second, etc. until the least predictive variable is last. The model is built progressively from greatest to least rather than by beginning with a full model and placing restrictions on it one at a time. The step-wise approach has the feature of being economical of computer time and also of rapidly providing the most parsimonious approach to prediction.

Summary — Inferential Statistics

Chi square is a statistic for determining whether certain frequencies of occurrences are greater than would be expected under normal conditions. When the probability of occurrence is not known it may be calculated.

Two types of t tests commonly used in research are the t_i test for independent samples and the t_c test for correlated samples. The t_i tells us if two groups differ whereas the t_c tells us if change occurs between observation one and observation two on the same group.

The one-way analysis of variance analyzes one independent variable in relation to one dependent variable and is appropriate for judging differences between or among two or more means simultaneously. The two-way and n-way classifications have main effects and interaction effects which answer different questions but must be interpreted within the relationship of one to the other.

Multivariate analysis of variance involves more than one dependent variable simultaneously and any number of independent variables. MANOVA is impractical through hand calculations as is the case with two-way and n-way ANOVA.

Multiple comparison techniques must be used following a significant F test to determine exactly which means differ. Performing a series of t tests leads to increased Type I errors and is not a recommended procedure.

Regression analysis is a technique for looking at percentages of variance accounted for in the criterion variable by various predictors. The full and restricted models approach and the step-wise approach may be used.

PRACTICAL APPLICATIONS OF STATISTICAL TECHNIQUES IN PHYSICAL EDUCATION SETTINGS

Both descriptive and inferential statistics are used in the studies typically reported in the literature of physical education; therefore the differences between descriptive and experimental research and between descriptive and inferential statistics should be understood before designing a study.

Difference Between Descriptive and Experimental Research

Briefly, the difference between descriptive and experimental research is that in descriptive research the investigator describes the behavior or characteritics of the subjects, or a situation, without attempting to manipulate the variables. In the case of experimental research the investigator introduces an experimental variable to observe the effects of this variable under very strictly controlled conditions. When conditions cannot be controlled, experimental research should not be attempted.

Difference Between Descriptive and Inferential Statistics

Descriptive statistics portray traits or characteristics of the subject group, whereas inferential statistics predict the similarity of the sample(s) to the parent population. Descriptive statistics are always appropriate for use in any study. Inferential statistics are truly most appropriate under the conditions of sampling, preferably simple random; however, Sage and Loudermilk[14] suggested that sample representativeness is not critical when the intent of the study is to establish variable interrelationships rather than parameter estimation.

Whereas inferential statistics were designed for use in experimental research, it is a common practice to use both inferential and descriptive techniques in either kind of research. A review of the most recent year of the *RQES* at this writing (1983) will serve to illustrate the point. Not all of the studies are reported since some did not utilize statistics. The analysis is presented in Tables 4-7 and 4-8 in Appendix A.

The author apologizes for any misclassifications which may have occurred. Some indistinctions are possible as a result of choices of words. For example, in some cases the words "informed consent" are used instead of "volunteers." In some cases the subjects are volunteers who came from some select group such as athletes, and in this case "selected volunteers" was utilized. As much consistency as possible was attempted, but some misjudgments may have occurred as a result of some of the arguments for classification being academic. See Tables 4-7 and 4-8 in Appendix A for these data.

In the foregoing analysis of the 1983 *RQES*, the 52 studies were classified as follows:

26 Descriptive
21 Experimental
 5 Other
——
52

An analysis of earlier issues would show that research in our discipline has moved from almost totally descriptive to almost equal emphasis on descriptive and experimental approaches. A more detailed discussion of the methods of research will appear in a later chapter. The topic is introduced here only as method relates to the statistics used.

Of the 52 studies analyzed, the classification of the statistics used and reported was the following:

16 Descriptive
 4 Inferential
32 Both
——
52

It is much more often the practice to use both descriptive and inferential statistics in descriptive and experimental studies. When a study is experimental but n's are unusually small, the use of inferential statistics is usually inappropriate. It leads to disappointment in not confirming one's research hypotheses in most cases.

Appropriate uses of Statistical Techniques

A general discussion of the application of the descriptive and inferential statistics discussed in this chapter will be presented first; and some actual studies from the *RQES* will be presented next, in order to give the reader some potential models for her/his own research.

General Discussion

Means and standard deviations are almost always appropriate if statistical data have been collected. Variance which is simply the standard deviation squared is also just as appropriate for describing fluctuations in performance. The standard deviation may be shown on a normal curve, whereas the variance cannot be graphically displayed. Graphs seem to help the reader who is not statistically-oriented and also are useful when numbers of subjects are insufficient, and only trends in the data can be discussed. Graphs are particularly appropriate for presenting interaction effects in the ANOVA, learning curves, pre and post test results, and performance on repeated measures in general. Scattergrams should accompany correlation procedures so that the reader can associate the concepts of the perfect line with the size of the r or Rho in question (See Figure 4-8 in Appendix B). Percentages, like means and standard deviations, are useful in most studies; but the researcher should take caution in judging these statistics at face value. Two percentages which differ numerically may well not be different statistically. Tests for statistical difference between two percentages (proportions) can be made, and chi square may also be applied for this purpose for two or more percentages.

Chi square is a test for differences among frequencies in various categories, and is useful with discrete data. The t tests (independent and correlated) provide tests between two means. For the t_i the two groups tested are not the same subjects. For the t_c one group is observed twice. The t_c is used predominantly to observe change. The ANOVA is similar to the t test in that it compares means, but ANOVA tests two or more groups simultaneously. If the ANOVA is more than a one-way comparison, a test of interaction between, or among, two or more variables provides additional information. Multiple comparison techniques identify where, among significantly different means, the actual significance exists.

MANOVA should be used for two or more dependent variables simultaneously observed in relation to the independent variables. Regression analysis is appropriate for explaining variance in a criterion variable. Predictors are set equal to the criterion measure, and the researcher's task is then to reduce the error which causes the prediction to be imperfect.

Actual Studies from RQES

The reader is referred to the foregoing analysis of the 1983 *RQES* in which the techniques used are identified. Often the title of the article does not identify for the reader the analysis used because usually some statistics are subsidiary to the primary statistical technique used in the analysis. Refer to Tables 4-7 and 4-8 in Appendix A and the *RQES* for 1983 for an example of this point.

TABLES FOR PRESENTING STATISTICAL DATA

Tables 4-9 through 4-24 which appear in Appendix A will furnish the reader with examples for presenting tabular data. The sources for these tables are referenced in reference notes 15 through 30 of this chapter.

SUMMARY OF STATISTICS CHAPTER

This summary is meant to be procedural because substantive summaries have followed the two major sections, descriptive and inferential statistics. In this chapter basic descriptive statistics were introduced, and examples and calculations were presented. The same was true for inferential statistics. An analysis of the *RQES* for 1983 was included for the purpose of relating descriptive-experimental research and descriptive-inferential statistics. Suggested projects followed at the end of the chapter. Answers to the problems are provided in Appendix B.

SUGGESTED PROJECTS

1. Calculate the standard deviation of the four sample means by using the 12 cases from Table 4-3, but use a table of random numbers to obtain the four sample groups. First pick group 1, then group 2, etc. Use the scores associated with the S_s as numbered in Table 4-3.
2. Calculate the standard deviation of the population of 12 cases from Table 4-3. Using this standard deviation, calculate the standard error of the mean.
3. Answer the following questions:
   a. Would you rather score a Z score of 2 or a T score of 75?
   b. Would you rather score a Z score of -1.0 or a T score of 30?
   c. Would you rather score a Z score of -2.5 or a T score of 25?
4. Plot the data on a scattergram.

		x	y			x	y
S_s	1	6	12	S_s	4	2	4
	2	4	10		5	3	7
	3	1	2		6	4	8

Estimate Pearson's *r* from the scattergram.

5. Calculate Pearson's *r* for the data in #4.
6. Calculate Spearman's Rho for the following data:

	x	*y*
S, 1	6	12
2	4	2
3	1	4

7. Calculate chi square for the following data:

Preference for Sports
Involving Vertigo

	SEX	
YES	2	8
NO	9	1

8. Calculate t_i for the following data:

Scores

Group 1		Group 2	
Ss 1	10	Ss 1	2
2	6	2	4
3	8	3	3
		4	1

9. Calculate t_c for the following data:

	Test 1	*Test 2*
Ss 1	10	20
2	5	8
3	2	9

10. Calculate a one-way ANOVA for the following data:

Gr. 1		Gr. 2		Gr. 3	
Ss 1	10	Ss 4	2	Ss 7	1
2	7	5	4	8	3
3	8	6	2	9	5

[ANSWERS ARE PROVIDED IN APPENDIX B.]

REFERENCE NOTES FOR CHAPTER IV

[1]Gene V. Glass and Julian C. Stanley, *Statistical Methods in Education and Psychology*, (Englewood Cliffs, NJ: Prentice-Hall, Inc., 1970), p. 1.
[2]Glass and Stanley, pp. 510-512.

[3] George A. Ferguson, *Statistical Analysis in Psychology and Education*, (New York: McGraw Hill Book Company, 1966), Chapter 9.

[4] Isaac and Michael, pp. 191-193.

[5] Helen M. Walker and Joseph Lev, *Elementary Statistical Methods*, Revised ed. (New York: Holt, Rinehart and Winston, 1958), p. 98.

[6] Ferguson, p. 67.

[7] Margaret J. Safrit, *Evaluation in Physical Education*, 2nd ed. (Englewood Cliffs, NJ: Prentice-Hall, Inc., 1981), p. 31.

[8] Harold M. Barrow and Rosemary McGee, *A Practical Approach to Measurement in Physical Education*, 3rd ed. (Philadelphia: Lea & Febiger, 1979), p. 38.

[9] Safrit, pp. 32-34.

[10] Francis J. Kelly, Donald L. Beggs, and Keith McNeil, *Research Design in the Behavioral Sciences Multiple Regression Approach* (Southern Illinois University Press: Carbondale, Illinois, 1969), pp. 47-53.

[11] Allen L. Edwards, *Experimental Design in Psychological research*, Revised edition (New York: Holt, Reinhart and Winston, 1964), pp. 136-157.

[12] A. J. Barr, J. H. Goodnight, and J. T. Helwig, *A User's Guide to S.A.S.* (Raleigh, N.C.: S.A.S. Institute, M.C., 1982).

[13] Kelly, Beggs, and McNeil.

[14] G. Sage and S. Loudermilk, "The Female Athlete and Role Conflict," *RQES*, 50 (March, 1979):88-96.

[15] Derouin, p. 41.

[16] Kildea, p. 117.

[17] Barrow and McGee, pp. 168-169.

[18] Acero, p. 112.

[19] O'Hare, p. 52.

[20] Kildea, p. 113.

[21] Kildea, p. 115.

[22] Ferrer, p. 58.

[23] *RQES* 47 (May, 1976):293.

[24] Mize, p. 74.

[25] Kildea, p. 118.

[26] Kildea, p. 120.

[27] Suellentrop, p. 48.

[28] *RQES* 54 (September, 1983):258.

[29] Mary Jane Dameron, "Augmented Knowledge of Results as an Aid to the Development of Velocity in the Overhand Softball Throw," (Master's Thesis, Southern Illinois University at Carbondale, 1971), p. 53.

[30] Walters, p. 88.

Chapter V

TECHNIQUES FOR GATHERING DATA

THE TECHNIQUES (tools) for gathering data are numerous; therefore only the most widely used will be discussed here. Statistical techniques have been presented in a separate chapter because each specific statistical technique requires extensive explanation. The bibliographic, questionnaire, interview, observation, attitude scale, rating scale, and six other techniques will be discussed in this chapter.

BIBLIOGRAPHIC TECHNIQUE

The bibliographic technique is essentially "library research," and is sometimes referred to as "documentary analysis." In the use of the bibliographic technique the application of internal and external criticism is always assumed. (Refer to the definitions in Chapter I for a review of these terms.)

General Categories of Sources

Sources are generally classified as either primary or secondary. In historical research it is particularly critical that attention be given to these classifications. This is not meant to imply that it is not important to judge the relative use of primary and secondary sources in other than historical research. Primary sources are always preferable because they are judged to be most free of distortion. The child's game of "rumor" will illustrate this point.

Primary

Primary sources are generally considered to be eyewitness accounts. An article in *RQES* would be primary. A letter, speech, essay, thesis, tape, position paper, minutes from a meeting, etc. would also be primary.

Secondary

Secondary sources generally include books, abstracts, newspaper accounts, interviews with people who did not actually observe the event(s) under consideration, photographs of some original object, etc. The discussion of primary vs. secondary sources will be expanded in the section on the historical method of research.

Appropriate Types of Entries

The predominance of entries should be in the general category of primary and technically-oriented sources, but the appropriate types of entries generally include the following, not all of which are primary:

1. Books
2. Articles
3. Theses and dissertations
4. Microforms
5. Documents
6. Unpublished materials
7. Abstracts
8. Interviews
9. Conferences
10. Class notes, etc.

Steps in Collecting Bibliographic Data

If you are in a situation where the library identifies °reference librarians," it would be well worth your time to seek some advice from this person, or persons, before engaging upon a search of the literature related to your topic. In comprehensive universities the library often has an educational program in which a highly qualified reference librarian will offer a class, or classes, to acquaint the inexperienced user(s) with appropriate sources for searching a topic. It is invaluable for new students in a university to apprise themselves of opportunities to understand, from a qualified professional, the library and its referencing system in a brief period of time.

If the service previously described is not available, the student or beginning researcher should embark upon the use of the bibliographic technique alone. (It is similar to climbing Mt. Everest without a guide.)

Probably a first step would be to peruse the card catalog and the *Encyclopedia of Educational Research* in order to make a working bibliography of articles or books to be read. Other sources include the Indexes of Education and that of Periodical Literature. The abstracts from *Completed Research in HPERD*, and *Dissertation Abstracts International* are also helpful.

The two prominent cataloging classifications are the Dewey and the Library of Congress systems. They are generally the following:[1]

Dewey Decimal System

000		General references, periodicals, encyclopedias, biography
100		Philosophy, psychology
200		Religion
300		Social Sciences
	310	Statistics
	320	Political Science
	330	Economics
	340	Law
	350	Administration
	360	Welfare Assns. and Institutions
	370	Education (General)
	370.1	Theory and Philosophy of Education
	370.9	History of Education
	371	Teachers—Methods
	372	Elementary Education
	373	Secondary Education
	374	Adult Education
	375	Curriculum
	376	Education of Women
	377	Religious, Ethical Education
	378	Higher Education
	379	Public Schools (Relation of State to Education)
	379.14	School Law
	379.15	Supervision and Control
	380	Commerce, Communications
	390	Customs
400		Linguistics
500		Pure Science
600		Applied Science
700		Arts and Recreation

| 800 | Literature |
| 900 | History |

Library of Congress System

A		General Works
B		Philosophy, Religion
C		History
D		World History
EF		American History
G		Geography, Anthropology
H		Social Sciences
I		vacant
J		Political Science
K		Law
L		Education
	LA	History of Education
	LB	Theory of Education
	LC	Special forms and applications
	LD	U.S. Schools
	LE	American Education (Outside U.S.)
	LF	European Education
	LG	Asia, Africa, Oceania
	LH	School of Periodicals
	LI	vacant
	LJ	Fraternities, Societies
	LT	Textbooks
M		Music
N		Fine Arts
O		vacant
P		Language, Literature
Q		Science
R		Medicine
S		Agriculture
T		Technology
U		Military Science
V		Naval Science
W		vacant
X		vacant
Y		vacant
Z		Library Science-Bibliography

For an annotated bibliography of reference materials see Best, Chapter 9, pp. 309-369.[2] See also "A Selected Bibliography of Research Aids in Education"[3] prepared by Ruth Bauner and "A Bibliography of Physical Education and Recreation Materials"[4] compiled by Cathy Cook both for the Education/Psychology Division at Southern Illinois University at Carbondale. The bibliographic aids by Bauner and Cook appear in Appendix C.

See Chapter II in this text for further details on the use of bibliographic technique.

Judging the Adequacy of the Bibliography

The bibliography should show evidence of primary sources and scientific and technical entries in the cases of experimental and descriptive research. For other methods appropriate sources vary. These will be discussed under those various methods. Whatever the general approach (method) the reader should be convinced that the researcher is well-read and thoroughly familiar with all aspects of the topic.

QUESTIONNAIRE TECHNIQUE

The questionnaire was a much over-used tool for gathering data in the early part of the twentieth century. It still suffers somewhat from overuse in educational research but often is the most appropriate avenue for obtaining information which is available in no other form.

Definition

The questionnaire is an instrument used to seek *factual* information. It consists of a series of questions which are arranged in a logical sequence. Normally the possible answers are fixed into defined categories, but open-ended or free responses are also often used.

Characteristics of Good Questionnaires

Good questionnaires:

1. Require a minimum of time
2. Have well-constructed direct questions
3. Are used only because the data are available only through this source

4. Are used to ascertain a state of affairs or a practice in effect
5. Are used only if you have a group of interested respondents
6. Are judged partially by the percentage of return
7. Seek factual information, not opinion
8. Do not ask questions, the answers to which would place the respondent in a poor light
9. Are well organized and have a logical order to the questioning
10. Seek results that can be used
11. Are preceded by a letter with an enclosed postcard for indicating willingness to respond
12. Have been tried on a pilot group
13. State that answers will be treated impersonally and confidentially
14. Have endorsement of an adviser or professional group
15. Promise a summary, and one is delivered
16. Contain a self-addressed stamped envelope for returning the completed questionnaire
17. Have well timed arrivals: avoid Christmas or other holidays, examination periods, summer, etc.
18. Are followed up when no response is received within two weeks
19. Are addressed to a specific person
20. Show consideration for the respondent at all times
21. Have an appearance which indicates professional preparation.

Construction of Questionnaires

One of the most substantive lists of "do's" for the construction of questionnaires was suggested by Best.[5] They are the following:

1. Define or qualify terms that could be easily misinterpreted
2. Be careful in using descriptive adjectives and adverbs that have no agreed-upon meaning
3. Beware of double negatives, and underline negatives for clarity
4. Avoid the double-barreled question
5. Underline a word if you wish to indicate special emphasis
6. Use a point of reference when asking for ratings or comparisons
7. Avoid unwarranted assumptions
8. Phrase questions so that they are appropriate for all respondents
9. Design questions that will give a complete response
10. Provide for the systematic quantification of responses.

The following numbers relate to the foregoing ten points suggested by Best and offer some examples:

1. Terms which are used regularly in physical education but which do not have universally accepted meanings are words such as flick, screen, pitch, dodge, tackle, bump, shank, blitz, block, smash, press, zip, etc. Best mentioned "value" as one of those words which generally has an imprecise meaning such as in the sentence, "What is the value of your home?"

2. Descriptive adjectives such as rarely, frequently, aesthetic, and beautiful all are relative and should be placed in some definite context.

3. When a double negative is used the negative should be underlined for example: It is unwise to teach players not to use "honor calls" in volleyball.

4. The querie of two issues in one statement is a prominent mistake. Consider the following: Honor calls place an undue burden on the players, and therefore should not be used. One may agree that honor calls place an undue burden upon the player but still believe that they should be used. The reverse situations might also be true.

5. Underlining for emphasis can give added meaning to the way in which a question is read. For example, "Do you know whether the rules of volleyball allude to honor calls?" This way of stating the question is more than a casual inquiry.

6. The point of reference tends to objectify ratings. If we say, "Which errors or fouls are players capable of calling on themselves?", this may be too general. If, however, we say "In which of the following types of fouls would the referee or umpire be more able than a player to judge whether a foul occurred?" we have provided a point of reference.

7. The unwarranted assumption often emanates from the investigator's bias, or belief that certain things not substantiated are, nevertheless, true. An example of such a question is the following: Which fouls should not be placed in the category of "honor calls?" The question assumes that the respondent believes that some fouls should be "honor calls." The person who believes that none should be cannot answer. The two questions should be divided so that if the respondent believes in honor calls, he or she can then say which ones.

8. Certain words (while simple) are just not often used; and the majority of readers, or even researchers, would not find them common. Just to use one example, let us refer to a thesaurus[6] for a reasonably uncommon word: anachronism. Its synonyms are even more uncommon. They include the following:
   1. Parachronism
   2. Metachronism
   3. Prochronism
   4. Prolepsis
   The point of this example is to suggest that one must phrase the questions so that the least well-informed of the respondents will be able to answer the item.
9. When several alternative answers are possible, do not try to force one or two dichotomies. For example, if we wish to know whether or not the respondent is an athlete or not, we should leave some ground in-between such as in the following definition from the questionnaire designed by Kildea:[7]

SPORT PARTICIPATION QUESTIONNAIRE

Directions: Please check the one most appropriate response in each section.

Section I:

☐ I participate in sports every day.
☐ I participate in sports almost every day.
☐ I participate in sports occasionally.
☐ I almost never participate in sports.
☐ I never participate in sports.

Section II:

If I had to say, I consider myself:
☐ a nonathlete
☐ an athlete

Class: _____
Instructor: _____
I.D..: _____
Name: _____   Phone Number: _____

10. The tabulation sheet should be planned well in advance of the collection of data. When possible, the tabulation should be adjacent to the questions so that an early assessment of the results and a "feel for the data" can be acquired. An example follows:[8]

TABLE 5-1
SUGGESTED TABULATION FOR EARLY
VISUAL INSPECTION OF THE DATA

Suggested tabulation is:					
Q. 13 Do you believe that Title IX is having any impact on the administrative structure of athletic departments?					
YES	BBBBB[a]	LLLLL LLLLL[b] LLLLL LLLLL	SSSSS SSSSS[c] SSSSS SSSSS SSSSS SSSSS SS		N = 57
SOME	BB	LLLLL LLLLL	SSSSS SSSSS SSSSS S		N = 21
NO	—	LLLLL LLLLL L	SSSSS SSSSS SSSSS SSSSS SS		N = 33
[a] B = Big 10		[b] L = Large		[c] S = Small	

If the responses are in categories of importance, colors can be used to indicate the frequencies by category. In Table 5-1 a letter symbolism was used instead of colors.

Some other suggestions for the construction of questionnaires include the following:

1. Outline the material to be asked so that the questions proceed in a logical order.
2. Use subheadings if necessary to clarify the frame of reference if the outline is somewhat complex.
3. Test each question against the foregoing suggestions made by Best.
4. Include sample questions and specific directions.
5. Conserve space to the extent possible but allow sufficient space for obtaining complete responses.
6. Print long questionnaires and have them reduced.
7. Place your name and address for returning the completed form on each page.
8. Use the front and back of the page(s) to conserve on postage.
9. Use open-ended or free response items when the lack of prior knowledge disenables you to plan the possible categories, and categorize the data later.

10. When sending a follow-up letter, include the questionnaire again and subtly suggest that you are enclosing another because it may not have been received. This will save time in searching and will maximize your chances for getting a response.
11. If appropriate, code each questionnaire for identification, in the event that the respondent does not sign it upon returning and/or you are not able to read the postmark.
12. An excellent and detailed article by Nixon[9] outlines the mechanics for constructing a questionnaire. Refer to that source for additional suggestions.

Tables for Presenting Data from Questionnaires

Some conventional tables for presenting data from questionnaires appear in Appendix A (Tables 4-9 through 4-24).

Statistical Analysis of Questionnaires

Frequencies, percentages, means, standard deviations, and chi square are most often used to describe the results from a questionnaire. The analysis of variance may also be applied. See Ferguson[10] for a more detailed discussion on this topic.

INTERVIEW TECHNIQUE

The interview is usually considered to be an oral questionnaire; however, the interview and the questionnaire are not necessarily interchangeable. Whereas the questionnaire is fixed in terms of the questions, the interview may be structured or unstructured. The interview is valuable for obtaining information about desires, goals, values, personality, attitudes, perceptions, personal history, family life, and other types of opinion. The family history which a physician seeks on a first visit is an interview.

Although various authors refer to the interview as an oral questionnaire, it is also a generally accepted concept that the questionnaire seeks fact and that interviews are more appropriate for obtaining not only fact, but opinion; therefore, the interview may be likened also to the opinionnaire. The distinctions are not necessarily important except as they relate to the construction of the instrument, the tabulation of the data, and the quantification of the data. Factual questions are easier than opinion to deal with in all ways, but some studies require opinion; and therefore, the researcher must be prepared to solve the problems associated.

Interviews are used in guidance, therapy, and research situations with individuals or groups, but one should remember that, whereas group therapy is effective with some persons, it intimidates others.

Structured Versus Unstructured Interviews

The structured interview is one which contains the same questions posed in the same manner to everyone. It is more rigid than the unstructured, but permits a more objective analysis.

The advantage of the unstructured is that it is more flexible and that there are no restrictions on the answers. Also, opportunities to probe initial answers make this type of interview attractive, but the reader is reminded that conducting any type of interview requires considerable experience; therefore, the person not adequately trained in the interview technique should probably choose the structured form or be prepared to enroll in a course for becoming prepared.

The particular difficulties with the unstructured form are in:

1. Quantifying data
2. Preventing the emergence of irrelevant variables
3. Comparing data from one subject to another.

Advantages of the Interview

1. A higher percentage of return than with the questionnaire is typical. Normally there are fewer than 5 percent refusals.
2. The interviewer can explain the purpose better than can be done in writing.
3. No problems of literacy exist.
4. Speed can be controlled, whereas questionnaires are often answered hurriedly.
5. The person interviewed may need a personal stimulus to become involved in answering.
6. Some people do not like to write.
7. Indefinite answers and leads can be followed up.
8. The interviewer can influence attitudes on the part of the respondent.
9. Respondents cannot read through all of the questions and decide on a line of answering.
10. Questions not understood can be explained.

Disadvantages of the Interview

1. When anyone conducts an inquiry into the personal life of another, the situation becomes exceedingly more complex than can be reported in a simple way.
2. Small changes in behavior may go unnoticed but may be extremely important.
3. The interviewer must be extremely well-trained.
4. The interviewer can rarely act in the same way to each person interviewed.
5. It is difficult to quantify data.
6. The respondent may agree to be interviewed but refuse to convey the information which is sought.
7. Interviewing is an art, and few persons would have the art.
8. Several different interviewers would be necessary to eliminate possible interview bias.

Suggestions for Planning Interviews

Many carefully taken steps in preparing an interview can make it go smoothly. Only a brief list will be suggested here. For greater detail see Kidder[11] and Stewart and Cash.[12]

1. Use a list of carefully-worded questions
2. Interpret the questions but do not embellish the explanations in order to avoid leading the interviewee to a biased answer
3. Ask questions which are nonthreatening to the extent possible, at least in the beginning
4. Turn irrelevant remarks into fruitful discussion by probing
5. Precode answers so that tabulation is facilitated
6. Use a tape recorder if the respondent is comfortable with it
7. Try the interview out in a pilot study in order to assess ambiguous or inadequate questions
8. Assess the objectivity of the interviewee by comparing two persons' answers on several subjects
9. Get permission for quotes
10. Turn back questions from the respondent
11. Tread lightly on sensitive topics
12. Do not prolong the interview when the respondent seems to be tired or bored
13. Use questions of a duplicative nature, not identically worded, for a check on reliability.

Tabulation of the Interview

The interviewer must be aware of the importance of complete and verbatim reporting. In order to do this, precoded answer sheets are a must. The time consumed in writing long answers tends to make the interview "bog down" and become boring. Even when a tape recorder is used, a precoded answer sheet can facilitate the accuracy of the record; and facial expressions, which the tape recorder cannot provide, can be noted.

Statistical Analysis of the Interview

The same statistics mentioned for the questionnaire are appropriate for the interview, since the frequencies of answers in certain categories are the type of data collected through both techniques. Primarily frequencies, percentages, chi square, and the ANOVA (if n's are large) could be used.

OBSERVATION TECHNIQUE

The observation technique is an unusually convenient tool for use by the beginning researcher. It requires no approval for the use of human subjects and may even be executed without the subjects' knowledge (if appropriate and/or necessary). It is often used in combination with many other techniques and all methods of research. In recording any event, for example, the observation technique is used to obtain the score. The precise definition of the word, "observe," includes one synonym which is "to take note." If we took that definition literally we would have to realize some imbrication among the definitions of the bibliographic, questionnaire, opinionnaire, interview, etc. techniques. For the purposes of use in research, the observation implies a rigorously planned and scientifically executed technique for gathering data.

Problems to Be Considered

A major problem with the observation technique, unless carefully considered, may be poor reliability. This enigmatic situation may result from any or all of the following:

1. Inadequate sampling
2. Lack of precision in defining the behavior to be observed
3. Complexity of the method of scoring
4. Rapid and/or complex interaction being observed

5. The difference in the perspective of the observers
6. Individual differences in the degree of decisiveness of the activity of the subjects being observed
7. Observer "bias" (overweighting, timing, the halo effect)
8. Necessity for a high order of classification of behavior
9. The simultaneous observation of too many variables
10. Long periods without rest
11. Inadequate training
12. The effect of the observer upon the subjects
13. Too much acquaintance with the subjects.

Dimensions of Naturalistic Research

Kidder,[13] under the rubric of "Observational and Archival Data," discussed at length naturalistic research and identified three primary dimensions:

1. Natural behavior: a behavior that is not established or maintained for the sole purpose of conducting research.
2. Natural setting: the recording behavior in a context that is not established solely for conducting research.
3. Natural treatment: a naturally occurring incident that has some social-psychological consequences.

In the first dimension, natural behavior, the observation is of things that exist with no attempt at any kind of intervention. Observing who have "Beware of the Dog" signs on their homes or how often and how meticulously they cut their grass is an example of this kind of observation.

Natural settings include libraries, student centers, playing fields, restaurants, airports, etc. These observations center on recording public behavior.

Natural treatment involves the recording of an event in which the people would have encountered it with or without the presence of a researcher. Examples are natural disasters, riots, economic changes, and the like.

In a physical education setting, we might observe the natural behavior of dressing in appropriate gym wear. The natural setting would be the class situation (gym, field, court, etc.). We could invoke natural treatment by determining the relationship between the proper dress and grade received in the class. The foregoing example is not to suggest that this research question is terribly exciting. It merely furnishes an accurate example.

Suggestions for Conducting Observations

The following suggestions would be helpful when planning a formal observation:

1. Arrange for an appropriate group of subjects and go for "big game"
2. Make prior arrangements and obtain permission for any special conditions necessary
3. Plan carefully the length(s) of the sessions, rest periods, etc.
4. Test the physical conditions and the position of the observer(s) prior to the collection of the data
5. Define very precisely the specific behavior or activity to be observed
6. Plan carefully the recording of the observation, and consider using a tape recorder, frequency tabulations, video taping, and/or filming
7. Plan to use one or more assistants, particularly if taping is to be done, so that one person can observe and another can be concerned with the mechanics of the operation
8. Consider whether time, or periods of time, are important to note
9. Carefully delimit the scope of the observation so that the observer(s) are not encumbered with too much complex activity to be observed simultaneously
10. Train the observers carefully in more than one session until objectivity in observing the behavior specified is confirmed
11. Plan the analysis of the data prior to collecting the data.

RATING SCALE TECHNIQUE

One feature in common to all types of rating scales is that the attribute being judged is placed on a continuum of ordered categories. The types of scales vary in terms of the number of categories, the method of construction, the interpretation, the physical appearance, etc. For example, whereas the questionnaire was discussed as a separate technique for gathering data, almost all questionnaires have the rating scale built in, as is true of the interview and the observation techniques. While free responses or unstructured notations are extremely useful, continuous and discrete data provide a greater opportunity than free responses for an orderly scientific analysis.

Types of Scales

The types of scales vary considerably, and Barrow and McGee[14] dealt with this subject in considerable detail. They enumerated the following types:

1. Student-to-studet
2. Comparison
3. Graphic
4. Percentage
5. Descriptive
6. Numerical
7. Combinations of 1 through 6.

For the researcher who intends to use the rating scale as a primary means for gathering data he/she should study the reference by Barrow and McGee and the reference by Kidder.[15]

Uses of the Rating Scale

The rating scale is useful for dichotomizing behavior. It may be particularly valuable in recording the responses in questionnaires, interviews, and observations. In physical education settings we use rating scales very often in judging complex behavior for which we have no skill tests. For example, we have no objective measures for judging performance in dance, so we resort to the use of rating scales. We also have no precise tests in gymnastics, and therefore, the entire procedure of judging in gymnastics consists of a rating system. In golf, bowling, and archery we often resort to the use of ratings, although scores are possible to obtain. This is because the normal lengths of our teaching units do not provide reliable scores, with the possible exception of bowling. Ratings are also widely used to test attitudes.

Because human judgments must enter into the use of a rating scale, the disadvantages of its use must be considered. Although a scale can be made highly objective, the lack of objectivity which occurs in many situations ultimately results in poor reliability. Care must be taken in the construction and use of the rating scale in order to avoid the problems that may be associated.

Certain problems are consistent threats to reliability. Some are the following:

1. Halo effect
2. Generosity error

3. Contrast error
4. Placebo effect
5. Hawthorne effect
6. Prejudices
7. Personality conflicts
8. Imprecise descriptors

The halo effect is looking too favorably on certain subjects for one reason or another. The generosity error is one of failing consistently to use the poor end of the scale; and the contrast error is that of tending to see others in an opposite manner to that of themselves, therefore over or underestimating that particular quality in others. For example, if one is neat, he/she might be overly severe in rating another's neatness.

Steps in Construction and Use of Rating Scales

The following steps in constructing rating scales were suggested by Barrow and McGee:[16]

1. Determine the precise purpose of the rating
2. Determine the traits to be measured and propose exact definitions of those traits
3. Divide the traits into subtraits if they are too complex to deal with globally
4. Select the kinds and numbers of categories
5. Use number values, if appropriate, so that a summated single score can be obtained
6. Prepare the rating sheet.

When using ratings with more than one observer or when using several traits such as might occur in rating one's form in golf, the best estimate of that performance is the sum or average of the observers' scores on the repeated trials. In general, discarding scores leads to discrepant data.

Take seriously the previously mentioned threats to reliability. A carefully prepared, well-defined, and tested rating scale can avoid many of the problems usually associated with this kind of measurement.

Other suggestions by Barrow and McGee[17] include the following:

1. Adding to the normal scoring a "degree of assurance" rating and weighting more heavily the very sure decisions
2. Conducting the ratings during a real performance as opposed to one which is staged or is merely a practice situation
3. Rating multiple items one at a time for all subjects

4. Discussing the ratings initially to determine the sources of lack of agreement, but conducting the rest of the session independently
5. Equalizing the opponents in competitive situations so as not to create impressions that one person or group is much better or worse than they actually are
6. Training observers and practicing in situations as similar to the real situations as possible

Use of Visual Aids

When pictorial representations can be used to clarify the definitions of the various distinctions on the scale this should be done. McDonald's study involved determining the frequency of occurrence and the effectiveness of serves in racquetball.[18] Because of the speed of the ball and the small court area, racquetball is a difficult sport to observe; therefore she used diagrams for training her observers to distinguish the various serves and record them quickly. See Figure 5-1 in Appendix D for an example. Whyman[19] used stick figures to objectify her rating scale which was used by student partners to correct errors in beginning swimming. See Figure 5-2 in Appendix D. Rogers[20] employed a similar system to train raters to observe different angles of projection of the spike in volleyball (Figure 5-3, in Appendix D).

The rating scale is a useful technique which is well within the grasp of most researchers, beginning and otherwise. The statistical analysis would be similar to those suggested for the questionnaire and the interview.

ATTITUDE SCALE TECHNIQUE

The measurement of attitude is important since attitude is directly related to behavior, in most situations. Attitudes are a person's belief, posture, opinion, view, feeling, or mood toward a concept, theory, issue, or another person or persons. The problem that the researcher faces, however, is the validity of the attitude reported.

Limitations

The following are limitations that the use of attitude scales involve:

1. Attitude is difficult to describe and measure
2. The researcher is dependent upon what the subjects *say* their beliefs and feelings are

3. What one says at a given time is only an estimate of her/his attitude and what he/she really believes
4. An individual may conceal her/his real attitude
5. A person may express only socially acceptable opinions
6. A person may not know how he/she really feels about an issue
7. The person may never have considered the issue before
8. Respondents may not have had a personal experience with the attitude in question
9. Behavior is not always a true expression of feeling
10. Social custom may produce artifacts in the data.

Methods Used

Best[21] listed four methods generally used to obtain measures of attitude:

1. Asking the subjects directly how he or she feels about a topic
2. Asking the subjects to check statements
3. Asking the subjects to indicate the degree of agreement or disagreement with the statements
4. Inferring attitude from one's reaction to projective devices.

Two very popular procedures are the Thurstone and the Likert techniques. The Thurstone technique utilizes the system of agreement or disagreement with certain statements, and the Likert approach consists of asking subjects to choose a value on a scale. A newer but also popular technique is the semantic differential approach. The forced choice comparison also has had wide usage.

Thurstone

A number of statements which express viewpoints are assembled. They are then submitted to qualified judges who rate the validity of the statement for predicting the attitude in question. To do this, the statements are placed on cards or pieces of paper, and the judge uses a Q-sort technique to place the statements usually into 1 to 11 categories. A number other than 11 may be used. Items for which there is serious disagreement are discarded. All items retained are assigned the median score of the judges. For example, if three judges were used and an item had been assigned 3, 5, and 6, the 5 would be used as the value of the item. The subject when given the statement would check "agree" or "disagree," and if he or she agreed, a 5 would be scored. The subjects do not know the value of the statements, and the score is registered only for "agree" items. If one agrees mostly with statements of low predictability, the total score would be low, whereas if the more powerful items were checked more often, the attitude score would be high.

Likert

The Likert and the Thurstone techniques have been found to correlate as high as +.92;[22] therefore, since the Thurstone approach is more mechanically complicated, the Likert has been used more frequently in the literature of physical education. In the Likert technique a number of positive and negative statements about an attitude are collected. Usually approximately 50 percent should be positive and 50 percent negative. The respondent then checks a scale such as from 1 to 5 as to her or his agreement with the item. The correctness of a statement is not a problem as long as a sufficient number of people hold the attitude, both negatively and positively.

While a panel of judges is not necessary when using the Likert technique, one should, nevertheless, use expert opinion when developing the statements. For example, if one wishes to test attitudes toward some aspect of intense athletic competition, interviews with coaches and/or players might be the best source for obtaining some initial statements. If attitudes toward administrators were sought, perhaps administrators and their immediate subordinates should be solicited for the original ideas for the statements. Medford[23] used the Likert approach in the development of the Player-Coach Interaction Inventory. She obtained her original list of adjectives from experienced coaches. See Appendix E for a copy of the Medford Scale.

Scoring for the Likert Scale involves reversing the scale for negative items so that the most positive scores yield the most positive attitude for the summated ratings. If on a 5-point scale the statement is positive, a 5 indicating strong agreement would be the most positive. If a statement is negative, strongly agreeing would be reversed so that the score is 1.

Semantic Differential

The semantic differential was developed by Osgood, Suci, and Tannenbaum[24] strictly for focusing on the measurement of the effective domain. The scale has three characteristics:

1. A concept or concepts
2. Two bi-polar adjectives for each concept
3. A series of undefined positions on a scale. (Seven positions was rec-

ommended by the originators.)

An example of the sample item from the "Attitude Toward Physical Activity" scale by Kenyon[25] will illustrate the semantic differential technique.

Sample Page Chart for Test Administration

What Does the Idea in the Box Mean to You?

> REFEREE

Always Think About the Idea in the Box.

good	_ : _ : _ : _ : _ : _ : _ 1 2 3 4 5 6 7	bad
of no use	_ : _ : _ : _ : _ : _ : _ 1 2 3 4 5 6 7	useful
not pleasant	_ : _ : _ : _ : _ : _ : _ 1 2 3 4 5 6 7	pleasant
bitter	_ : _ : _ : _ : _ : _ : _ 1 2 3 4 5 6 7	sweet
nice	_ : _ : _ : _ : _ : _ : _ 1 2 3 4 5 6 7	awful
happy	_ : _ : _ : _ : _ : _ : _ 1 2 3 4 5 6 7	sad
dirty	_ : _ : _ : _ : _ : _ : _ 1 2 3 4 5 6 7	clean
steady	_ : _ : _ : _ : _ : _ : _ 1 2 3 4 5 6 7	nervous

First Page of CATPA Instrument:

What Does the Idea in the Box Mean to You?

> PHYSICAL ACTIVITY AS A SOCIAL EXPERIENCE
> Physical activities which give you a chance to
> meet new people and be with your friends.

Always Think About the Idea in The Box.

good   _ : _ : _ : _ : _ : _ : _   bad
     1   2   3   4   5   6   7

of no use __ : __ : __ : __ : __ : __ : __ useful
                1   2   3   4   5   6   7

not pleasant __ : __ : __ : __ : __ : __ : __ pleasant
                   1   2   3   4   5   6   7

bitter __ : __ : __ : __ : __ : __ : __ sweet
            1   2   3   4   5   6   7

nice __ : __ : __ : __ : __ : __ : __ awful
          1   2   3   4   5   6   7

happy __ : __ : __ : __ : __ : __ : __ sad
           1   2   3   4   5   6   7

dirty __ : __ : __ : __ : __ : __ : __ clean
           1   2   3   4   5   6   7

steady __ : __ : __ : __ : __ : __ : __ nervous
            1   2   3   4   5   6   7

Idea to go in box on second page of booklet:

PHYSICAL ACTIVITY FOR HEALTH AND FITNESS
Taking part in physical activities to make your health
better and to get your body in better condition.

A concise description of the semantic differential was presented by Isaac and Michael.[26] The profile comparison suggested there and presented as follows offers an interesting way of displaying results.

Profile Comparison of Mean Responses of Eighth
Grade Achievers and Nonachievers to Concept 'School'

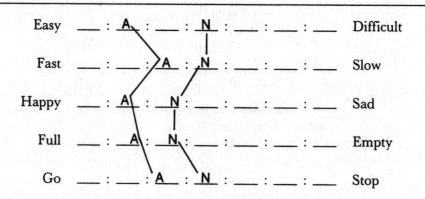

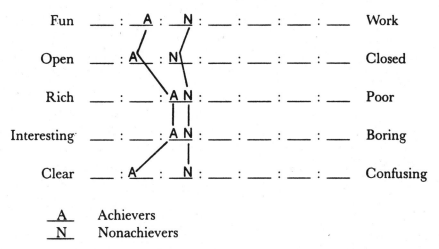

A	Achievers
N	Nonachievers

The Sign Test of the Profile Pattern: The probability that all of the response means of the Achiever group would fall to one side of all of the response means of the Nonachiever group (no cross-over patterns) is $P = .001$; an occurrence of 9 out of 10 is $P = .011$; an occurrence of 8 out of 10 is $P = .055$.

Forced-Choice Comparison

The method of paired comparisons is thoroughly discussed in Edwards.[27] An item to illustrate this technique is:

"I would prefer exercising to reading."

The subject makes choices on statements designed to force descriptions about herself or himself on certain variables. A well-known and widely used instrument of this type is the personality scale developed by Edwards, the Edwards Personal Preference Schedule.[28]

A section concerning the statistics of attitude scaling appears in Kerlinger.[29] He warns that the usual statistics may not be applicable. The use of this technique, just as other techniques, requires expert judgment and advice. The beginning researcher should seek this advice whether or not course work has been taken in the area.

OTHER TECHNIQUES

The tools for collecting data are extensive, making it possible for this chapter to continue in an endless fashion. The more often used techniques in addition to those described in detail previously are: apparatus, choreography, objective tests, diary-anecdotal records, cinematography, and electromyography.

Apparatus

The instruments used in the laboratory are considered apparatus. The dictionary definition suggests that apparatus is any complex instrument. A stop watch might even be placed in this category, but more often we think of treadmills, force platforms, ergometers, and the like.

The researcher should exercise extreme caution in the use of apparatus since the reliability of the instrument itself can create artifacts in the data. Stopwatches should be checked for calibration. Scales should be checked for proper adjustments, and studies of both the objectivity in taking readings and the reliability of subjects' performances should be made.

The fact that an instrument has just arrived from a manufacturer is no assurance that it is reliable. Without reliability the measures taken cannot be valid. Objectivity of scoring, reliability of subject performance, and validity of the measures should be established in that order. The factors are interdependent and are a basic necessity for stating findings.

Choreography

The choreographic technique is used most often in the creative method of research in dance. The method will be discussed in greater detail in a later chapter. Much more than simply composing a dance is involved in the use of this technique. The elements of dance which include form, level, space, tempo, rhythm, variation, etc. must be incorporated into the composition in order for it to fulfill the requirements of creative research. Considerable experience in theory and technique is necessary; and the tutelage of a professor of dance is requisite to the creation of a significant composition.

Objective Tests

Objective tests include tests in the categories of both skill and knowledge. The use of skill tests for collecting data is considered in detail in the texts devoted to the general area of tests and measurements and evaluation in physical education. Once again the selection of any of these tests for data gathering should be based upon their objectivity, reliability, and validity.

The work of Bloom[30] and his associates is unsurpassed in its contribution to the classification of educational goals and testing in the cognitive domain. A taxonomy for testing knowledge is presented, and sample questions are provided. The researcher who plans to use knowledge tests as a means of collecting data must study this source carefully. In physical education Scott and French,[31] Baumgartner and Jackson,[32] Barrow and McGee,[33] and Safrit[34] devote considerable attention to the construction of knowledge tests. If the researcher wishes to use an already constructed knowledge test its validity should, nevertheless, be evaluated. See Safrit[35] for suggestions in this endeavor.

Cumulative and Anecdotal Records

Cumulative and anecdotal records are most often used in the case study approach in research, but they may also be useful in clinical work, counseling, and instructional situations. It has been a practice for some time to report the performance of children, particularly in grammar school, through dialogue rather than through letter grades. Cumulative records are the longitudinally-collected anecdotes.

Positive and Negative Features

Some positive features in using anecdotal records are the following:

1. The observer has unlimited freedom as to what is being observed and recorded.
2. No restrictions exist on the length of the narrative.
3. The record does not have to be made on the spot; it can be written later.
4. The report may be taped and transcribed later.
5. No special training is required in the use of this technique.

Just as with any technique the anecdotal record also suffers from some negative aspects which include the following:

1. The perceptions may be highly subjective.
2. The halo effect, generosity error, and contrast error are dangerous threats to objectivity, reliability, and validity. (See the earlier discussion in this chapter.)
3. Data cannot be verified statistically because they usually cannot be quantified or replicated.
4. A bias toward recording only negative events often exists.
5. If the record is not made proximately to the observation, some forgetting will distort the results.
6. If the record is being handwritten and becomes lengthy, some temptation to shorten the report and be selective, rather than complete, may occur.

Suggestions

Good[36] suggested 15 points to consider when attempting to use anecdotal records. Among them were the following:

1. Keep the number and length reasonable
2. Use prepared forms
3. Try to concentrate on *significant* behavior rather than on *all* behavior
4. Separate opinion from the report of the incident itself
5. Do not allow the anecdote to become a self-justification technique in an instructional situation
6. Use a brief description of the background of the incident as a help in avoiding misinterpretation as a result of isolating a single incident which was a small part of a social setting
7. Do not accept a small number of anecdotes as an accurate representation of total behavior
8. Treat records confidentially
9. Develop a workable plan for handling the clerical work
10. Avoid hasty generalizations
11. Record favorable as well as unfavorable behavior
12. Look for repeated incidents rather than single incidents.

See Good[37] also for a discussion of ethical standards in conducting case studies involving the use of anecdotal records.

Cinematography

A detailed presentation of the cinematographic technique is beyond the scope of this text. The researcher who anticipates doing research in Kinesiology-Biomechanics will find it necessary to do course work in the area. For a brief description of the technique, see Cooper, Adrien, and Glassow.[38] See also Hay,[39] Miller and Petak,[40] Cureton,[41] and Plagenhoef.[42]

Electromyography

Course work in electromyographic techniques will be necessary for learning this procedure for gathering data. For obtaining a basic understanding of the technique, see Winter,[43] Grieve et al.,[44] and MacConaill and Basmajian.[45]

EXAMPLES OF TECHNIQUES FROM RECENT RQES'S

An analysis of some recent *RQES*'s will provide examples of the practical application of the various techniques discussed in this chapter. The analysis was restricted to 1980-1983. See Table 5-2 for these examples.

TABLE 5-2

EXAMPLES OF TECHNIQUES FROM RECENT RQES

Techniques	*Author(s)*	*RQES*
1. Bibliographic	Note: Each study containing a review of related literature employs the bibliographic technique.	
2. Questionnaire	Williams & Miller	Dec. 1983, p. 398
	Southard	Dec. 1983, p. 383
3. Interviews	Harris	Dec. 1983, p. 330
	Kleiber & Roberts	June 1983, p. 200
	Snyder & Purdy	Sept. 1982, p. 263
4. Observation	Vogler & French	Sept. 1983, p. 273
	Godbout, Brunnelle, and Tousignant	March 1983, p.11
5. Attitude	Cox	Sept. 1983, p. 223
	Anthrop & Allison	June 1983, p. 104
6. Rating	Brennan	Sept. 1983, p. 293
	Iso-Ahola & Allen	June 1982, p. 141.
7. Other a. apparatus	Note: Almost every study which involves testing employs apparatus	
b. Choreographic	None reported since 1980	
c. Objective Tests (1) Skill	Morris, Williams Atwater, & Wilmore	Sept. 1982, p. 214
	Chapman	Sept. 1982, p. 239

TABLE 5-2 (Continued)

Techniques	Author(s)	RQES
(2) Knowledge	None reported since 1980	
d. Anecdotal Record	None reported since 1980	
e. Cinematography	Marino	Sept. 1983, p. 234
	Higgs	Sept. 1983, p. 229
f. Electromyography	Balog	June 1983, p. 119
	Englehorn	Dec. 1983, p. 315

SUMMARY OF TECHNIQUES FOR GATHERING DATA

The techniques for obtaining data in research are numerous. Thirteen techniques were discussed in this chapter. The bibliographic technique is used in all research either for a review of literature or for explaining the theoretical framework for the problem. The questionnaire, opinionnaire, interview, observation, rating scales, and attitude scales are often used in combination. Study, in addition to the material in this chapter, is recommended.

Other techniques, considered in less detail, were apparatus, choreography, objective tests, anecdotal records, cinematography, and electromyography. Additional course work would be necessary in order to use these techniques effectively.

A physical educator is an expert in the discipline of teaching motor skills. He or she cannot be expected to be a master also of the use of the techniques of research. Reputable research can, therefore, only result from reading, studying, and talking with those who are experts.

SUGGESTED PROJECTS

1. Bibliographic technique. Write a report on a topic of interest from the sources suggested in this chapter under the heading, "Appropriate Types of Entries." Use at least one entry from each type of source.
2. Questionnaire
   a. Construct a 1-page questionnaire on a topic of interest.

b. Prepare a tabulation sheet.
c. Administer, tabulate, and evaluate your questionnaire. Use at least ten subjects.
3. Interview
a. Develop a structured 10-minute interview.
b. Formulate a method or sheet for tabulation.
c. Interview at least three persons and tabulate the results.
d. Evaluate the interview yourself and ask the respondents also to do so.
4. Observation
a. Plan an observation on any activity you wish. (Overt behavior is easier to observe.)
b. Formulate a method for recording the observation.
c. Conduct the observation.
d. Record the results and evaluate the experience.
5. Rating Scale
a. Make a list of the attributes to be judged.
b. Decide upon the type of scale. (See the section on types in this chapter.)
c. Select the kind and number of categories.
d. Construct the scale.
e. Ask observers to use the scale to judge at least ten subjects, and evaluate the experience.
6. Attitude Scale
a. Choose an attitude to measure.
b. Construct the scale to conform to not more than ten questions.
c. Construct the scale in any of the following formats: Thurstone, Likert, semantic differential, or forced-choice comparison.
d. For the three types not chosen, make a sample question from the scale constructed to demonstrate your understanding of the other forms.
e. Administer the scale to at least ten subjects and evaluate the exercise.
7. Other Techniques. Choose any number of the following as specified by your professor.
a. Interview the dance instructor for more detail concerning how he/she goes about using the choreographic technique in producing a composition in dance.
b. Choose an objective, reliable, and valid skill or knowledge test in

  any sport, and administer it to at least ten subjects. Summarize the results.

 c. Use an anecdotal record to note the results of an observation. Observe the subject or setting on at least three occasions.

 d. Observe a filming session which is for the purpose of cinematographical analysis.

 e. Observe a testing session which is for the purpose of gathering electromyographic data.

REFERENCE NOTES FOR CHAPTER V

[1] Best, pp. 314-315.

[2] Best, pp.309-369.

[3] Ruth Bauner, compiler, "A Selected Bibliography of Research Aids in Education," Education/Psychology Division of the Morris Library, Southern Illinois University at Carbondale, June 1984.

[4] Cathy Cook, compiler, "Bibliography of Physical Education and Recreation Materials," Education/Psychology Division of the Morris Library, Southern Illinois University at Carbondale, January, 1981.

[5] Best, pp. 170-176.

[6] *Roget's International Thesaurus*, 3rd edition (New York: Thomas Y. Crowell Company, 1962), p. 53.

[7] Kildea, p. 165.

[8] Derouin, p. 92.

[9] John E. Nixon, "The Mechanics of Questionnaire Construction," *Journal of Educational Research* 67 (March, 1954):481-487.

[10] Ferguson, p. 319.

[11] Kidder, pp. 146-197.

[12] Charles J. Stewart and William B. Cash, Jr., *Interviewing*, 2nd edition (Dubuque, Iowa: Wm. C. Brown, 1974).

[13] Kidder, pp. 263-266.

[14] Barrow and McGee, pp. 544-547.

[15] Kidder, pp. 202-206.

[16] Barrow and McGee, pp. 537-541.

[17] Barrow and McGee, pp. 542-547.

[18] McDonald, p. 14.

[19] Dee Wyman, "Two Methods of Evaluating the Front Crawl in Swimming" (Master's Thesis, Southern Illinois University at Carbondale, 1970), pp. 123-126.

[20] Virginia Rogers, "Three Methods of Assessing Velocity and Angle of Projection of the Volleyball Spike" (Master's Thesis, Southern Illinois University at Carbondale, 1969), pp. 119-120.

[21] Best, p. 180.

[22] Best, p. 181.

[23] Pam Medford, "The Construction of an Inventory for Measuring Player-Coach Interaction" (Master's Thesis, Southern Illinois University at Carbondale, 1980), pp. 84-86.

[24] C. E. Osgood, G. J. Suci, and P. H. Tannenbaum, *The Measurement of Meaning* (Urbana, Illinois: The University of Illinois Press, 1957).

[25] G. S. Kenyon, "Values Held for Physical Activity by Selected Urban Secondary Students in Canada, Australia, England, and the United States" (Washington, D.C.: United States Office of Education, 1978, K0029).

[26] Isaac and Michael, pp. 144-148.

[27] Allen L. Edwards, *Techniques of Attitude Scale Construction* (New York: Appleton-Century-Crofts, 1957), pp. 19-30.

[28] Allen L. Edwards, *Manual for the Edwards Personal Preference Schedule* (New York: The Psychological Corporation, 1954).

[29] Kerlinger, pp. 495-509.

[30] Benjamin S. Bloom, ed. *Taxonomy of Educational Objectives* (New York: David McKay Company, Inc., 1956).

[31] M. Gladys Scott and Esther French, *Measurement and Evaluation in Physical Education* (Dubuque, Iowa: Wm. C. Brown Company, 1959), pp. 97-116.

[32] T. A. Baumgartner and A. S. Jackson, *Measurement for Evaluation in Physical Education*, (Dubuque, Iowa: Wm. C. Brown Company, 1982), pp. 412-454.

[33] Barrow and McGee, pp. 343-391.

[34] Safrit, pp. 166-189.

[35] Safrit, pp. 143-144.

[36] Good, pp. 348-351.

[37] Good, pp. 351-353.

[38] John M. Cooper, Marlene Adrian, and Ruth B. Glassow, *Kinesiology*, 5th edition (St. Louis: The C. V. Mosby Co., 1982), pp. 174-187.

[39] J. G. Hay, *The Biomechanics of Sports Techniques*, 2nd edition (Englewood Cliffs, N.J.: Prentice-Hall, Inc., 1978).

[40] D. I. Miller and K. L. Petak, "Three-Dimensional Cinematography," in *Kinesiology 1973* (Washington, D.C.: AAHPER).

[41] T. K. Cureton, "Elementary Principles and Techniques of Cinematographic Analysis as Aids in Athletic Research," *Research Quarterly* 10 (May, 1939):3-24.

[42] S. Plagenhoef, *Patterns of Human Motion* (Englewood Cliffs: Prentice-Hall, Inc., 1971).

[43] D. A. Winter, *Biomechanics of Human Movement* (New York: John Wiley and Sons, 1979).

[44] D. W. Grieve, *et al.*, *Techniques for the Analysis of Human Movement* (London: Lepus Books, 1975).

[45] M. A. MacConaill and J. V. Basmajian, *Muscles and Movement: A Basis for Kinesiology* (Huntington, N.Y.: Robert E. Krieger Publishing Co., 1977).

Chapter VI

THE DESIGN OF STUDIES

THIS CHAPTER will acquaint the reader with definitions related to various research designs, problems in designs, and types of designs. In addition, hypothetical studies and published studies in the *RQES* will be discussed.

DEFINITIONS

The treatment of design varies considerably with various authors. Probably the most comprehensive presentation is that of Campbell and Stanley[1] which addresses the experimental and quasi-experimental methods. The following definitions may clarify what is meant by the methods of research as they relate to design:

1. Experiment: a scientific investigation in which the researcher controls one or more independent variables in order to observe the result upon the dependent variable.[2]
2. Experimental design: a design in which the investigator manipulates at least one independent variable.[3]
3. True experimental design: a design in which the investigator has the privilege of randomly selecting and assigning subjects to experimental groups.[4]
4. Ex post facto design: a design in which something done or occurring after an event is studied in relation to its retroactive effect on the event.[5]
5. Quasi-experimental design: a design for the experimental approach to causal research in field settings.[6]
6. Pre-experimental design: a design which is not truly experimental, in that no control group(s) or means of equating groups are employed.[7]

7. Factorial designs: models in which more than single variables (independent and/or dependent) are utilized.

CRITERIA FOR RESEARCH DESIGNS

Kerlinger[8] enumerated principles which should guide the researcher in planning the design of a study. They are the following:

1. The design should permit answering the research questions
2. The design should permit the adequate testing of the hypotheses
3. Subjects should be selected at random, assigned to group at random, and assigned to experimental treatments at random when possible
4. Independent variables should be controlled so that extraneous and unwanted sources of systematic variance have a minimal opportunity to operate
5. The results should be generalizable to other subjects, other groups, and other conditions.

An exhaustive coverage of experimental and/or quasi-experimental design is not possible in this general text, but some of the more widely used designs will be discussed. The symbolism used to express these designs in this text is the following:

Gr.	= Group
PrT	= Pretest
PoT	= Post test
X	= Experimental treatment
X	= Experimental variable removed
R	= Random selection
T	= Test or observation
T (3)	= 3 different tests or T (2) = 2 different tests
C	= Control Treatment
O	= No experimental variable

The least sophisticated and least acceptable design is the one-time case study such as a teacher might use on a single class. No control group and no equivalence of a control group is used. The symbolism for such a design is as follows:

$$X \quad O \quad T$$

The teacher may use an experimental approach to teaching some physical skill such as a lay-up shot in basketball, for example, then test the group to determine their level of performance on the lay-up shot. Almost no generalizability exists in this design. The teacher may have certain perceptions about the effectiveness of the method, especially if he or she has taught basketball for some time, but caution is urged about this kind of research. It is tempting to become evangelical over what might result in spurious results.

The one-group pretest-posttest differs from the one-group case study only in that pre and posttests are given. That symbolism would be:

$$\text{PrT} \quad \text{X} \quad \text{PoT}$$

This design is somewhat stronger than the first design, but still no comparison is possible because there is no control group. Whatever improvement occurs could be attributable to many sources of variance other than the experimental variable. Among these artifacts might be individual differences, the teacher's personality, the Hawthorne or halo effects, or the motivation for learning this particular skill, to name a few.

The static-group comparison is an improvement upon both of the first two designs in that it employs a control group. It is represented graphically as follows:

$$\text{Gr}_1 \quad \text{X} \quad \text{O} \quad \text{T}$$
$$\text{Gr}_2 \quad \text{C} \quad \text{O} \quad \text{T}$$

Without a pretest, however, it is not possible to know whether or not the groups were equivalent at the beginning of the experiment. Serious misjudgments can, therefore, occur without this knowledge of initial equivalence.

Almost all authors who have written on research design minimize the value of the preexperimental approach. This is unfortunate because any type of experimentation is better than none at all, provided sweeping generalizations are avoided. The teacher who experiments is at least alert enough to care about her or his methods and the students' progress. These kinds of studies provide excellent approaches in pilot work and other problems for a beginning researcher.

TRUE EXPERIMENTAL DESIGNS

The true experimental designs discussed in this section are the following:

> Posttest only, equivalent groups
> Pretest-Posttest, equivalent groups
> Solomon, four-group

Posttest Only, Equivalent Groups

The symbolism for the posttest only design is:

$$Gr_1 \quad R \quad X \quad PoT$$
$$Gr_2 \quad R \quad C \quad PoT$$

The subjects are randomly selected and are randomly assigned to treatment groups. Equivalence of the groups is assumed because of the random selection and the random assignment. This may, or may not, be the actual state of affairs.

Pretest-Posttest, Equivalent Groups

An improved design over the "posttest only design" is that of the pretest-posttest equivalent groups which is graphically displayed as follows:

$$Gr_1 \quad R \quad PrT \quad X \quad PoT$$
$$Gr_2 \quad R \quad PrT \quad C \quad PoT$$

In this design equivalence can be measured; and if random procedures have not resulted in equivalence, statistical techniques such as the analysis of covariance can be utilized to correct for the initial inequities. The possibility for resampling also exists.

Solomon Four-Group

In certain studies the effect merely of taking a pretest can confound the results in a posttest. For example, consider the novel task of juggling. Let us say that the pretest is of juggling two balls twice, and the ultimate task or posttest is to juggle each ball 10 times. Two different approaches are used. Assume that the subjects do not know how to juggle; therefore learning to do the pretest may have a profound influence on performance on the posttest. The Solomon design is proposed to account for pretest influence on posttest results. The graphic representation is as follows:

$$Gr_1 \quad R \quad PrT \quad X \quad PoT$$
$$Gr_2 \quad R \quad PrT \quad C \quad PoT$$
$$Gr_3 \quad R \qquad\quad X \quad PoT$$
$$Gr_4 \quad R \qquad\quad C \quad PoT$$

Something must be said here about pretest measures in physical education. In some instances it is not possible to find a suitable pretest. For example, if a study utilizes nonswimmers it may be impossible to test them on initial swimming ability. The same might be true in gymnastics, golf, archery, bowling, tennis, badminton, dance, and other activities where the structure of the motor skills involved are not so fundamental as running, jumping, and throwing. In these instances other approaches to judging equivalence are warranted.

One approach might be to use a general motor ability test if the study involves general motor performance, or an I.Q. test if the study involves cognitive performance. Still another approach might be to use an experience questionnaire. See the one by Walters[9] which appears in Appendix E. In a step-wise regression procedure this experience score was the best predictor of the dependent variable. If carefully constructed, this type of instrument can be invaluable for equating groups.

QUASI-EXPERIMENTAL DESIGNS

The most comprehensive and complete discourse on quasi-experimentation may be found in Cook and Campbell.[10] The book, according to the authors, is addressed to two audiences: persons trained in laboratory research who wish to conduct their work in the real world, and social scientists who are acquainted primarily with descriptive research.

The presentations in the various texts concerning quasi-experimental designs vary considerably. Best[11] differentiates the true experimental from the quasi-experimental only in that the former includes random sampling whereas the latter does not. Good[12] tends to suggest that the difference between true experimental and quasi-experimental is solely a matter of controls. Isaac and Michael[13] give considerable attention to eight designs but do not make distinctions among preexperimental, true experimental, and quasi-experimental (at least in this section).

Cook and Campbell devoted their text to the following designs:

1. Non-equivalent control group
2. Interrupted time series
3. Passive observation
4. Randomized experiments

The nonequivalent control group designs were presented earlier under the heading of "preexperimental designs." The interrupted time series will be considered now.

Simple Interrupted Time Series

The most basic of these designs requires one experimental group and repeated measures. An example of the symbolism follows:

$$T_1 \ T_2 \ T_3 \ T_4 \ X \ T_5 \ T_6 \ T_7 \ T_8$$

This design might be used in physical education to observe four days of practice followed by an intervention of some experimental variable and four succeeding days of practice after the intervention. The trend before the introduction of the X variable and after its introduction can be studied in this design.

Interrupted Time Series With Nonequivalent Dependent Variables

This design enables the investigator to examine history and the effect of the introduction of an experimental variable that should be influential and another that should not be. It is diagrammed as follows:

Dependent Variables	Time	Days of Testing
Running + Attitude	Early Morning	$T_1 \ T_2 \ T_3$
Running + Attitude	Midday	$T_1 \ T_2 \ T_3$
	Material introduced to nullify attitude	X
Running + Attitude	Early morning	$T_4 \ T_5 \ T_6$
Running + Attitude	Midday	$T_4 \ T_5 \ T_6$

The observations (or tests) are made at two different times. For example and application, let us use a situation of runners performing in a setting where our hypothesis is that time of day has an influence on running time and attitude toward the workout. We test the subjects on three consecutive days both on running time and on attitude toward the workout early in the morning and at midday. We introduce material designed to nullify the effects of time of day, and then test them on three consecutive days, both in early morning and at midday.

Interrupted Time Series With Removed Treatment

This design is represented as follows:

Day 1		Day 2		Day 3
$T_1 \ T_2 \ T_3$	×	$T_4 \ T_5 \ T_6$	×	$T_7 \ T_8 \ T_9$

We may wish to test the psychological effect of some motivational device as it might affect running time. We could even use a placebo which is purported to be some sort of energy-producing agent. We test the runners for three trials on Day 1. On Day 2 we administer a placebo, then test for three trials. On Day 3 we announce that we are not using the energy-producing agent today, and test for three more trials. This design is considered to be two interrupted time series.

The "interrupted time series multiple replications" and the "interrupted time series with switching replications" are also discussed by Cook and Campbell[14] but will not be elaborated here.

Passive Observation

The passive observation studies have, in the past, been referred to as correlational studies, but the term "nonexperimental" seems now to be more appropriate since inferential statistics are widely used, although the study is descriptive in nature. The adjective "passive" was added by Cook and Campbell[15] since the procedures of description and observation may also be used in experimental studies.

Cook and Campbell[16] devote some discussion to causal modeling by path analysis, but only present basic ideas. Readers and potential users of path analysis are directed to Blalock,[17,18] Duncan,[19] and Heise,[20] for acquainting themselves with path analysis and to Goldberger and Duncan[21] for more advanced information on the subject.

"Cross-lagged panel correlation" and the "causal analysis of concomitants in time series" are also discussed prior to the final section of Cook and Campbell.[22] In this section they give suggestions for moving from passive observation to deliberate manipulation. They recommend cross-validation studies and discussion of any differences between the causal variable as it has had its impact in the natural setting and how it might have had an effect when deliberately manipulated. Cook and Campbell also warn that random assignment is not necessarily a panacea for ruling out all threats to internal validity, and they present a comprehensive discussion of validity.

FACTORIAL DESIGNS

Earlier in the physical sciences single variables were plausible, but in the behavioral sciences human events are rarely attributable to single causes.[23] More than one independent variable tends to affect the dependent variable(s); and often it is necessary to employ more than one dependent variable. At this point, once again, we must refer to the relationships among designs, techniques, and methods of research. The analysis of variance is a statistical technique which is used in both descriptive and experimental research to respond to the necessity for factorial designs. The textbooks on design use a different graphic symbolism for these studies. See the chapter in this text on Basic Statistics (inferential) for these examples.

THREATS TO INTERNAL AND EXTERNAL VALIDITY

A list of threats to internal validity as cited by Isaac and Michael[24] are the following:

1. History: specific events occurring between the first and second measurement in addition to the experimental variable
2. Maturation: processes within the subjects operating as a function of the passage of time, per se (growing older, hungrier, fatigued, or less attentive)
3. Testing: the effects of testing upon the scores of a subsequent testing
4. Instrumentation: changes in obtained measurement due to changes in instrument calibration or changes in the observers or judges
5. Statistical Regression: a phenomenon occurring when groups have been selected on the basis of extreme scores
6. Selection: biases resulting from the differential selection of subjects for the comparison groups
7. Experimental Mortality: the differential loss of subjects from the comparison groups
8. Selection-Maturation Interaction, etc.: interaction effects between the aforementioned variables which can be mistaken for the effects of the experimental variable

They also list four jeopardizing factors to external validity. They are the following:

1. Interaction effects of selection biases and the experimental variable.
2. Reactive or interaction effect of pretesting: The pretesting modifies the subject in such a way that he responds to the experimental treatment differently than will unpretested persons in the same population.
3. Reactive effects of experimental procedures: effects arising from the experimental setting which will not occur in nonexperimental settings.

4. Multiple-treatment interference: effects due to multiple treatments applied to the same subjects where prior treatments influence subsequent treatments in the series because their effects are not erasable.

A NOTE ABOUT DESIGN

When we speak of the design of a study we actually are referring to two kinds of design — overall and statistical. This section has been intended to address overall design, but the reader must be reminded that the overall design usually includes more than the symbolism which is used and is more than can be portrayed graphically.

For example, consider the following design:

$$Gr_1 \quad R \quad X \quad PoT$$
$$Gr_2 \quad R \quad C \quad PoT$$

We have two groups, one experimental and one control. There is no pretest but subjects were randomly assigned to the two groups. What this symbolism may not show is that a pilot study or perhaps the administration of an ex post facto experience questionnaire was applied in order to assist in interpreting the results. Some procedures do not emerge in the graphic representation but must be explained as a part of the overall "Design of the Study."

Cook and Campbell[25] devote 58 pages to the discussion of validity and offer some additions to the foregoing "threats" suggested by Isaac and Michael. For more detail, see the original sources by Cook and Campbell and Isaac and Michael.

Hypothetical examples were incorporated with the designs presented. A brief analysis of the designs in the published research notes of *RQES* will follow.

Designs Used in 1983 RQES Research Notes

Author(s)	*RQES*		*Design*
1. Corbin, et al.	Dec., '83	Gr.1	X PoT
		Gr.2	O PoT
2. Langefeld	Dec., '83	Gr.1	T1 X T2 X T3 X T4
		Gr.2	T1 O T2 O T3 O T4
3. Brennan	Sept., '83	Gr.1	T1 T2 T3
4. Byrd & Thomas	Sept., '83	Gr.1	T1 T2 T3
5. Sady, et al.	Sept., '83	Gr.1	T1 T2 T3
		Gr.2	T4 T5 T6

6.	Gabbard, Gibbons,	June, '83	G1	T1 T2 T3
	& Elledge		G1	T4 T5 T6
7.	Shick, Stoner,			
	& Jette	March, '83	Gr1	T1 T2 T3
			Gr2	T1 T2 T3
			Gr3	T1 T2 T3
8.	Upton, et al.	March, '83	Gr1	T(17)
			Gr2	T(17)

The reader will note that an analysis of the *RQES* for 1983 was limited to the articles refered to as research notes. This choice was made because the designs of the notes tend to be more elementary than those of the longer articles. This text is designed to acquaint the researcher with basic ideas about design, rather than to present an exhaustive coverage. For more sophisticated designs, see Campbell and Stanley,[26] Cook and Campbell,[27] and Edwards.[28]

SUGGESTED PROJECTS

1. Propose a study on the *same* topic using the following designs, and give their symbolic representations:
   a. Preexperimental
   b. True-experimental
   c. Quasi-experimental
   d. Factorial
2. Suggest a research question and propose any of the foregoing designs (stated in #1) as the most appropriate approach to answering the question. Justify your answer.
3. Choose an article from the *RQES* within the last three years. Classify it as to research design. Identify any extraneous or possibly unwarranted sources of variance. Recommend a correction.
4. Determine for the year 1981 the number of studies reported in *RQES* which were generalizable: state to which population they were generalizable. Present this in tabular form.
5. Analyze the 1982 Research Notes from *RQES* in the same fashion, as was done for 1983 in this chapter.

   Note: When possible these projects should be related to the proposed theses or dissertation. By accepting this concept at an early stage, the student of the methods of research may avoid the common graduate student malaise of malingering and/or procrastination.

REFERENCE NOTES FOR CHAPTER VI

[1] D. Campbell and J. Stanley, *Experimental and Quasi-Experimental Designs for Research* (Chicago, IL: Rand McNally, 1966).
[2] Kerlinger, p. 315.
[3] Kerlinger, p. 315.
[4] Kerlinger, p. 315.
[5] Kerlinger, p. 315.
[6] Thomas D. Cook and Donald T. Campbell, *Quasi-Experimentation* (Boston: Houghton Mifflin Company, 1979), p. 1.
[7] Best, p. 69.
[8] Kerlinger, pp. 322-326.
[9] Walters, pp. 109-112.
[10] Cook and Campbell, p. 1.
[11] Best, pp. 72-80.
[12] Good, pp. 379-389.
[13] Isaac and Michael, pp. 63-75.
[14] Cook and Campbell, pp. 222-225.
[15] Cook and Campbell, pp. 295-296.
[16] Cook and Campbell, pp. 301-309.
[17] H. M. Blalock, Jr., *Causal Inferences in Non-Experimental Research*, 1st ed. (Chapel Hill, N.C.: The University of North Carolina Press, 1961).
[18] H. M. Blalock, Jr., *Causal Models in the Social Sciences* (Chicago: Aldine, 1971).
[19] O. D. Duncan, *Introduction to Structural Equation Models* (New York: Academic Press, 1975).
[20] D. R. Heise, *Causal Analysis* (New York: Wiley, 1975).
[21] A. S. Goldberger and O. D. Duncan, Structural Equation Models in the Social Sciences (New York: Seminar Press, 1973).
[22] Cook and Campbell, p. 339.
[23] Best, pp. 58-59.
[24] Isaac and Michael, p. 59.
[25] Cook and Campbell, pp. 37-94.
[26] Campbell and Stanley.
[27] Cook and Campbell.
[28] Allen L. Edwards, *Experimental Design in Psychological Research* (New York: Holt, Rinehart, and Winston, 1963).

Chapter VII

METHODS OF RESEARCH SPECIFICALLY APPLIED TO PHYSICAL EDUCATION

THE METHODS of research are classified differently by various authors; however, three general categories are mentioned in all texts, and some writers mention additional special categories.

GENERAL CLASSIFICATIONS

The widely accepted general methods of research include descriptive, experimental, and historical. The following definitions are from Isaac and Michael.[1]

1. Historical: To reconstruct the past objectively and accurately, often in relation to the tenability of an hypothesis
2. Descriptive: To describe systematically a situation or area of interest factually and accurately
3. Developmental: To investigate patterns and sequences of growth and/or change as a function of time
4. Case and Field: To study intensively the background, current status, and environmental interactions of a given social unit: an individual, group, institution, or community
5. Correlational: To investigate the extent to which variations in one factor correspond with variations in one or more other factors based on correlation coefficients
6. Causal-Comparative or "Ex Post Facto": To investigate possible cause-and-effect relationships by observing some existing consequence and searching back through the data for plausible causal factors
7. True Experimental: To investigate possible cause-and-effect relationships by exposing one or more experimental groups to one or

more treatment conditions and comparing the results to one or more control groups not receiving the treatment (random assignment being essential)

8. Quasi-Experimental: To approximate the conditions of the true experiment in a setting which does not allow the control and/or manipulation of all relevant variables. (The researcher must clearly understand what compromises exist in the internal and external validity of her/his design and proceed with these limitations.)

9. Action: To develop new skills or new approaches and to solve problems with direct application to the classroom or other applied setting. (This method is in need of some assurance of external validity.)

Descriptive

In the descriptive approach to a study, the researcher describes a state of affairs with no attempt at inference to some parent population. Both descriptive and inferential statistics may be utilized. A distinction between the descriptive and experimental methods is the absence of an experimental variable which is introduced under carefully controlled conditions. Another distinction is the *necessity* for random sampling in the experimental method and the *desirability* for it in the descriptive method. In all kinds of research, research hypotheses are appropriate. The descriptive approach is no exception.

The descriptive method is a catch-all category. In some textbooks the special cases mentioned by Isaac and Michael are simply referred to as descriptive. These are the following from that preceding reference: developmental, case and field, correlational, causal comparative or ex post facto, quasi-experimental, and action.

Best[2] presented even some different special cases of the descriptive method. They are the following:

1. General survey
2. Social survey
3. Public-opinion survey
4. National assessment
5. International assessment
6. Activity analysis
7. Trend studies
8. School surveys
9. Assessment and evaluation in problem solving
10. Follow-up study

11. Document or content analysis
12. Case study
13. Ethnographic studies
14. Ex post facto or explanatory observation studies
15. Replication and secondary analysis

These, in addition to those mentioned by Isaac and Michael, offer a reasonably comprehensive list of the special cases of approaches to descriptive research. In general, the descriptive method is concerned with conditions, relationships, practices, beliefs, attitudes, processes, and trends.

The investigator using the descriptive approach is reminded that it is not enough simply to describe a situation. Some significance to the interpretation must be provided.

Experimental and Quasi-Experimental

Experimental and quasi-experimental methods have been discussed in the previous chapter in detail as they relate to design. The earliest experiments were performed with one experimental variable. Soon the concept of the necessity for factorial designs emerged. Now it is rare when studies do not involve more than one independent variable, and it is becoming increasingly more typical that two or more dependent variables are being utilized.

Easy access to the use of computers and packaged programs have facilitated the liberation of researchers who have more than simple questions to ask. It is now possible to find answers quickly to complex problems; however, one difficulty still seems to exist. Some researchers with an exuberance for asking questions do not have sufficient enthusiasm for involving an adequate number of subjects for answering those questions. The design may be correct; the computer program may be flawless; but without appropriate n's nothing can be concluded. The various packages which seem to fit the kinds of studies being conducted currently in physical education will be discussed in a section of the appendix. (They are the SAS, SPSSX, and BIO-MED.)

Internal and external validity are extremely important in all studies; but particularly in experimental studies when random sampling is not utilized, the situation becomes increasingly critical. Without a high degree of internal validity, there can be only limited external validity. Certain "threats" to both internal and external validity have been suggested by several authors. Among them, was the list proposed by Isaac and Michael[3] earlier in Chapter VI.

Four jeopardizing factors (according to Isaac and Michael) are:[4]

1. Interaction effects of selection biases and the experimental variable
2. Reactive or interaction effect of pretesting: The pretesting modifies the subject in such a way that he or she responds to the experimental treatment differently than unpretested persons in the same population
3. Reactive effects of experimental procedures: effects arising from the experimental setting which will not occur in nonexperimental settings
4. Multiple-treatment interference: effects resulting from multiple treatments applied to the same subjects where prior treatments influence subsequent treatments in the series because their effects are not erasable.

Whereas random sampling has sometimes been purported to be a cure for all problems in design, it does not assure that initial comparability of groups will be maintained throughout the experiment. Because conclusions are made upon the posttest comparability of groups on all variables other than treatment, it is reasonable that many kinds of changes which were not present at the time of the pretest can occur. These changes were referred to as "attrition" by Cook and Campbell[5] who suggested that if attrition is random, one can continue with the analysis as coming from a randomized experiment. They, however, suggested that if the attrition is systematic, the experimenter must attempt to describe the ways in which the changes are systematic and must try to control for these factors in the statistical analysis.

An interesting explanation of a way in which to understand what random assignment does not do was offered by Cook and Campbell.[6] They suggested that one think of this concept as part of the experimental design, which is itself only *part* of the *overall* research design. Research design is broader than experimental design. The latter involves the scheduling of observations, the choice of treatments and comparisons, the selection of measured control variables, and the manner of assigning subjects or units of treatments. Random assignment has only to do with the manner of assigning subjects or units to treatments. Assigning at random is, therefore, only a small part of the experimental design and an even smaller part of the research design which is concerned with formulating relevant research questions, selecting the variables, and selecting the proper respondents.

Additional information concerning random sampling appears in the same section of Cook and Campbell.[7] The researcher who plans to use a randomized experiment should spend considerable time in studying that chapter.

Some experimental studies suffer from the following consistent errors:

1. The failure to study the reliability of the measures
2. The use of numbers of subjects which are too small
3. The use of inappropriate statistics or none at all
4. The discussion of correlations which are not different from zero
5. The discussion of numerical differences which are not statistically significant
6. The use of elaborate instrumentation which is not reliable but is automatically assumed to be.

Historical

A concise, but complete, definition of historical research is given by Best[8] as follows:

> Historical research describes what was. The process involves investigating, recording, analyzing, and interpreting the events of the past for the purpose of discovering generalizations that are helpful in understanding the past, understanding the present, and to a limited extent, in anticipating the future.

The subjects of historical research may be people, events, movements, costumes, organizations, traditions, customs, equipment, myths, institutions, games, automobiles, etc. An attempt to name the potential subjects of historical research is futile folly, for they may be anything with an interesting, or even uninteresting, past. Best[9] goes on to suggest that "practices hailed as innovative are often old ideas that have previously been tried and replaced with something new."

Historical research, regardless of the topic, is one of the most rigorous of methods. The researcher must be particularly well founded in the bibliographical technique, documentary analysis, and the interview technique (in the case of oral history).

WRITING THE HISTORICAL REPORT

The divisions of the historical report usually do not follow the traditional headings discussed earlier in the chapter on "Writing the Report." Hypotheses are appropriate and should be utilized, and procedures are similar to other studies.

HISTORICAL HYPOTHESES

Research hypotheses of an historical nature might be the following:

1. M. Gladys Scott contributed significantly to the sub-discipline of measurement and evaluation in physical education.
2. The Association for Intercollegiate Athletics for Women (AIAW) was responsible for the emergence of Women's Intercollegiate Athletics.
3. Physical education attire has had a significant impact upon dress in the United States.

HISTORICAL PROCEDURES

The procedures include the following:

1. Select the problem
2. Formulate hypotheses
3. Collect the source materials
4. Criticize the source materials through both external and internal criticism
5. Interpret the findings
6. Formulate the conclusions
7. Accept or reject the hypotheses.

SOURCE MATERIALS

The sources of data for historical research include both primary and secondary sources, but primary are by far the more preferred. Primary sources include eyewitness accounts, first-hand information, original documents, pictures, articles, oral testimony, costumes, pieces of equipment, etc. Secondary sources include reports by a second or third party, reports based upon, but paraphrasing, some original document or account, etc.

Primary sources should far exceed secondary sources in valid historical research. Relics and remains are extremely trustworthy because they are tangible and can, therefore, be examined.

The following are examples of primary and secondary sources which were suggested by Best.[10]

Primary are:

1. Official records and other documentary materials: Included in this category are records and reports of legislative bodies and state departments of public instruction, city superintendents, principals, presidents, deans, department heads, educational committees, minutes of school boards and boards of trustees, surveys, charters, deeds, wills, professional and lay periodicals, school newspapers,

annuals, bulletins, catalogs, courses of study, curriculum guides, athletic game records, programs (for graduation, dramatic, musical, and athletic events), licenses, certificates, textbooks, examinations, report cards, drawings, maps, letters, diaries, autobiographies, teacher and pupil personnel files, samples of students' work, and recordings.

2. Oral testimony: Included here are interviews with administrators,, teachers and other school employees, students and relatives, school patrons or lay citizens, and members of governing bodies.

3. Relics: Included in this category are buildings, furniture, teaching materials, equipment, murals, decorative pictures, textbooks, examinations, and samples of students' work.

Most history textbooks and encyclopedias are examples of secondary sources, for they are often several times removed from the original, first-hand account of events.

Some material may be secondary sources for some purposes and primary sources for another. For example, a high school textbook in American history is ordinarily a secondary source. But if one were making a study of the changing emphasis on nationalism in high school American history textbooks, the book would be a primary document or source of data.

Secondary sources generally are:

1. Textbooks
2. Encyclopedias
3. Current newspaper articles about past historical events
4. Paraphrasing of passages of the original by another person
5. Tales passed on for generations.

EXTERNAL AND INTERNAL CRITICISM

External criticism involves establishing the authenticity or genuineness of the data. Some questions that may be answered during this process are: Is the relic, document, letter, etc. an original, forgery, or copy? Is it counterfeit? Problems associated with external criticism may be resolved through various techniques such as comparing signatures, locating birth certificates, analyzing writing style, making chemical tests, comparing a relic with one the age of which has already been established, comparing spelling, etc.

Once external criticism has been completed, the writer of history must then apply internal criticism which is an analysis of the validity of the data. Some questions to be answered in this procedure are: Do the data reveal the truth or do distortions exist? Were the sources, if human sources, competent to comment or write on the topic? Did pressures or fears enter in to cause inaccuracies? Could forgetting have occurred as a result of long periods of time, or other events, between the observation and the recording? Was the method of recording (in the case of oral testimony) complete or open to interpretation? Is a position taken that of the writer or some collective opinion of an appropriate group? Do other accounts agree? Did he or she wish to please a later generation? See Best[11] for examples on this topic of internal criticism.

ORGANIZATION OF THE HISTORICAL REPORT

As mentioned earlier in the chapter on Writing the Report, the historical study is usually organized under headings which do not follow the traditional sections such as review of literature, procedures, collection and analysis of data, conclusions, etc. It is true, however, that the historical study may need some traditional sections such as an introduction, statement of hypotheses, delimitations and limitations, some description of procedures, summaries, and final acceptance or rejection of the hypotheses. The data of the historical study are usually the review of literature, and the analysis is the section(s) on external and internal criticism.

For some studies it may be necessary to have a separate review of literature. The following example of a study by Ermler[12] will illustrate the separate review of literature and conformance to more traditional headings whereas the study of Martin[13] is illustrative of the review being presented as the data. The title of the Ermler study was "The History of Intercollegiate Athletics for Women at Southern Illinois University from 1921-1977," and the title of the Martin study was "The Football Helmet: A Historical Perspective from 1860 Through 1979."

Ermler: Chapters IV through VII

Ermler used the review for purposes of establishing background information and a frame of reference for her analysis of the situation at Southern Illinois University at Carbondale, whereas Martin incorporated his review as his data for the chronological sections 1860-1892, 1893-1938, and 1939-1979. Ermler chose to use descriptive captions for her time periods whereas Martin used strictly the time periods. Either approach is acceptable. The Ermler approach tends to be more widely used for its descriptive appeal. Since topics and purposes vary widely, individual choice rather than precise convention tends to characterize the organization of the historical report.

Problems with Historical Research

Historical research, and particularly that of graduate students, may be subject to some of the following faults, according to Best.[14]

1. Stating the problem too broadly
2. Overuse of secondary sources
3. Inadequate use of external and internal criticism
4. Poor logical analysis
5. Introduction of personal bias
6. Poor reporting style

Other problems may also be:

1. Inability to deal with the necessarily voluminous sources of historical research
2. Inability to organize the sources into meaningful, but still an interesting product
3. Lack of interest
4. Lack of economic resources
5. Lack of time
6. Inability to conceptualize the ramifications of the data
7. Inaccessibility to the required primary, and even secondary, sources
8. Lack of experience with the historical method and the associated techniques.

Historical research is one of the more rigorous and demanding approaches; and, therefore, is not often undertaken by students, particularly at the master's level. With some course work, however, and/or the tutelage of a professor of historical research, this method is within the grasp of all graduate students.

The reader is reminded that the reporting of history is not just a chronological list of events. Interpretations, relationships, and the significance of events must be provided.

For the would-be historical researcher, the text by Barzun and Graff[15] is essential reading. Particularly useful in this text is a quite complete section on writing. See also the bibliography in Best,[16] and Van Dalen.[17]

SPECIAL CLASSIFICATIONS

Certain of the special classifications to be mentioned in this section can be classified under the general categories of descriptive, experimental, or historical research; however, some seem not to fit the standard categories. These are the measurement, creative, and philosophical approaches. The curriculum and case study methods are normally included as special classifications although they might be placed under the descriptive method, and the biography is a special case of the historical method.

Biographical

The foregoing discussion of the historical method also applies to biographical research. Biographical research is sometimes referred to as "life history." More often the researcher is other than the person being studied, but autobiography is not uncommon among persons who have made outstanding contributions to society, nations, the world, or mankind in general..

The techniques widely used are those mentioned earlier under the historical method, but especially oral testimony is important. In the case of the autobiography, the diary and personal effects, as well as letters, are exceedingly necessary.

Basic criteria for evaluating life history approaches were suggested by Dollard[18] and appear in Good.[19] They are the following:

1. The subject must be viewed as a specimen in a cultural series
2. The organic motors of action ascribed must be socially relevant
3. The peculiar role of the family group in transmitting the culture must be recognized
4. The specific method of elaboration of organic materials into social behavior must be shown
5. The continuous related character of experience from childhood through adulthood must be stressed
6. The social situation must be carefully and continuously specified as a factor
7. The life-history material itself must be organized and conceptualized.

The purposes and procedures of a classic life history or autobiography may be helpful as background for understanding this approach. These purposes might be:

1. To prepare a relatively full and reliable account of an individual's experience and development from birth on, or a comprehensive life history emphasizing personality problems
2. To accumulate and arrange in natural order a socially and culturally-oriented record of an individual in a "primitive society" for the purpose of developing and checking certain hypotheses in the field of culture
3. To attempt at least a partial interpretation of the individual's development and behavior
4. To utilize the investigation for the formulation of generalizations and the testing of theories in the field of individual behavior with respect to society and culture (reserved for further study).

Measurement

The measurement method is devoted to test construction and includes both a creative approach and a descriptive approach. It is creative in that the test must be developed by the investigator and descriptive both in surveying previous tests and in performing a field test of the final product.

General Criteria for Tests

General criteria suggested by a number of authors are objectivity, reliability, validity, and practicality. Objectivity is scorer agreement or accuracy in scoring. Reliability is repeatability of subject performance, and validity is the degree to which a test can be used to measure the behavior for which it was designed. The factors are interdependent. Objectivity, reliability, and validity must be established in that order. For additional information on these procedures consult measurement and evaluation textbooks.

Steps in the Measurement Method

1. Identify an area of need
2. Establish that need
3. Define good performance
4. Propose the test
5. Study subject response with a small group
6. Refine the test
7. Study reliability, if objectivity was acceptable
8. Administer the test to a large number of subjects
9. Study reliability with the large number of subjects
10. Establish statistical validity
11. Revise the test if necessary
12. Subject the test to comparison of the test with the criteria established for:

    Objectivity   Validity
    Reliability   Practicality
13. Establish norms
14. Publish the test
15. Evaluate the test after some extended use.

With respect to practicality, the test should compare favorably with the following criteria:

1. Be easy to administer
2. Have reusable targets or other equipment (where appropriate)
3. Have mass testability

4. Be economical in terms of costs and time for the organization and set-up
5. Provide easily interpreted scores.

Philosophical

As stated earlier in another chapter in this text, the physical educator is primarily a specialist in the methodology and sciences associated with motor skilled learning and performance. He or she can rarely also be a physiologist, psychologist, sociologist, statistician, computer scientist, inventor, historian, philosopher, etc. It was with this concept in mind that the author sought the assistance of Professor Elizabeth Eames[20] for the development of this section which she has chosen to entitle "Kinds of Analysis Within the Philosophical Method." This section is presented with extreme appreciation to Professor Eames.

Throughout its 25 centuries western philosophy has had an intimate relation with the science of its day.[21] Aristotle was the leading scientist of his day, and Descartes and others generalized the mathematical method of Galilean mechanics. Hume and others adapted the observational aspect of Newtonian astronomy. Not only have philosophers tried to adapt the methods of science to their uses, but also they have tried to found their own hypotheses on successful scientific theories. Scientists also have found the methods and ideas of philosophers suggestive, as 19th century atomic theory owed much to the fifth B.C. work of Democritus. Hence, it would not be surprising if the method of philosophical analysis should provide some analogues to, and hints and models for, the contemporary work in the research of Physical Education.

Kinds of Analysis

The philosophical methods used today which are closest to those of science, and hence the most promising for this text, are those of philosophical analysis, or conceptual analysis. In what follows, sketches of some of the models of philosophical analysis are provided, along with some analogies for research in our field.

DIALECTICAL ANALYSIS

The most time-honored method of analysis is that known as the dialectical method.[22] This method was used by Plato and a version of it is in use in contemporary continental philosophy. The idea behind this method is that one way of clarifying meanings and getting rid of confusions and muddles is to seek a definition of one's subject. The tentative definition is then submitted to successive criticism, amendments or redefinitions, and new objections and criticisms until all of the relevant considerations are brought out. The concept, entity, or hypothesis is then clear and can be used with an unequivocal and universally understood meaning. This process of ongoing argument—definition, criticism, new proposals to meet the criticism, and then further criticism, is thought to be characteristic of all human thought processes present in dialogues between inquirers, and even, perhaps, to be a reflection of the ebb and flow of opposing and interacting forces in nature. It may be that this dialectical and critical method can be useful in conceptual analysis in our field, as in many others. Example: Can physical education be defined as a discipline? If so, what distinguishes it as a discipline? And does this distinctness leave out the aspect of physical education as a profession?

ANALYSIS INTO SIMPLES

A second and similar method of analysis is analysis into simples.[23] The idea here is that an inquiry starts with something complex, confused, and tentative and that to reach the truth one should resolve the complex into its parts. When each part of the complex has been separated and identified, one can then test each simple component, or unit, to see if it is fully understood and if what is believed about it is true. In this way one can locate and discard any dubious or uncertain elements and reconstruct one's theory with units which have survived in the testing of the doubt. It was by a method of analysis into simples that Marie Curie isolated the element which alone was not known to be incapable of producing exposure on the photographic plate, and this resulted in the identification of radium. It was by identifying and discarding the doubtful element of phlogiston in the theory of heat that scientists cleared the way for the emergence of the theory of kinetics.[24] Every inquiry incorporates some elements from its past which require analysis into parts and the testing of doubt. Example: What constitutes the general ability currently labeled "athletic ability"? The research in physical education has resulted in an identification of at least the following basic physical abilities which, together, constitute athletic ability: agility, balance, coordination, endurance, flexibility, kinesthesis, rhythm, speed, strength, and power. Thorpe and West[25,26,27,28] attempted an examination of the construct of "game sense" as an addition to the understanding of the cognitive aspects of athletic ability, but much room for additional explorations still exists in this area.

EMPIRICAL ANALYSIS

One of the most influential philosophical methods of the last 200 years may be called that of empirical or obervational analysis.[29] Here, the philosophers, impressed by the progress of science and its reliance on observational data, attempted to curb their own tendency to reach hasty conclusions and to speculate far beyond the scope of human knowledge. The question asked by empirical analysis is, "Where is the warrant in experience for the proposition which is put forth? Or can the proposed concept or assertion be tested observationally?" If the philosophical concept cannot be brought to such an observational test, at least in the forseeable future; and if it cannot be interpreted as a purely logical or mathematical concept, such as zero or infinity, then they say with Hume, "Cast it into the flames." They say that such a concept is not meaningful in a rational sense and belongs to the realm of mythology or poetry. Such an untested, yet accepted, concept which has had too long an immunity from empirical analysis is that of the fundamental and inherent differences between feminine and masculine gender-types. Persons in each field of inquiry, who claim to be scientific, try to use such an empirical critique; and this approach is what many modern philosophers have self consciously practiced. Example: Sampson[30] realized that textbooks in Physical Education are often written by good coaches and/or good players who are expert but may not be those same persons who are scientifically-oriented toward a knowledge of the game, sport, or activity. She, therefore, proposed to determine: "Does film analysis (cinematography) confirm or deny textbook descriptions of a skill in field hockey?"

LOGICAL ANALYSIS

The counterpart of empirical analysis is logical analysis.[31] Here the focus is on the consistency, or absence of contradictions in a system of symbols. Mathematicians and logicians have been concerned with this kind of analysis since mathematics and logic were invented. For instance, a problem may occur in a mathematical or logical system if it appears that some of the symbols cannot be converted into other symbols of the system. The scandals in ancient mathematics and philosophy included the incommensurability of the radius of a circle and the paradoxes connected with the mathematical postulate of the infinite divisibility of space and time. For example, Xeno argued that Achilles can never win the race with the tortoise.[32] In our own century the contradiction of classes that are not members of themselves (Russell's paradox) presented similar difficulties.[33] Of course, scientists can use mathematical and logical systems of symbols even when internal contradictions and unproven theories are present, but it remains a goal for thought that all systems of symbols should be free of such problems. The empirical and logical methods of analysis together have been the basis of the criteria for the philosophic resolution of ancient philosophical puzzles. While the language for a particular science may never conform exactly to Tarski's[34] requirement, "language with a specified structure" may provide an ideal toward which we strive. At any rate, the employment of logical analysis may help us test our scientific theory for the existence of contradictions and inconsistencies. Example: In regression analysis we attempt to explain maximally the variance in some criterion variable, and so we construct an equation which we believe to be hypothetically capable of decreasing error and increasing prediction to the greatest extent possible. The criterion variable should be uncontaminated by having one of the chosen predictors as an *a priori* known part of it.

ANALYSIS THROUGH ORDINARY LANGUAGE

A method of philosophical analysis in fashion in the present period is that of ordinary language.[35] In this method the goal of an "artificial language," that is, a specified language such as that of mathematics or chemistry, is rejected. It is said that our ordinary natural language has embedded in it fine discriminations, and usage rules which guide us away from talking nonsense. It is claimed that we lose the richness and subtlety of communication when we resort to "jargon" or invented words or symbols. What we ought to do, according to these linguistic analysts, is to examine our own language habits and find in them clues for understanding our concepts. Unlike other analysts, ordinary language analysts see philosophy as differing from science and as having its own method. Example: Conn[36] studied responses of physical education majors and nonmajors with respect to sports jargon. Some of these words (15 in all) were the following: "fan," "dive," "ace," "pickle," "kill," "slide," and "steal." He found that the two groups understood the words "dive," "ace," and "slide" in different ways.

The fourth and fifth analytic methods of logic and ordinary language thus are in conflict, and philosophy may be seen to be giving contradictory guidance to other inquiry which may be endangered by a lack of specified structure and clearly defined terms. Or is our inquiry endangered by a technical jargon which makes the inquiry appear scientific when it is not? Perhaps we may find examples of both difficulties in our area of research. We have been taught to be careful with numbers and the quantification of data, but we also need to be aware of the necessity for care in the interpretation of the language in our discipline and our choice of methods of analysis. A conscious awareness of meanings is involved in the sixth of the methods of philosophical analysis — pragmatic analysis.

PRAGMATIC ANALYSIS

Pragmatic analysis is the name given to a philosophical method formulated by C. S. Peirce, William James, John Dewey, and George Herbert Mead during the late 19th and early 20th centuries.[37] These philosophers inquired as to the meaning of a term, idea, or concept. In essence, to say that a body is heavy is to say that (in the absence of opposing forces) it will fall. The concept is that body weight means falling under certain circumstances. A single symbol may serve to represent a concept which is variable in different contexts, and a full tracing out of its consequences in each context is required to understand it.

If we are speaking of "parent" in the context of genetics, for instance, we would need to trace out the actual biological lines of descent and define "parent" in terms of this descent. If, however, we are speaking of "parent" in the context of family structures and relationships, we will need to define "parent" as a responsible adult living with a child. The employment of concepts in an ongoing inquiry is of central concern in this method. Perhaps the pragmatic analysis, in terms of the consequence of the use of the concept in inquiry, may provide a way of mediating the previously stated fourth and fifth methods of analysis. From a pragmatic viewpoint what matters is not whether one invents a new precise term as part of a specified language or whether one chooses to use terms in our natural language; rather what matters is that the full meanings of the concept are worked out in terms of how they are to be used in the given inquiry. Example: Because the word "athlete" can have many interpretations, it was necessary for Kildea[38] to clarify the meaning of "athlete" and "nonathlete" as they were to be utilized in her study. The resulting definitions were:

1. Athlete: A female student involved in one or more competitive sports offered by the Women's Intercollegiate Athletic Program at Southern Illinois University during the 1978-1979 school year.
2. Nonathlete: A female student of Southern Illinois University not involved in the Women's Intercollegiate Athletic Program during the 1978-1979 school year and also only occasionally involved in sport, if involved at all.

Contrast Conn's exploration of verbal usage with Kildea's stipulated definition of athlete and nonathlete. Bandy's[39] conceptual analysis of play, game, sport, and athletics is an example in which common language is analyzed to reveal important distinctions.

SUMMARY

We might review the different methods of analysis by looking at the direction of the analysis in each case. Dialectical analysis proceeds from the confused to the clear, as, for instance, when we attempt to give a clear meaning to "physical education." Analysis into simple moves from the complex to the simple component, as we saw in the example of "athletic ability" broken down into agility, endurance, balance, coordination, and so forth. Empirical analysis moves from the unwarranted to the warranted, from what is assumed, or guessed, or theorized about to what can be observed and verified. The example is the film analysis by which the performance theory developed by coaches is tested by direct observation of the activity. The method of logical analysis proceeds from the disordered to the ordered. The use of numbers, quantitative measures, and statistics attempts to achieve the goal of order and to solve any problems of inconsistency by the use of mathematical techniques. Regression analysis is an example. The method of ordinary language moves from the unselfconscious and imprecise use of language to careful attention to common usage. The analysis of terms applying to athletics, such as "fan," "dive," "ace," and so forth, provides an example. The method of pragmatic analysis moves from the concept and terms taken in isolation to a study of their use in specific contexts of inquiry. An example is the attempt to analyze the way in which terms such as "play," "game," "sport," and "athletics" are employed in different contexts.

Case Study

Case studies have been reported frequently in the *RQES* and *Completed Research in Health, Physical Education, and Recreation*. It is, however, a very important method for the study of individuals, institutions, communities, organizations, curriculum, and other social units.

Case history, case study, and case work are commonly used terms which have quite different meanings and should be contrasted here. Records which are kept, but not subjected to formal evaluation, are case histories. Case work is a process of therapy and follow-up to remedy some problematic situation. A case study in research must incorporate all of the formality of other methods. For example, the divisions of the study would normally be the same as a study under the descriptive or experimental methods. The study should have hypotheses, a review of literature, procedures, data, an analysis of data, and conclusions. A contrast between the case study and other descriptive studies is the in-depth concentration on small numbers of units in the case, as opposed to the study of large n's, in the descriptive and experimental methods.

The case study is appropriate for use in any discipline when maximum information is needed about a unit. We could obtain an almost total picture of all variables which motivate a single person to overcome fear of water if we limited our probing to one fear case. If we wanted to use a descriptive approach we could take 40 fear cases, but the number of contacts would have to be limited; and the information would have to be more superficial. Lest it sound like the case method is a panacea, it is fair to point out that generalizability is not possible unless there is more than one unit. In other words, the factors that were responsible for getting one case over fear of water may not work at all with another.

The following evaluation criteria for conducting case studies were suggested by Good[40]:

1. Continuity of data and procedure, and use of longitudinal data, although a logical sequence is not always possible in life situations where the movement of examination, diagnosis, and therapy may be shuttlelike

2. Completeness and validity of data, critical evaluation of evidence, and consideration of individual idiosyncrasies, covering initial status, examination results, and history

3. Synthesis in the form of adequate diagnosis and prognosis, in the concept of nondirective, or client-centered therapy, tend to minimize the process of diagnosis as a basis for therapy

4. Relationships with the client and case recording may not be maintained on a confidential basis.

Rothney[41] recommended 20 questions for evaluating a case study of an individual but also with some applications to case studies of other social units. The questions are:

1. Are there any serious omissions in the data?

2. Was more than one method employed in the collection of the data?

3. Has more than one school of thought been considered in the interpretation of the data?

4. Are the sources of all data specified?

5. Have independent judgments been made by use of tests, judges, and those who provided behavior descriptions?

6. Have reference points for statistics been given?
7. Has consideration been given to the possibility of deception by the subject?
8. Is the cultural situation given in enough detail?
9. Is a description of the family situation presented?
10. Is the developmental story told as far as it is relevant?
11. Has adequate attention been given to current trends in behavior?
12. Are future plans given enough consideration?
13. Are data presented as evidence when predictions are made?
14. Has due care been exercised in the interpretation of the motivation of the subject?
15. Are concrete illustrations of general categories presented?
16. Have censorial terms been avoided?
17. Is the writing good?
18. Has maximum brevity been sought?
19. Does the opening paragraph set the tone for the study?
20. Do you feel that you really know the person when you have finished reading the case study?

For examples of two case studies conducted in physical education settings see Schultze[42] and Sherrill.[43]

Creative

The creative method involves the production of an original composition, whether it be music, painting, dance, a mechanical invention, or a mathematical formula. Some of the criteria for judging creative research are the following:

1. It must be original to whatever extent possible, given the fact that nothing is every really new
2. It must be performed, staged, and shown before an audience if it is a dance or other work of art
3. It must be accompanied by a written report
4. It must be evaluated by a panel of qualified judges
5. It must be preserved
6. It must be criticized with respect to its artistic qualities and/or its contributions to the appropriate body of knowledge.

The written report should not necessarily conform to the traditional chapter headings. A creative study in dance, for example, might have the following for chapter headings and/or sub-headings:

Chapter I.   Introduction
                A. Need
                B. Purpose(s) or hypotheses
                C. Definition of terms
                D. Delimitations
                E. Limitations
Chapter II.   Review of literature (particularly for dances based upon literary themes). The extent of this review would vary greatly from study to study and would be brief in some and lengthy in others.
Chapter III.   Procedures
                All studies have procedures, irrespective of the method of research being utilized; and these procedures must be specified for the reader.
Chapter IV.   Internal and External Criticism
                This section has some similarity to an analysis of data and involves a thorough criticism of the work. The criticism should be that of both the creator and the panel of expert judges.
Chapter V.   Conclusions

Some of the techniques of research typically employed in creative studies are the following:

1. Bibliographic
2. Choreographic
3. Cinematographic
4. Apparatus
5. Documentary analysis
6. Composition

Programmed Learning

The development of a programmed text does not seem to fit clearly into any of the other methods of research mentioned thus far. There is a creative aspect and a descriptive aspect to the development of a program. The development is accomplished through analysis and creativity; and the field test of the program is descriptive in nature.

Principles of programmed learning which must be incorporated require that the program have the following characteristics:

1. Cause the learner to make an active response

2. Provide the learner with immediate knowledge of results
3. Have small steps in a logically ordered progression
4. Allow the learner to progress at her/his own rate.

Once the program is developed, it must be field tested, and certain dependent variables which are typically studied are time to learn the skill or acquire the knowledge, error rates for various sequences and the total program, and subject response to the experience. An analysis of the effectiveness of the program is often accomplished through the comparison of groups who learned by the traditional teacher-directed method with those who learned by the programmed text method. The research hypothesis for these comparisons is usually the assumption that the programmed text method will be as effective as the teacher-directed method. When this hypothesis is confirmed, the validity of the program is established.

SUGGESTED PROJECTS

1. Analyze the most current year available of the *RQES*. Classify each article as to the method of research utilized.
2. Choose a topic of personal interest. Design a study of the topic of interest under three different methods.

REFERENCE NOTES FOR CHAPTER VII

[1] Isaac and Michael, pp. 42-43.
[2] Best, pp. 93-128.
[3] Isaac and Michael, pp. 60-61.
[4] Isaac and Michael, pp. 60-61.
[5] Cook and Campbell, pp. 342-344.
[6] Cook and Campbell, pp. 343-344.
[7] Cook and Campbell, pp. 344-386.
[8] Best, p. 25.
[9] Best, pp. 132-133.
[10] Best, pp. 139-141.
[11] Best, pp. 142-146.
[12] Kathy L. Ermler, "The History of Intercollegiate Athletics for Women at Southern Illinois University from 1921-1977" (Master's thesis, Southern Illinois University at Carbondale, 1978), pp. iv-vi.
[13] Robert G. Martin, "The Football Helmet: A Historical Perspective from 1860 Through 1979" (Master's thesis, Southern Illinois University at Carbondale, 1980), p. iv.
[14] Best, pp. 147-148.

[15] Jacques Barzun and Henry F. Graff, *The Modern Researcher*, 3rd ed. (New York: Harcourt, Brace, Jovanovic, Inc. 1977).

[16] Best, pp. 149-150.

[17] D. B. Van Dalen, *Understanding Educational Research* (New York: McGraw-Hill Book Company, 1979).

[18] John Dollard, *Criteria for Life History* (New Haven, Conn.: Yale University Press, 1935). Reprinted in 1949 by Peter Smith.

[19] Good, p. 336.

[20] Elizabeth R. Eames is a student of Bertrand Russell's philosophy and is also Professor and Chair of the Department of Philosophy at Southern Illinois University at Carbondale. The section to which Dr. Eames contributed was entitled "Philosophical Methods."

[21] Bertrand Russell, *A History of Western Philosophy* (New York: Simon and Schuster, 1945); References in this paragraph can be found on the following pages, successively, pp. xiv, 203, 525, 546, and 568.

[22] Russell, pp. 92, 784.

[23] Frank Thilly and Ledger Wood, *A History of Philosophy*, 3rd ed. (London: Allen and Unwin, Ltd., 1919), pp. 302-3.

[24] Sir William Cecil Dampier, *A History of Science and its Relations with Philosophy and Religion* (Cambridge University Press, 1929, 4th ed., 1948), pp. 182-4.

[25] J. Thorpe and C. West, "Game Sense and Intelligence," *Perceptual and Motor Skills*, 1969, *29*, p. 326.

[26] J. Thorpe and C. West, "A Test of Game Sense in Badminton," *Perceptual and Motor Skills*, 1969, *28*, pp. 159-169.

[27] J. Thorpe and C. West, "Reliability of a Test of Game Sense," *Perceptual and Motor Skills*, 1970, *31*, p. 582.

[28] J. Thorpe and C. West, "Estimation of Validity for a Test of Game Sense," *Perceptual and Motor Skills*, 1970, *31*, pp. 933-934.

[29] Russell, *A History of Western Philosophy*, pp. 604-674.

[30] Barbara Sampson, "Description and Comparison of Performances for the Straight Drive in Field Hockey," (Master's thesis, Southern Illinois University at Carbondale, 1972).

[31] Russell, pp. 828, ff.

[32] Dampier, *A History of Science*, pp. 17-20.

[33] Bertrand Russell, *Introduction to Mathematical Philosophy* (London: Allen and Unwin, Ltd., 1919), pp. 135, ff.

[34] Alfred Tarski, "Logical Empiricism" in *Readings in Philosophical Analysis* (New York: Appleton-Century-Crofts, 1949), p. 5.

[35] Gilbert Ryle, "Ordinary Language" in *Collected Papers 1929-1968* (New York: Barnes and Noble, 1971).

[36] James Conn, "Response of Physical Education Majors and Non-Physical Education Majors to Sport Jargon," (unpublished paper, P. E. 530, Southern Illinois University at Carbondale, Spring 1979).

[37] S. Morris Eames, *Pragmatic Naturalism* (Carbondale and Edwardsville: Southern Illinois Press, 1977), Ch. 8.

[38] Alice Kildea, p. 16.

[39]Nancy Bandy, "A Conceptual Analysis of Play, Game, Sport, and Athletics," (unpublished paper, P.E. 530, Southern Illinois University at Carbondale, Spring 1980).

[40]Good, pp. 331-333.

[41]John W. Rothney, *Methods of Studying the Individual Child: The Psychological Case Study* (Waltham, Mass.: Blaisdell Publishing Company, 1968), pp. 86-89.

[42]Jacquelyn Schultze, "A Case Study of a Remedial Swimmer," (unpublished master's thesis, Southern Illinois University at Carbondale, 1969).

[43]Claudine Sherrill, "The Case Method Approach to the Professional Preparation of College Teachers in the General Education Program of Physical Education," (unpublished doctoral dissertation, Teacher's College, Columbia University, 1961).

Chapter VIII

CRITICISM OF RESEARCH

ALTHOUGH "criticism," by exact definition, is not necessarily negative it has come to mean that to most people. The dictionary definition of "careful judgment" is probably the most appropriate description of
criticism of research; since if it is research, there must be something good;
but there could be something bad about the work. A thesaurus, by listing
synonyms such as "discriminating," "exacting," and "particular," confirms
the fact that criticism need not be all negative. Criticism, then, must be
understood to be an exercise in evaluation; and evaluation always encompasses an overall assessment from which both positive and negative aspects emerge.

MECHANICAL FACTORS

Certain mechanicl parts should be present regardless of the journal (if
an article), or University (if a thesis). A checklist such as the following
might serve the purpose of an initial mechanical assessment; and the substantive issues of content may be jusdged secondly. The mechanical check
should consist of the presence of the following:

1. Abstract
2. Introduction
3. Statement of Problem
4. Definitions
5. Purposes
6. Review of Literature
7. Procedures
8. Analysis
9. Discussion
10. Conclusions

11. References
12. Summaries
13. Footnotes or reference notes

SUBSTANTIVE QUESTIONS

After the mechanical check has been made, the more substantive issues may be judged by answering the following questions.

1. is the title sufficiently and accurately descriptive?
2. Is the grammar correct?
3. Are paragraph and sentence structures correct?
4. Does the introduction properly set in context the study?
5. Is interest created in the need for the study?
6. Does the statement of the problem delineate the purpose(s), subjects, and how the data were collected and analyzed?
7. Are the purposes very specific?
8. Does the review of literature cover the topic, have many kinds of references, critique other studies, and show the need for the study by pointing out voids in the literature?
9. Are the procedures and the design of the study appropriate and clear?
10. Does the analysis of data utilize appropriate techniques?
11. Are tables clear, tables explained, and findings explained?
12. Are findings parallel with purposes?
13. Are conclusions warranted by the data?
14. Do conclusions relate in a parallel way to the purposes?
15. Are conclusions stated as absolutes?
16. Are the findings and conclusions of the study related and discussed in relation to previous findings in other studies?
17. Are the references wisely chosen and adequate?
18. Are the references predominantly primary sources?
19. Are there many variations and kinds of references with no unwarranted imbalance?
20. Is there an appropiate amount of material appended or footnotes indicating where one can obtain material, if this applies?
21. Are there voids in the design?
22. Did the analysis answer the purposes? Did the study need to be done?
23. Is there some overall meaningfulness to the study?

24. Does the study add some theoretical dimension to what we already know?
25. Do we need to know what the study is about?
26. Is this study serious research?
27. Would we be pleased for reviewers outside of our discipline to see this study?

In addition to the suggestions cited previously the reader is referred to three additional sources. Best[1] offers a "Research Reprt Evaluation Form," which is comprehensive in that it contains the adjectival descriptions necessary for interpretation of the criteria. Isaac and Michael[2] approach this subjec with a section on "Criteria for Evaluation of a Research Report, Article, or Thesis." They elaborate on the criteria in a comprehensive manner. A rating scale employed by Thorpe[3], in addition to those of Best, and Isaac and Michael, appears in Appendix F.

Many of the suggestions offered earlier in the chapter on writing the report relate to criticism. If those recommendations are not followed, they become points of criticism. In addition to the three references mentioned previously (Best; Isaac and Michael; and Thorpe), Barzun and Graff[4] devoted considerable attention to criticism, not in the form of criticism per se, but by way of their coverage on writing the report. For criticism of research, in general, in the discipline of physical education see Dotson's[4] article in the 50th anniversary issue of the *RQES*.

When reviewing and/or criticizing research, whether it is for the *RQES* or as an adviser, it is incumbent upon the reviewer not just to say what is wrong but to offer constructive suggestions as to how the problem(s) may be corrected. This places the burden of proof upon the critical person who knows how to criticize but unfortunately does not know more than the writer. It is quite simple to criticize, but suggestions coming from someone who does not know more than the writer should be taken lightly.

SUMMARY

Criticism is a process of evaluation and should result in both positive and negative comments. A mechanical check should be made first, then an evaluation of the substance of the work should follow. When the researcher receives the results of a review, he/she should insist upon instructive comments in order to judge the validity of the review.

SUGGESTED PROJECTS

1. Using any of the sources recommended, evaluate an article a thesis, or a research report which has been published.
2. Act as a reviewer for an article which has been submitted to the *RQES*.
3. Analyze two to three articles in the recent volume of *RQES* for consistent points of criticism.
4. Criticize abstracts provided by classmates or colleagues.
5. Suggest ways in which the *RQES* could be improved and ways in which it is superior.
6. Read Dotson's article in the 50th anniversary issue of the *RQES*; write a brief summary; and state how research in the profession should change according to Dotson.

REFERENCE NOTES FOR CHAPTER VIII

[1] Best, p. 414.
[2] Isaac and Michael, pp. 223-225.
[3] Jo Anne L. Thorpe, "Rating Scale for Evaluating Thesis Briefs," (unpublished material, PE 500, Southern Illinois University at Carbondale, Illinois, 1985).
[4] Barzun and Graff, pp. 209-279.
[5] Dotson, pp. 23-36.

Chapter IX

ABSTRACTING, ORAL REPORTING, WRITING THE PROSPECTUS

Abstracting

A SAMPLE of acceptable abstracts can readily be found in "Research Completed in HPERD," which is subscribed to by most advanced-degree-granting universities. The guidelines are available from the editor and are quite specific.

The first rule is that the abstract be no more than 200 words. Other journals may allow as much as 500 or more. If the submitter does not adhere to this rule, the editors will cut, and will not necessarily cut where the submitter wishes.

The guidelines suggest accepted abbreviations. These abbreviations reduce the number of words and should be used when possible.

The contents of an abstract should include: the need, purpose(s), subjects, how the data were collected, how the data were analyzed, and the results. If the length is not binding, other important topics such as a brief review of literature and a discussion should be included.

Two sample abstracts follow, one from *Completed Research in HPERD* and one from *Dissertation Abstracts International.* The guidelines for other publications should be obtained from the editor(s).

Example 1: Research Completed in HPER[1]

586. Rogers, Virginia A. Three methods of assessing velocity and angle of projection of the volleyball spike. M.S. in Education, 1969. 129 p. (J.A. Thorpe).

College women students (N = 59) in beginning classes of volleyball and 14 members of the women's varsity volleyball team at SIU were tested on 5 trials of the volleyball spike. Each spike was scored for distance and time and was subjectively assessed for velocity (using a 10-point scale) and for angle of projection (using an independent 5-point scale). The fourth trial of the spike was filmed. Velocity and angle of projection of the spike were determined by the three following methods: the timer-distance method in which the two components were determined by calculation from measures of horizontal distance that the ball traveled, time of ball flight, and height of contact point; the film analysis method in which the two components were determined from the measures described previsouly; and the subjective method. The film analysis, timer-distance, and subjective methods were comparable in assessing the velocity and angle of projection of the volleyball spike (r's ranged from -.91 to .45). The timer-distance method appeared to be the most accurate of the three methods.

Example 2: Dissertation Abstracts International[2]

MEANINGFULNESS IN LIFE, LOCUS OF CONTROL AND SEX-ROLE ORIENTATION OF SELECTED FEMALE ATHLETES AND NON-ATHLETES Order No. 8004057

Kildea, Alice E., Ph.D., Southern Illinois University at Carbondale, 1979, 188 pp. Major Professor: Jo Anne Thorpe

The purpose of this study was to investigate the inter-relationships among meaningfulness in life (MIL), locus of control (LC), and sex-role orientation (SRO) of selected female athletes andnon-athletes.

The subjects were 100 female intercollegiate athletes and one hundred women students who were not athletes. All subjects were undergraduate students of Southern Illinois University, Carbondale.

Data were collected in the spring semester of 1979 by means of the Purpose in Life Test, the Nowicki-Strickland Internal-External Scale and the Bem Sex-Role Inventory. Data were analyzed through correlations, chi-square, and analysis of variance techniques.All statistical techniques were derived through the Statistical Analysis System (SAS); and Duncan's Multiple Range Test was used to test the differences among the means. The critical level for rejection of the null-hypothesis was established at an alpha of .10.

The analyses revealed the following findings: Athletes scored significantly higher on meaningfulness in life than non-athletes.

There was no significant difference between athletes and non-athletes on locus of control.

In sex-role orientation categories the distribution of athletes and non-athletes were significantly different. The percentage of androgynous and masculinely-oriented athletes was musch greater than the percentage of non-athletes in those categories. More than three times more non-athletes than athletes were categorized feminine while the percentage of undifferentiated subjects of the two samples was similar.

Assignment of subjects to sex-role orientation categories when using Bem medians or Kildea medians resulted in no significant difference.

Each level of locus of control was found to be significantly different for athletes with internals (low locus of control) corresponding with high meansingfulness in life, the medium level of locus control corresponding with the middle mean value of meaningfulness in life and the externals (high locus of control) corresponding with low meaningfulness in life. Internal and medium locus of control non-athletes scored significantly higher on meaningfulness in life than external (high locus of control) non-athletes.

For athletes, all levels of meaningfulness in life on locus of control were significantly different with each level inversely corresponding. Non-athletes of the medium and high levels of meaningfulness in life scored significantly higher on meaningfulness in life than non-athletes of the feminine and undifferentiated sex-role orientation categories.

Of all subjects in the study only masculinely-oriented athletes demonstrated a significant difference on locus of control. Masculinely-oriented athletes were more internal (low locus of control) than subjects of all other sex-role orientation categories.

ORAL REPORTING

The three types of oral reports most frequently used are: a specific piece of research which is underway or completed, a review and synthesis of what has been done on a certain topic, or an essay on some theoretical topic. The first type is by far the most used, at least in physical education. The second and third types are most predominant for the guest lecture which normally provides for more time than the format used at convention meetings. For examplesof the second and third types see.

Example of Essay:

Roberta J. Park, "Research and Scholarship in the History of Physical Education and Sport: The Current State of Affairs," *RQES* 54 (June, 1983), pp. 93-103.

Example of Review:

Waneen W. Spirduso, "Exercise and the Aging Brain," *RQES* 54 (June, 1983), pp. 208-218.

The parts of a report on a specific piece of research consists of an introduction, purpose of the study, a review of literature, an account of procedures, introduction and analysis of data, conclusions, and a summary. For any oral presentation the speaker should tell the audience what he/she is going to tell them, tell them, and tell them what he/she has told them.

In preparation for the presentation the speaker should always write out the report. It should then be typed, edited, and retyped. Last-minute changes can still be inserted, but they should be minimal by the time of the presentation.

Most speakers use double-spacing; however, the writer finds that triple-spaced pages with normal margins amount to one minute of speaking time, facilitate the ease of reading, and provides moee space for last-minute changes. These mechanical factors are a matter of preference and relate somewhat to speed in presenting and whether or not the paper is being read.

It is preferable to read a paper when the time is dictated. There is usually no time for rambling, joking, and reminiscing in research-oriented programs. Light, clever comments can be worked in, however, to add humor and to prevent the presentation from being a dull mechanical utterance.

Practice and timing is essential if the speaker does not wish to be embarrassed by having the presentation interrupted and stopped before he/she has completed the report. If questions are to be allowed, a set amount of time should be planned for these in the timing. The normal format for the programs of research for HPERD is 12 minutes per presentation with three minutes for questions. It is frustrating for the presenters and for the audience whent ime schedules are not adhered to.

Many speakers rely heavily on the use of mechanical and electrical visual aids. If not overdone,this can be helpful; however, many an audience has been put to sleep during these dark moments. If visual aids are a must, be prepared for many mechanical factors that may go wrong, such as a burned out bulb, no extension cord, bad focus, and the like. In some convention sites problems exist with union rules about who can install and operate these aids. It is always wise to consider, at least, the failure of mechanical devices.

One can readily see that the writer would rather avoid electrical equipment at a presentation. For most studies the need for visual aids can be satisfied by having handouts that contain tables, graphs, drawings, figures, etc. Whether or not abstracts are printed and distributed prior to the session, it is an excellent plan to offer handouts. These handouts put the listener at ease because note-taking is minimized, data can be studied later,and these written accounts normally contain more than an abstract. Also, the name and address of the presenter can be provided for additional correspondence if necessary or desirable.

Johnson[3] suggested a list of 11 common errors in oral presentations. They are the following:

1. To much review of literature
2. Failure to state the purposes
3. Too much material to cover; therefore rushing
4. Extemporaneous speaking

5. Failure to synthesize the results and relate them to the literature
6. Extrapolation
7. Poor visual aids (see examples in Johnson, pp.340-341)
8. Failure to rehearse adequately
9. Waste of time on slides
10. Hurried speaking
11. Reading with no interest

The author should add also inadequate explanation of procedures and reluctance to yield the podium when time is called.

WRITING THE PROSPECTUS

In research, a prospectus is generally considered to be a proposal for conducting a project, thesis, or dissertation. The purpose of writing a prospectus is usually to convince someone (whose approval is needed) that the project is worthwhile, rests on sound theory, will contribute to some void in a body of knowledge, and really needs to be done.

The parts of a prospectus may vary according to the rules of the university, college, department, agency, or organization in control. It is, however, more or less standard that the parts consist, at least, of the following:

1. An introcution which resembles an introductory chapter in a thesis or dissertation (see the chapter in this text on "Writing the Report")
2. A statement of purposes of the study and hypotheses (if appropriate)
3. A review of literature which is at least sufficiently extensive to show the theoretical basis for the study and where a void exists in the literature
4. Some proposed procedures in order to judge the adequacy of the investigator's experience for dealing with the techniques required; also to determine the availability of the subject group
5. Anticipated results and results from pilot work if available
6. References
7. Appendix material, including preliminary work such as questionnaires, interviews, test directions, diagrams, etc.

Because a prospectus involves something planned rather than something which has already occurred, it seems correct to write in the future tense, with the exception of the review of literature. Although this approach is logical, a student who is writing a thesis or a dissertation will find that writing in the past tense will enable her/him to utilize much of the prospectus to insert later into the thesis or dissertation. The extent to which this can be done is integrally tied to how thorough the work has been in preparing the prospectus.

The length of a prospectus varies considerably; however, because the purpose is to convince someone of worthiness, the longer approach usually results in better acceptance and fewer changes which are necessary in the final work. There is the chance, of course, that the prospectus of great length can be "shot down" with as great ease as the brief one. This is not usually the case and can be avoided to a certain extent by good communication and regular consultation with those persons who are to approve the prospectus. Too often the paper is written in too much isolation from the people in authority.

A word of advice to the graduate student here is probably a bit out of context as a part of writing a prospectus, but it is given anyway. Asceticism, which is a way of making students suffer, still lurks in the minds of many professors. Those who ascribe to this point of view believe that this is the way in which a graduate student should learn. A student of research may believe that he or she has produced the perfect piece of work only to have it shredded. Cheer up, do careful preparation, and work hard on communication. It is the quickest way to soften an ascetic.

SUMMARY

Abstracts vary according to the rules of certain journals but in general give purpose(s), a brief review of literature, procedures, and findings. The length usually varies from 200 words to 500 or more.

Oral reports may be for different purposes but in physical education the most widely used is that of a specific research project. The parts are the same as those of a thesis. Typing, rehearsing, and timing the paper are essential. If mechanical and electrical visual aids are to be used, anticipate potential problems so that the presentation can go on. Giving handouts is a good way to avoid using electrical visual aids and also is very useful for the listener.

Since a prospectus is designed to convince someone whose approval is needed, it should contain all of the parts of a thesis except, of course, the data and the final results. The more complete the prospectus, the better the outcome usually. Writing in the past tense can save some re-writing later. Careful preparation and good communication can offset the rejection rate of a prospectus.

SUGGESTED PROJECTS

1. Prepare an abstract consistent with the requirements of "Completed Research in HPER." Use a topic in your area of interest for a thesis. Fabricate the results to be consistent with your research hypothesis.
2. Prepare and give a 3-minute oral report based on a pilot study which you have conducted. Give handouts and/or use electrical visual aids.
3. Write a prospectus for a thesis or dissertation. This may be a final project for a course in research methodology.

REFERENCE NOTES FOR CHAPTER IX

[1]Virginia A. Rogers, "The Methods of Assessing Velocity and Angle of Projection of the Volleyball Spike," *Research Completed in HPER,* 12 (1970):215.
[2]Alice E. Kildea, "Meaningfulness in Life, Locus of Control, and Sex-Role Orientation of Selected Female Athletes and Non-Athletes," *Dissertation Abstracts International,* 40 (February, 1980):4519-A and 4520-A.
[3]Perry Johnson in AAHPER, *Research Methods,* pp. 339-342.

APPENDIX A
TABLES

TABLE 4-1

TABLE OF RANDOM DIGITS[a]

03 99 11 04 61	93 71 61 68 94	66 08 32 46 53	84 60 95 82 32	88 61 81 91 61
38 55 59 55 54	32 88 65 97 80	08 35 56 08 60	29 73 54 77 62	71 29 92 38 53
17 54 67 37 04	92 05 24 62 15	55 12 12 92 81	59 07 60 79 36	27 95 45 89 09
32 64 35 28 61	95 81 90 68 31	00 91 19 89 36	76 35 59 37 79	80 86 30 05 14
69 57 26 87 77	39 51 03 59 05	14 06 04 06 19	29 54 96 96 16	33 56 46 07 80
24 12 26 65 91	27 69 90 64 94	14 84 54 66 72	61 95 87 71 00	90 89 97 57 54
61 19 63 02 31	92 96 26 17 73	41 83 95 53 82	17 26 77 09 43	78 03 87 02 67
30 53 22 17 04	10 27 41 22 02	39 68 52 33 09	10 06 16 88 29	55 98 66 64 85
03 78 89 75 99	75 86 72 07 17	74 41 65 31 66	35 20 83 33 74	87 53 90 88 23
48 22 86 33 79	85 78 34 76 19	53 15 26 74 33	35 66 35 29 72	16 81 86 03 11

[a]This table is an excerpt printed by permission of the Rand Corporation.

TABLE 4-4

CRITICAL VALUES OF CHI SQUARE[a]

df	Probability under H_a that $X^2 \geq$ chi square													
	.99	.98	.95	.90	.80	.70	.50	.30	.20	.10	.05	.02	.01	.001
1	.00016	.00063	.0039	.016	.064	.15	.46	1.07	1.64	2.71	3.84	5.41	6.64	10.83
2	.02	.04	.10	.21	.45	.71	1.39	2.41	3.22	4.60	5.99	7.82	9.21	13.82
3	.12	.18	.35	.58	1.00	1.42	2.37	3.66	4.64	6.25	7.82	9.84	11.34	16.27
4	.30	.43	.71	1.06	1.65	2.20	3.36	4.88	5.99	7.78	9.49	11.67	13.28	18.46
5	.55	.75	1.14	1.61	2.34	3.00	4.35	6.06	7.29	9.24	11.07	13.39	15.09	20.52

[a]This table is an excerpt. It contains figures for only 5 degrees of freedom for illustrative purpose for problem number 7. Chapter IV.

TABLE 4-5

CRITICAL VALUES OF t^a

df	Level of significance of one-tailed test					
	.10	.05	.025	.01	.005	.0005
	Level of significance for two-tailed test					
	.20	.10	.05	.02	.01	.001
1	3.078	6.314	12.706	31.821	63.657	636.619
2	1.886	2.920	4.303	6.965	9.925	31.598
3	1.638	2.353	3.182	4.541	5.841	12.941
4	1.533	2.132	2.776	3.747	4.604	8.610
5	1.476	2.015	2.571	3.365	4.032	6.859
6	1.440	1.943	2.447	3.143	3.707	5.959
7	1.415	1.895	2.365	2.998	3.499	5.405
8	1.397	1.850	2.306	2.896	3.355	5.041
9	1.383	1.833	2.262	2.821	3.250	4.781
10	1.372	1.812	2.228	2.764	3.169	4.587
40	1.303	1.684	2.021	2.423	2.704	3.551
60	1.296	1.671	2.000	2.390	2.660	3.460
120	1.289	1.658	1.980	2.358	2.617	3.373
∞	1.282	1.645	1.960	2.326	2.576	3.291

[a]This table is an excerpt for degrees of freedom 1 - 10 and 40 - infinity. It is illustrative for problems number 8 and 9, Chapter IV.

TABLE 4-6

CRITICAL VALUES OF F

5 PERCENT AND 1 PERCENT POINTS FOR THE DISTRIBUTION OF F*

Each cell gives two values: the smaller (upper) is for the .05 level, the larger (lower) is for the .01 level.

Degrees of freedom for greater mean square

df (lesser)	1	2	3	4	5	6	7	8	9	10	11	12	14	16	20	24	30	40	50	75	100	200	500	∞
1	161 / 4062	200 / 4999	216 / 5403	225 / 5625	230 / 5764	234 / 5859	237 / 5928	239 / 5981	241 / 6022	242 / 6056	243 / 6082	244 / 6106	245 / 6142	246 / 6159	248 / 6208	249 / 6234	250 / 6258	251 / 6286	252 / 6302	253 / 6323	253 / 6334	254 / 6352	254 / 6361	254 / 6366
2	18.51 / 98.49	19.00 / 99.01	19.16 / 99.17	19.25 / 99.25	19.30 / 99.30	19.33 / 99.33	19.36 / 99.34	19.37 / 99.36	19.38 / 99.38	19.39 / 99.40	19.40 / 99.41	19.41 / 99.42	19.42 / 99.43	19.43 / 99.44	19.44 / 99.45	19.45 / 99.46	19.46 / 99.47	19.47 / 99.48	19.47 / 99.48	19.48 / 99.49	19.49 / 99.49	19.49 / 99.49	19.50 / 99.50	19.50 / 99.50
3	10.13 / 34.12	9.55 / 30.81	9.28 / 29.46	9.12 / 28.71	9.01 / 28.24	8.94 / 27.91	8.88 / 27.67	8.84 / 27.49	8.81 / 27.34	8.78 / 27.23	8.76 / 27.13	8.74 / 27.05	8.71 / 26.92	8.69 / 26.83	8.66 / 26.69	8.64 / 26.60	8.62 / 26.50	8.60 / 26.41	8.58 / 26.35	8.57 / 26.27	8.56 / 26.23	8.54 / 26.18	8.54 / 26.14	8.53 / 26.12
4	7.71 / 21.20	6.94 / 18.00	6.59 / 15.69	6.39 / 15.98	6.26 / 15.52	6.16 / 15.21	6.09 / 14.98	6.04 / 14.80	6.00 / 14.66	5.96 / 14.54	5.93 / 14.45	5.91 / 14.37	5.87 / 14.24	5.84 / 14.18	5.80 / 14.02	5.77 / 13.93	5.74 / 13.83	5.71 / 13.74	5.70 / 13.69	5.68 / 13.61	5.66 / 13.57	5.65 / 13.52	5.64 / 13.48	5.63 / 13.45
5	6.61 / 16.26	5.79 / 13.27	5.41 / 12.06	5.19 / 11.39	5.05 / 10.97	4.95 / 10.67	4.88 / 10.45	4.82 / 10.27	4.78 / 10.15	4.74 / 10.05	4.70 / 9.96	4.68 / 9.89	4.64 / 9.77	4.60 / 9.68	4.56 / 9.55	4.53 / 9.47	4.50 / 9.38	4.46 / 9.29	4.44 / 9.24	4.42 / 9.17	4.40 / 9.13	4.38 / 9.07	4.37 / 9.04	4.36 / 9.02
6	5.99 / 13.74	5.14 / 10.92	4.76 / 9.78	4.53 / 9.15	4.39 / 8.75	4.28 / 8.47	4.21 / 8.26	4.15 / 8.10	4.10 / 7.98	4.06 / 7.87	4.03 / 7.79	4.00 / 7.72	3.96 / 7.60	3.92 / 7.52	3.87 / 7.39	3.84 / 7.31	3.81 / 7.23	3.77 / 7.14	3.75 / 7.09	3.72 / 7.02	3.71 / 6.99	3.69 / 6.94	3.68 / 6.90	3.67 / 6.88
7	5.59 / 12.25	4.74 / 9.55	4.35 / 8.45	4.12 / 7.85	3.97 / 7.46	3.87 / 7.19	3.79 / 7.00	3.73 / 6.84	3.68 / 6.71	3.63 / 6.62	3.60 / 6.54	3.57 / 6.47	3.52 / 6.35	3.49 / 6.27	3.44 / 6.15	3.41 / 6.07	3.38 / 5.98	3.34 / 5.90	3.32 / 5.88	3.29 / 5.78	3.28 / 5.75	3.25 / 5.70	3.24 / 5.67	3.23 / 5.65
8	5.32 / 11.26	4.46 / 8.65	4.07 / 7.59	3.84 / 7.01	3.69 / 6.63	3.58 / 6.37	3.50 / 6.19	3.44 / 6.03	3.39 / 5.91	3.34 / 5.82	3.31 / 5.74	3.28 / 5.67	3.23 / 5.56	3.20 / 5.48	3.15 / 5.36	3.12 / 5.28	3.08 / 5.20	3.05 / 5.11	3.03 / 5.06	3.00 / 5.00	2.98 / 4.96	2.96 / 4.91	2.94 / 4.88	2.93 / 4.86
9	5.12 / 10.56	4.26 / 8.02	3.86 / 6.99	3.63 / 6.42	3.48 / 6.06	3.37 / 5.80	3.29 / 5.62	3.23 / 5.47	3.18 / 5.35	3.13 / 5.26	3.10 / 5.18	3.07 / 5.11	3.02 / 5.00	2.98 / 4.92	2.93 / 4.80	2.90 / 4.73	2.86 / 4.64	2.82 / 4.56	2.80 / 4.51	2.77 / 4.45	2.76 / 4.41	2.73 / 4.36	2.72 / 4.33	2.71 / 4.31

*This excerpt is illustrative for problem number 10, Chapter IV. The smaller of the F ratios in the set of 2 is for the .05 level. The larger is for the .01 level.

TABLE 4-7

ANALYSIS OF *RZES*, 1983, FOR
METHODS, STATISTICAL TECHNIQUES, AND SUBJECTS

Reference	Method of Research	Primary Statistical Techniques	Type of Statistics Used	Type of Subjects
Englehorn	Experimental	ANOVA, graphs, multiple comparisons, means, standard deviations (S.D.'s)	B[a]	Volunteers
Felt and Spray	Descriptive	means, S.D.'s, standard error, percentages	D[a]	Hypothetical distributions
Lee and Magill	Experimental	Graphs, ANOVA, MANOVA, multiple comparisons, means, S.D.'s	B	Selected Psychology classes
Magill and Parks	Experimental	ANOVA, multiple comparisons	I[a]	Volunteers
Reeve and Mainor	Experimental	graphs, ANOVA, means	B	Selected volunteers
Roche, Tyleshevski and Rogers	Descriptive	correlations, graphs, means, S.D.'s	D	Volunteer parents and their children
Southard	Descriptive	correlations, means	D	Volunteers
Tucker	Experimental	means, S.D.'s, ANOVA, MANOVA	B	Cluster sample 5 classes in Weight Training, 5 in health
Williams and Miller	Descriptive Survey	means, S.D.'s, percentages, chi square	B	Athletic directors responding to a questionnaire
Corbin, et al.	Experimental	means, S.D.'s, ANOVA	B	Volunteers
Langenfeld	Descriptive	percentages, S.D.'s means, graphs	D	Selected volunteers
Cox	Experimental	means, S.D.'s graphs, ANOVA	B	Volunteers

[a]D = descriptive, I = inferential, B = both

TABLE 4-7 *(Continued)*

Reference	Method of Research	Primary Statistical Techniques	Type of Statistics Used	Type of Subjects
Higgs	Descriptive	means, S.D.'s	D	Wheelchairs
Marino	Descriptive	means, S.D.'s correlation	D	Selected volunteers
Mihevic	Experimental	graphs, ANOVA, S.D.'s	B	Selected volunteers
Noble and Cox	Measurement	means, correlation, regression	B	A selected class
Schutz, Smoll, and Gessaroli	Descriptive	MANOVA, ANOVA, means, S.D.'s, regression, correlation	B	Stratified random
Thomas, et al.	Experimental	means, S.D.'s, ANOVA, MANOVA, graphs	B	Stratified random
Vogler and Ford	Experimental	graphs, ANOVA, multiple comparisons	B	Selected students
Brennan	Measurement	ANOVA, percentages	B	Selected students
Byrd and Thomas	Descriptive	correlation, ANOVA, means, standard errors	B	Volunteers
Sady, et al.	Descriptive	means, S.D.'s, ANOVA standard errors, graphs	B	Volunteers
Tangen-Foster and Lathen	Descriptive Survey	percentages	D	Selected department heads
Anthrop and Allen	Descriptive	percentages, X^2, ANOVA, means	B	Selected female athletes
Bain and Wendt	Descriptive	correlation, means, S.D.'s, ANOVA, regression, X^2	B	Selected volunteers
Balog	Experimental	graphs, ANOVA, multiple comparisons	B	Volunteers

TABLE 4–7 *(Continued)*

Reference	Method of Research	Primary Statistical Techniques	Type of Statistics Used	Type of Subjects
Fortney	Descriptive	ANOVA, graphs, means	B	Volunteers
Gagnon, Doré, and Lamontagne	Creative	graphs, means, S.D.'s	D	One selected subject
Hardy	Experimental	means, S.D.'s, correlation	D	Volunteers
Imwold and Hoffman	Descriptive	means, S.D.'s, graphs	D	Selected teachers
McMurray, Wilson, and Kitchell	Experimental	means, standard errors, graphs	D	Selected volunteers
Morris, Clarke, and Dainis	Descriptive	means, S.D.'s, graphs	D	Volunteers
Plagenhoff	Descriptive	percentages, means, S.D.'s	D	One cadaver
Powers, et al.	Descriptive	regression, means, correlation, standard errors	D	Selected volunteers
Schempp, Cheffers, and Zaichkowsky	Experimental	ANOVA, MANOVA, means, graphs, correlation	B	Selected volunteers
Weiss	Experimental	MANOVA, ANOVA, means, S.D.'s	B	Random sample
Gabbard, Gibbons, and Elledge	Descriptive	graphs, ANOVA, multiple comparisons	B	Volunteers
Kleiber and Roberts	Descriptive	percentages χ^2	B	Selected volunteers
Safrit and Wood	Measurement	percentages	D	All Physical Education teachers in Madison, WI

TABLE 4–7 *(Continued)*

Reference	Method of Research	Primary Statistical Techniques	Types of Statistics Used	Type of Subjects
Bird and Rikli	Experimental	graphs, means, S.D.'s, ANOVA	B	Volunteers
Clutch, et al.	Experimental	ANOVA, graph, S.D.'s, means	B	Volunteers, class V.B. team
Godbout, Brunelle, and Tousignant	Descriptive	means, S.D.'s, *t* tests, graphs	B	Stratified random
Godbout and Schutz	Descriptive	ANOVA	I	Selected observers and subjects
Haywood	Experimental	means, S.D.'s, ANOVA, multiple comparisons	B	Volunteers
Hoffman, Imwold and Koller	Descriptive	graphs, ANOVA, means, multiple comparisons, percentages	B	Random selection
Puretz	Experimental	ANOVA	I	Volunteers
Sady, et al.	Experimental	means, standard errors, graphs, correlations, percentages, *t* tests, ANOVA	B	Volunteers
Sprague and Mann	Descriptive	correlation, means, S.D.'s, graphs	D	Selected volunteers
Wrisberg and Mead	Experimental	ANOVA, means, S.D.'s, multiple comparisons	B	Selected volunteers
Schick and Berg	Measurement	means, S.D.'s, correlation	D	Selected volunteers
Schick, Stoner, and Jette	Descriptive	ANOVA, means, multiple comparisons, percentages	B	Selected volunteers
Upton, et al.	Descriptive	*t* tests	I	Selected volunteers

TABLE 4-8

SUMMARY OF METHOD BY TYPE OF STATISTICS
FOR *RQES* 1983

Statistical Techniques by Category

Methods	Descriptive	Inferential	Both
Descriptive N = 26	11	2	13
Experimental N = 21	2	2	17
Other N = 5	3	0	2
TOTAL N = 52	N = 16	N = 4	N = 32

TABLE 4-9

PERCENTAGES FOR SEX OF CHIEF ADMINISTRATOR
OF ATHLETICS BY SIZE OF UNIVERSITY

	Males			Females			Total	
	f	%	% of Total	f	%	% of Total	f	%
Small	62	95.38	62.63	3	4.62	3.30	65	65.66
Large	29	96.67	29.29	1	3.33	1.01	30	30.30
Big 10	4	100.00	4.04	0	0.00	0.00	4	4.04
Total	95		95.96	4		4.04	99[a]	100.00

[a]Twelve institutions did not respond to the question and were not included in the total number of responses. Therefore, the total number was 99 instead of 111 for this analysis.

TABLE 4-10

MEANS AND STANDARD DEVIATIONS FOR MEANINGFULNESS IN LIFE FOR ATHLETES AND NONATHLETES

Variable	Mean	Standard Deviation	N
Meaningfulness in Life	111.01	13.75	200
Athletes	114.33	11.07	100
Nonathletes	107.69	15.98	100

TABLE 4-11

STANDARD SCORES FOR NINTH-GRADE BOYS[a]

T-Score	Basketball Throw (feet)	Broad Jump (inches)	Obstacle Race (Seconds)	T-Score
80	117		16.0	80
79			16.1	79
78		104	16.2	78
77	111		16.3	77
76	109	103	16.4	76
75	108	102	16.5	75
74	107	101	16.6	74
73	106		16.7	73
72	104	100	16.8	72
71	102		16.9	71
70	100	99	17.0	70
69	99	98	17.1	69
68	98	97	17.2	68
67	97	96	17.3	67
66	96	95	17.4	66
65	95	94	17.5	65
64	94	93	17.6	64
63	93	92	17.7	63
62	92	91	17.8	62
61	91	90	17.9	61
60	90	89	18.0	60
59	89	88	18.1	59
58	88	87	18.2	58
57	87	86	18.3	57
56	86	85	18.4	56
55	85	84	18.5	55
54	84	83	18.6	54
53	83	82	18.7	53
52	82	81	18.8	52
51	81	80	18.9	51
50	80	79	19.0	50
49	79	78	19.1	49
48	78	77	19.2	48
47	77	76	19.3	47
46	76	75	19.4	46

TABLE 4-11 *(Continued)*

T-Score	Basketball Throw (feet)	Broad Jump (inches)	Obstacle Race (Seconds)	T-Score
45	75	74	19.5	45
44	74	73	19.6	44
43	73	72	19.7	43
42	72	71	19.8	42
41	71	70	20.0	41
40	70	69	20.2	40
39	69	68	20.4	39
38	68	67	20.6	38
37	67	66	20.8	37
36	66	65	21.0	36
35	65	64	21.2	35
34	64	63	21.4	34
33	63	62	21.6	33
32	62	61	22.0	32
31	61	60	22.2	31
30	60	59		30
29	59	58		29
28	58	57		28
27	56	56	24.0	27
26	55	55		26
25	54	54		25
24	52	53		24
23	50			23
22	48			22
21	46			21

[a]From Kilday, K., and M. Latchaw, Study of Motor in Ninth Grade Boys. Unpublished studies, University of California, Los Angeles, 1961.
Adapted by permission of Dr. Marjorie Latchaw (originally) and Barrow and McGee (recently).

TABLE 4-12

CORRELATION COEFFICIENTS AMONG THE SEVEN VARIABLES INVOLVED IN THE STUDY OF RELATIONSHIPS

	Time	Vertical Difference	Effect. 1	Effect. 2	Horizontal Velocity	Vertical Velocity	Projection Velocity
time	1.00						
Vertical Difference	.17[a]	1.00					
Effect. 1	.12	.02	1.00				
Effect. 2	.10	.12	.94	1.00			
Horizontal Velocity	-.73	-.33	.18	.14	1.00		
Vertical Velocity	.94	-.16	-.10	-.13	-.61	1.00	
Projection Velocity	-.34	-.50	.19	.11	.87	.16	1.00

[a]The probability for $r > .0000$ for $n = 64$ at the .05 level is .211.

TABLE 4-13

ODD-EVEN RELIABILITY COEFFICIENTS
FOR DISTANCE AND VELOCITY IN THE ACTUAL STUDY

	No. of Observations[a]	Obtained r	Spearman-Brown (n = 2)
Standard Bat			
Distance	5	.42	.59
Velocity	5	.58	.73
Angular Bat			
Distance	5	.53	.69
Velocity	5	.50	.67

[a]Ten trials were given: 5 odd and 5 even.

TABLE 4-14

CONTINGENCY TABLES OF CHI-SQUARE FOR ASSIGNMENT TO SEX-ROLE ORIENTATION CATEGORIES OF NONATHLETES WITH BEM MEDIANS AND KILDEA MEDIANS

Bem Study	Present Study Nonathletes				Frequency
	A	M	F	U	
A	17	7	2	1	27
M	0	13	0	0	13
F	0	0	37	6	
U	0	0	0	17	17
Frequency	17	20	39	24	100

Total χ^2 = 193.527, *df* = 9, *P* = .0001

Total χ^2 value required at α = .10 level = 14.68

Contingency Coefficient = .81

TABLE 4-15

CONTINGENCY TABLE OF CHI-SQUARE FOR THE DIFFERENCE BETWEEN ATHLETES AND NONATHLETES IN THEIR DISTRIBUTIONS AMONG SEX-ROLE ORIENTATION CATEGORIES

	Androgynous	Masculine	Feminine	Undif-ferentiated	Marginal Total
Athlete					
Frequency	33.0	34.0	12.0	21.0	100
Expected	25.0	27.0	25.5	22.5	
Cell²	2.6	1.8	7.1	0.1	
Percent	16.50	17.00	6.00	10.50	50.00
Row Pct	33.00	34.00	12.00	21.00	
Col Pct	66.0	62.96	23.53	46.67	
Nonathlete					
Frequency	17.0	20.0	39.0	24.0	100
Expected	25.0	27.0	22.5		
Cell²	2.6	1.8	7.1	0.1	
Percent	8.50	10.00	19.50	12.00	50.00
Row Pct	17.00	20.00	39.00	24.00	
Col Pct	34.00	37.04	76.47	53.33	
Marginal	50	54	51	45	200
Total	25.00	37.00	25.50	22.50	100.00

Total $X^2 = 23.24$, $P = .0001$, $df = 3$
Total X^2 value required at $\alpha = .10$ level $= 6.251$
Contingency Coefficient $= .32$

TABLE 4-16

ANALYSIS OF TOTAL ERRORS FOR GAMES WON VS GAMES LOST

				t TEST FOR THE SET			
Independent Variable:	N	Mean	Standard Deviation	Variance	df	t	P<.10
Games Won	8	.25	1.58	Equal	14	2.50	.025
Games Lost	8	-1.88	1.80				

TABLE 4-17

PHYSICAL AND BODY COMPOSITION CHARACTERISTICS
PRE- AND POST-TRAINING

Variable		Pretraining	Posttraining	Paired t
Height (Ccm)	x	166.1	166.1	0.27
	SD	4.1	3.8	
Total body weight	x	62.5	62.1	1.47
	SD	7.8	7.2	
Density (g.m⁻³)	x	1.052	1.054	2.79*
	SD	.000	.000	
% fat	x	20.4	19.6	2.91*
	SD	7.5	6.7	
Fat weight (kg)	x	12.7	12.1	2.95*
	SD	6.2	5.4	
Lean body weight (kg)	x	49.8	50.0	0.68
	SD	4.1	3.9	
Residual volume (1)	x	1.40	1.42	0.68
	SD	.35	.32	
Weight in water (kg)	x	1.95	2.01	1.51
	SD	.59	.56	

*Significant at .05 level.

SKINFOLD (sf) AND CIRCUMFERENCE CHANGES RESULTING FROM SWIMMING

Variable		Pretraining	Posttraining	Paired t
Means sf of 3 sites (mm)	x	14.5	11.9	3.87*
	SD	4.5	3.1	
Triceps sf (mm)	x	14.3	13.2	2.05
	SD	3.6	2.5	
Scapulla sf (mm)	x	13.2	10.3	3.84*
	SD	4.7	2.6	
Supra iliac sf (mm)	x	15.9	12.1	4.07*
	SD	7.2	6.0	
Hip circumference (cm)	x	94.7	95.0	0.82
	SD	5.4	5.2	
Flexed biceps	x	29.7	30.0	0.69
circumference (cm)	SD	1.3	1.1	

*Significant at .05 level.

TABLE 4-18

ONE-WAY ANALYSES OF VARIANCE FOR THE CATEGORIES OF SEX-ROLE ORIENTATION ON ATPA (BEM MEDIANS)

Dependent Variables	Independent Variables Androgynous — Masculine — Feminine — Undifferentiated			
	Sum of Squares	Mean Squares	F[a]	p[b]
Social Experience	300.657	100.219	2.39	.0677[c]
Within Subjects	11014.084	41.879		
Health and Fitness	281.395	93.798	2.33	.0731[c]
Within Subjects	10570.792	40.193		
Vertigo	771.666	257.222	3.40	.0182[c]
Within Subjects	19809.633	75.629		
Aesthetic	368.031	122.677	2.38	.0684[c]
Within Subjects	13527.931	51.437		
Cathartic	485.281	161.760	2.98	.0315[c]
Within Subjects	14270.111	54.258		
Ascetic	530.618	176.872	2.42	.0655[c]
Within Subjects	19233.860	73.132		
Chance	95.140	31.713	0.35	.7926
Within Subjects	23907.451	90.902		

[a]df = 3/263 for all analyses
[b]Exact probabilities are reported
[c]Significant at the .10 level

TABLE 4-19

ANALYSIS OF VARIANCE FOR LOCUS OF CONTROL AND
SEX-ROLE ORIENTATION OF NONATHLETES
ON MEANINGFULNESS IN LIFE

Source of Variance	df	Sum of Squares	Mean Squares	F	Prob.[a]	R^2
Full Model	11	4942.41	449.31	1.94	.0400	.20
Within Subjects	88	20334.98	231.08			
Total	99	25277.39				
Full Model Sources						
SRO	3	1649.05	549.68	2.38	.0730[a]	.065
LC	2	2286.94	1143.47	4.95	.0090[a]	.090
SRO × LC	6	1006.41	167.41	0.73	.6290	.039

[a]Exact Probability

TABLE 4-20

DUNCAN'S MULTIPLE RANGE TEST FOR THREE GROUPS OF LOCUS OF CONTROL ON MEANINGFULNESS IN LIFE FOR NONATHLETES

Dependent Variable = MIL	Mean	Standard Deviation	Grouping	N
Nonathletes:				
LC Low	112.90	21.67	A	30
LC Medium	110.09	9.90	A	35
LC High	100.83	12.91	B	35

ªMeans with same grouping letters are not significantly different.

TABLE 4-21

ANOVA FOR REPEATED MEASURES — TRIAL 1 FOR 4 TESTS OF 100 YARDS EACH AT 0, 2, 4, and 6 WEEKS

Source	SS	df	MS	F	Prob. of F[a]
Main Effects and 2-way Interaction					
Class	158.39	1	158.39	0.20	0.6587
Method	1,295.07	1	1,295.07	1.62	0.2099
Class X Method	173.13	1	173.13	0.22	0.6442
Within Treatments	37,671.60	47	801.52		
Total	39,298.19	50			
Repeated Measures Over Time — 2-way and 3-way Interactions					
Four Tests	890.78	3	296.93	11.59	0.0001[b]
Test X Class	466.37	3	155.46	6.07	0.0007[b]
Test X Method	131.86	3	43.95	1.71	0.1667
Test X Class X Method	94.31	3	31.44	1.23	0.3024
Within Replicates	3,613.74	141	25.63		
Total	5,197.06	153			

[a]The .10 level of significance was selected as the critical level for rejection of the null-hypothesis; however, exact probabilities are reported.
[b]Statistically significant.

TABLE 4-22

MANOVA RESULTS

Effect	Multivariate F	P
Athlete-Nonathlete	7.00	.0001
Sex	30.83	.0001
A-NA × Sex	1.30	.24

Univariate ANOVA Followups

	A-NA	Sex
Social Growth	A > NA'	F > M
Social Continuation	A > NA	F > M
Health and Fitness: Value	A > NA	Non Sig
Health and Fitness: Enjoyment	A > NA	M > F
Vertigo	A > NA	M > F
Aesthetic	A > NA	F > M
Catharsis	Non Sig	F > M
Ascetic	A > NA	M > F

'To be interpreted as Athletes scoring significantly higher than Nonathletes on this subdomain. (p < .01).

TABLE 4-23

REGRESSION ANALYSIS FOR COMPARISON OF CLASSES ON THE PRETEST

Model	Criterion	Predictors	R^2	F Ratio	Probability
Full	Pretest Score	Unit vector + Classes 1-4	.04		
				1.41[a]	.24
Restricted	Pretest Score	Unit vector	.00		

[a]Degrees of freedom = 3 and 105 in the numerator and denominator, respectively.

TABLE 4-24

STEP-WISE REGRESSION ANALYSIS FOR FIVE PREDICTORS OF RESPONSE ACCURACY

Predictor	R^2 Full	Restriction	R^2 Restriction	R^2 Change	Partial[a] F	df	Overall F	df
T	.283	Zero	.283	.283			8.69[b]	1/22
T + MT	.373	T	.373	.090	3.02**	1/21	6.25*	2/21
T + MT + W	.409	T + MT	.409	.035	1.20	1/20	4.60**	3/20
T + MT + W + IQ	.417	T + MT + W	.417	.008	.27	1/19	3.40**	4/19
T + MT + W + IQ + RT	.425	T + MT + W + IA		.008	.26	1/18	2.66**	5/18

Legend

T = Thorpe Experience   IQ = Intelligence
MT = Movement Time   RT = Reaction Time
W = West Experience

[a]Partial F = the F ratio for the variance of the restriction only. Overall F ratio is the ratio for all predictors of the full model.
[b]The variable contributing the greatest variance to the predictionis tested against zero; therefore the partial and overall F's are the same for the first variable.
* P = <.05
** P = <.10

APPENDIX B
ANSWERS TO PROBLEMS IN CHAPTER IV

ANSWERS TO PROBLEMS IN CHAPTER IV

Problems No. 1

Four Samples Drawn from the 12 Scores in Table 4-2

	Drawn by Lot				Drawn by Using A Table Random Numbers		
	S_s No.	Score			S_s No.	Score	
Group I	1	6		Group I	3	5	
	2	9			11	3	
	3	5			4	6	
Group II	4	6		Group II	8	8	
	5	8			5	8	
	6	10			12	6	
Group III	7	2		Group III	7	2	
	8	8			9	7	
	9	7			6	10	
Group IV	10	5		Group IV	1	6	
	11	3			2	9	
	12	6			10	5	

Note: In choosing group 1 by using the table of random numbers we are reading all numbers of 12 and less. The first three numbers are 03, 11, and 04. They, therefore, become group 1. The next three become group 2, etc. There is no need to draw the final group.

Sample Means: Group 1   4.7
        2   7.3.
        3   6.3
        4   6.7

Standard Deviation of the Sample Means: 1.12

Problem No. 2
Population Standard Deviation: 2.34
Standard Error of the Mean: .68

Problem No. 3
A. *T* of 75
B. *Z* of -1.0
C. Either. They are the Same.

Problem No. 4

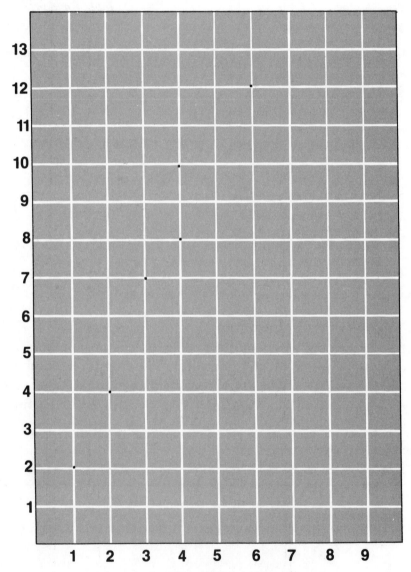

Figure 4.8 Scattergram for Problem No. 4

Pearson's *r* would range from .90 to .99.
(Actual *r* = .97)

Problem No. 5
Pearson's $r = .98$

Problem No. 6
Spearman's Rho $(\rho) = .50$

Problem No. 7
Chi Square $(\chi^2) = 9.90$ With df = 3, it is statistically significant at the .02 level (9.84 required).

Problem No. 8
$t_i = 4.17$. With df = 5, t_i is statistically significant at the .01 level (4.032 required).

Problem No. 9
$t_c = -3.29$. With df = 2, t_c is statistically non-significant at the .05 level (4.303 required). It is significant at the .10 level (2.92 required).

Problem No. 10
$F = 11.63$ For $\dfrac{df = 2}{df = 6}$, F is statistically significant at the .01 level (10.92 required).

APPENDIX C
BIBLIOGRAPHICAL AIDS

A SELECTED BIBLIOGRAPHY OF RESEARCH AIDS IN EDUCATION

Compiled by Ruth E. Bauner

Education and Psychology Division
Morris Library
Southern Illinois University at Carbondale
Revised June 1984

I. GUIDES FOR BOOKS

1. Educ. Office
   q015.73
   P976b and P976s

   Books in Print. Annual author, title, and subject index to *Publishers' Trade List Annual.*

2. 370.16
   B959d
   1967

   Burke, Arvid J. and Mary A. *Documentation in Education.* N.Y., Teachers College Press, 1967. (Revision of *How To Locate Education Information and Data,* by Carter Alexander and Arvid J. Burke.)

3. B015.73
   C972

   Cumulative Book Index. 1928-date. (Monthly. Successor to *United States Catalog.*)

4. qB018.1
   C356

   National Union Catalog, pre-1956 imprints. Chicago, Mansell.

5. B018.1
   N277

   National Union Catalog; a cumulative author list representing Library of Congress printed cards and titles reported by other American libraries. Washington, 1956-date. (Printed in 9 monthly issues, 3 quarterly cumulations, annual cumulations for four years and a quinquennial in the fifth.)

6. B015.73
   U58

   United States Catalog; Books in print. N.Y., Wilson, 1899-1928.

7. B018.1
   C357

   U.S. Library of Congress. *A Catalog of Books Represented by Library of Congress Printed Cards* to July 31, 1942. Author list. 167v.

8. B019.1
   U58s

   U.S. Library of Congress. *The Library of Congress Subject Catalog,* a cumulative list of works represented by Library of Congress printed cards, 1950-date.

9. R025.5
   S541g

   Sheehy, Eugene P. *Guide to Reference Books.* 9th ed. Chicago A.L.A., 1976 (and supplements).

II. BIBLIOGRAPHIES OF RESEARCH STUDIES

1. Index Table
   R082
   C737
   V.20-24

   Comprehensive Dissertation Index 1861-1972, V.20-24 (Education). Ann Arbor, Michigan, Xerox University Microfilms, 1973.

2. Index Table
   R082
   C737
   V.33-37

   Comprehensive Dissertation Index 1861-1972, V.33-37 (*Author Index*). Ann Arbor, Michigan, Xerox University Microfilms, 1973.

3. Index Table
   R082
   C737
   1973
   V.1-5

   Comprehensive Dissertations Index 1973. Ann Arbor, Michigan, Xerox University Microfilms, 1974 (V.3-4, Social Sciences and Humanities; V.5, Author Index). This is the beginning of an annual series.

4. Index Table
   R082
   M626

   Dissertation Abstracts. (Formerly Microfilm Abstracts) V.12-26. 1952-1966.

5. Index Table
   R082
   D613

   Dissertation Abstracts A; The Humanities and Social Sciences. V.27, July 1966-June 1969.

6. R501.6
   D613

   Dissertation Abstracts B; The Sciences and Engineering. V.27, July 1966-June 1969.

7. Index Table
   R082
   D613

   Dissertation Abstracts International A; The Humanities and Social Sciences. V.30, July 1969-date.

8. R501.6
   D613

   Dissertation Abstracts International B; The Sciences and Engineering. V.30, July 1969-date.

9. Ref.
   q370.3
   E562
   1982

   Encyclopedia of Educational Research. Ed. By Harold E. Mitzel. 5th ed. N.Y. Macmillan, 1982. (A critical evaluation, synthesis and interpretation of reported studies in the field of education.)

10. Periodical
    Education
    Library

    Review of Educational Research 1931-date. Has a cumulative index for volumes 1-12, 1931-52. (Supplements *Encyclopedia of Educational Research.*)

11. R370.16
    I64m

    Iowa State Teachers College, Cedar Falls. Bureau of Research. *Mater's Theses in Education.* Cedar Falls, 1951/1952-date. (Annual)

12. Reference
    Desk and
    Index Table

    A KWIC Index to Theses and Dissertations, 1949-1972, Southern Illinois University at Carbondale, Illinois, Morris Library, 1975.

13. Index Table
    R082
    M423

    Masters abstracts; a catalog of selected masters theses on microfilm with keyword and author index, Ann Arbor, Michigan, University Microfilms, V.1, 1962-date.

III. MAGAZINE AND NEWSPAPER INDEXES

1. R605
   I42

   Applied Science and Technology Index. 1958-date. (Successor to *Industrial Arts Index.*)

2. Index Table
   R370.5016
   B862

   British Education Index. 1954-date.

3. Index Table
   R650.16
   B979

   Business Periodicals Index. 1958-date. (Successor to *Industrial Arts Index*)

4. Social Studies
   Index Table
   qR071.3016
   N558

   Chicago Tribune Newspaper Index. V.1, 1972-date.

5. Index Table
   Education Library

   Child Development Abstracts and Bibliography. V.1, 1927-date.

6. Index Table
   R370.5
   C976

   Current Index to Journals in Education. V.1, 1969-date.

7. Periodical
   Education Library

   Education Abstracts. V.1-8, 1936-Oct. 1944. (No longer published.)

8. Periodical
   Education Library

   Education Abstracts. UNESCO. Education Clearing House, V.1-16, 1948-1964. (No longer published.)

9. Index Table
   R370.5
   E24

   Education Index. January 1929-date. (Includes periodicals, proceedings, and yearbooks.)

10. Index Table
    R340.05
    I38

    An Index to Legal Periodicals. V.1, 1926-date.

11. Index Table
    R977.866
    I38

    Index to St. Louis Newspapers. V.1, 1975-date.

12. Social Studies
    Index Table
    R050
    I61

    International Index to Periodicals. 1907-1964. (V.1-4 includes indexing of 22 education periodicals which were transferred to *Education Index* in 1929. Changed to *Social Sciences and Humanities Index.*)

13. Social Studies
    Index Table

    Management Research. V.1, 1968-date.

14. Social Studies
    Index Table
    R070
    N552

    New York Times Index. 1851-date.

15. Ref.
    150.3
    T413
    1982

    Thesaurus of Psychological Index Terms, 3rd ed. Washington, D.C., American Psychological Association 1982.

16.	Education Index Table
	Psychological Abstracts. 1927-date.
17.	Index Table qR150.16 C726a
	Author Index to Psychological Index 1894-1935 and Psychological Abstracts 1927-1958. Boston, G.K. Hall, 1960. 5 vols. (Supplements)
18.	Index Table qR150.16 P974c
	Cumulative Subject Index to Psychological Abstracts 1927-1960. Boston, G.K. Hall, 1966. 2 vols. (Supplements)
19.	Index Table R300.16 P976
	Public Affairs Information Service. 1915-date. (Includes books, periodicals, and pamphlets.)
20.	Ref. 050 R286 Social Studies, Humanities and Undergraduate Libraries
	Readers' Guide to Periodical Literature. 1900-date. (Indexes only periodicals.)
21.	Index Table R300.16 S6783
	Social Sciences Index. V.1, 1974-date.
22.	Index Table Social Studies
	Sociological Abstracts, V.1, 1953-date.
23.	Index Table R370.5016 S797
	State Education Journal Index. 1963-date.

IV. DIRECTORIES TO PERIODICALS

1. R072.058
   A976d

   Ayer, N.W. and sons. *Directory of Newspapers and Periodicals*. Philadelphia, Ayer, 1880-date. (Annual)

2. R370.5016
   C186g
   1975

   Camp, William L. and Bryan L. Schwark. *Guide to Periodicals in Education and Its Academic Disciplines*. 2nd ed. Scarecrow Press, 1975.

3. R370.16
   K92e

   Krepel, Wayne J. and DuVall, Charles R. *Education and Education Related Serials*; a directory. Littleton, Colorado, Libraries Unlimited, 1977.

4. Ref.
   370.78
   M274a

   Manera, Elizabeth S. and Wright, Robert E. *Annotated Writer's Guide to Professional Education Journals*. Scottsdate, Ariz., Bobets Pub. Co., 1982.

5. Education
   R050.16
   U45

   Ulrich's International Periodicals Directory. A classified guide to current periodicals, foreign and domestic. N.Y. Bowker. (Biennial)

6. qB050.16
   U584
   1965

   Union List of Serials in Libraries of the United States and Canada. 3rd ed. N.Y. Wilson, 1965. (This is supplemented by the following item.)

7. qB050.16
   N532

   New Serials Titles. Washington, DC, Library of Congress, Jan. 1950-date.

8. Education
   Library

   Southern Illinois University. Morris Library. *Current Periodicals List.* Carbondale, Illinois, 1978. (and *Supplement*)

9. R370.5
   W956

   The Writer's Guide to Educational Journals, edited by William L. Heward. Columbus, Ohio, Special Press, 1979.

V. DIRECTORIES TO ORGANIZATIONS AND ASSOCIATIONS

1. Education office
   q061.58
   N567f
   ed.9

   The Foundation Directory. 9th ed. N.Y., Foundation Center, 1983.

2. Education
   qR061

   Gale Research Co. *Encyclopedia of Associations.* Detroit, Gale, 1958-date. 2 vols. (Annual)

3. R370.5873
   G946
   1980

   Guide to American Educational Directories. 5th ed. Edited by Bernard Klein. N.Y., B. Klein & Co., 1980.

4. R370.6
   U58e

   U.S. Office of Education. *Education Directory.* Washington, G.P.O., 1912-date. (Annual)

VI. STATISTICS

1. R370.973
   H219d

   Hamilton, Malcolm C. *Directory of Educational Statistics;* a guide to sources. Ann Arbor, Michigan. Pierian Press, 1974.

2. R371.2
   W9721

   World Survey of Education. Paris, UNESCO, V.1-5, 1955-1971. (Successor to *World Handbook of Educational Organizations and Statistics.*)

3. K
   C3.223/
   (no.)

   U.S. Bureau of the Census. *Census of the Population:* 1980. Washington, G.P.O., 1981-82.

4. K
   ED1.113:
   982

   U.S. Department of Education. *Digest of Education Statistics,* Washington, G.P.O., 1962-date. (Annual)

5. K
ED1.112:
980

U.S. Department of Education. National Center for Education Statistics. *Elementary and Secondary Schools, Pupils and Staff.* Washington, G.P.O. 1982. (Annual)

6. K
ED1.112/2:
980-81

U.S. Department of Educational National Center for Education Statistics. *Public Elementary and Secondary Education in the United States, 1980-81: A Statistical Conpendium.* Washington, G.P.O., 1983

7. K
HE19.318/3:
973-74

U.S. Office of Education. *Statistics of State School Systems,* 1973-74. Washington, G.P.O., 1976. (Annual)

8. K
ED1.120:
990-91/v.1

U.S. Department of Education. *National Center for Education Statistics. Projections of Educational Statistics to 1990-91.*

See also *Montly Catalog of United States Publications* and general statistical sources such as *Information Please Almanac, World Almanac, Statistical Abstract, Historical Statistics of the United States,* encyclopedias, yearbooks, and periodical articles which can be located through the periodical indexes.

VII. SPECIALIZED ENCYCLOPEDIAS, DICTIONARIES, ETC.

1. Ref
q370.3
D326a

Dejnozka, Edward L. and Kapel, David E. *American Educators' Encyclopedia.* Westport, Conn, Greenwood Press, 1982.

2. R370.16
E242
1979

Education Literature, 1907-1932, ed. by Malcolm Hamilton. N.Y., Garland, 1979. 25v. in 12.

3. qR370.3
E565

The Encyclopedia of Education. Edited by Lee C. Deighton. N.Y., Macmillan, 1971. 10v.

4. R150.3
E562

Encyclopedia of Psychology, New York, Herder and Herder, 1972.

5. R150.3
E58c
1964

English, Horace B. and Ava C., *A Comprehensive Dictionary of Psychological and Psychoanalytical Terms.* N.Y., David McKay, 1964.

6. R370.3
G646d
1973

Good, C.V. *Dictionary of Education.* 3rd ed. N.Y., McGraw-Hill, 1973.

7. Ref
370.321
H391c

Hawes, Gene R. and Hawes, Lynne Salop *The Concise Dictionary of Education.* N.Y., Van Nostrand, 1982.

8. R378.003
I61

The International Encyclopedia of Higher Education. ed. by Asa S. Knowles. San Francisco, Calif., Jossey-

Bass, 1977. 10v

9. Education
qR616.89003
I61

International Encyclopedia of Psychiatry, Psychology, Psychoanalysis, and Neurology, ed. by Benjamin B. Wolman. N.Y., Aesculapius Publishers, 1977. 12v.

10. R370.59
S785

Standard Education Almanac. Los Angeles, Academic Media, 1968-date. (Annual)

11. R371
S445
1973

Travers, Robert M.W., ed. *Second Handbook of Research on Teaching;* a Project of the American Educational Research Association. Chicago, Rand McNally, 1973. (Successor to Nathaniel Gage's *Handbook of Research on Teaching.*)

VIII. GOVERNMENT PUBLICATIONS: INDEXES, BIBLIOGRAPHIES, AND DIRECTORIES, ETC.

For *U.S. Publications* consult the following:

1. Education
R015.73
M838i
1978

Morehead, Joe. *Introduction to United States Public Documents.* Littleton, Colo., Libraries Unlimited, 1978.

2. K
LC1.6/4:
Documents
Index Table Basement

Palic, Vladimir. *Government Publications; A Guide to Bibliographic Tools,* 4th ed. Washington, Library of Congress, 1975.

3. K
LG6.2:
G74/976
Documents
Index Table Basement

Popular Names of U.S. Government Reports; a catalog. Washington, Library of Congress, 1976.

4. 370.6
U58c
no. 736
Education Library
Office

U.S. Office of Education. *Cooperative Research Projects.* Washington, G.P.O., 1964, 1966.

5. 370.78
U58cp

U.S. Office of Education. *Cooperative Research Projects.* Supplement. Washington, G.P.O., 1964-1966.

6. Index Table
R370.78016
R432

U.S. Office of Education. *Resources in Education.* Washington, DC. 1975-date. (Published 12 times a year. Annual cumulative indexes.) Formerly *Research in Education,* Nov. 1966-Dec. 1974

7. Ref
025.49
E24t
ed.10

Thesaurus of ERIC Descriptors, 10th ed. Phoenix, Ariz., Oryx Press, 1984.

8. Index Table
R015.73
U58m
Education and
Documents Area
in Basement

U.S. Superintendent of Documents. *Monthly Catalog of United States Public Documents*, 1895-date

9. Documents
qR015.73
U58m
Subject Index

Cumulative Subject Index to the Monthly Catalog of United States Government Publications, 1900-1971, v.1-15. Washington, Carrollton Press, 1973.

For United Nations and UNESCO publications consult the following:

10. Documents
Index Table
Basement

Documents of Internal Organizations. V.1-3, 1947-50

11. Documents
Index Table
Basement

United Nations Documents Index. V.1, 1950-date.

12. Documents
Index Table

United Nations Documents Index. Cumulated Index, 1950-1962, V.1-13. N.Y., Kraus-Thomson Organization Limited, 1974.

13. Documents
Index Table
UN
ST/LIB/Ser.1
A. 28-37
Basement

Undex; United Nations Documents Index; Series A-Subject Index. New York, United Nations, 1974-date.

For *Illinois School Law* consult the following:

14. R379.14773
I29s
1983

Illinois. Department of Public Instruction. *The School Code of Illinois.* 1983.

IX. SOURCES FOR REVIEWS

1. Humanities
Index Table
R028.05
B724

Book Review Digest. N.Y., Wilson, 1905-date. (Monthly with annual cumulations.)

2. Humanities
Index Table
R028.5
B7243

Book Review Index. Detroit, Gale Research Co., 1965-1968, 1972-date. (Bi-monthly with annual cumulations.)

3. R151.2015
B967m

Buros, Oscar Krisen. *Mental Measurements Yearbook.* Highland Park, N.J., Gryphon Press, 1st, 1938-date.

4. Index Table
   R370.5
   E24

Education Index. January 1929-September 1961, July 1969-date. (By author under heading: "Book Reviews." Starting July 1975 in the back of each index.)

5. Periodical
   Humanities

New York Times Book Review Index. 1896-1970. 5v (Author, title, byline, subject, and category index to reviews appearing in the *New York Times Book Review.*)

X. STYLE MANUALS

1. R150.149
   A512p
   1983

American Psychological Assocation. *Publication Manual,* 3rd ed. Washington, 1983.

2. R378.242
   T929m
   1973

Turabian, Kate S. *A manual for Writing of Term Papers, Theses and Dissertations,* 4th ed. Chicago and London, University of Chicago Press, 1973.

Bound copies of all Southern Illinois University theses and dissertations are listed in the Morris Library Central Card Catalog under author and under the subject heading "Southern Illinois University. Theses." Subject files of education and psychology theses and dissertations may also be found in the Education/Psychology card catalog.

XI. EDUCATIONAL RESEARCH PERIODICALS

The following are some of the education periodicals which usually carry reports of education research:

African Journal of Educational Research
Alberta Journal of Educational Research
American Educational Research Journal
British Journal of Educational Psychology
CEDR Quarterly
College and Research Libraries
College Student Journal
ERQ: Educational Research Quarterly
Education Canada
Educational Administration Quarterly
Educational and Psychological Measurement

Educational Research
Elementary School Journal
Graduate Research in Urban Education and Related
  Disciplines
Illinois School of Research and Development
Journal for Research in Mathematics Education
Journal of Education Research
Journal of Educational Statistics
Journal of Experimental Education
Journal of Research and Development in Education
Journal of Research in Science Teaching
Journal of Vocational Education Research
Peabody Journal of Education
Research in Higher Education
Research Quarterly for Exercise and Sport
Review of Educational Research
Scandinavian Journal of Educational Research
Theory Into Practice
Viewpoints in Teaching and Learning

PHYSICAL EDUCATION AND RECREATION

1. R371.732 A5126c — American Association for Health, Physical Education and Recreation. Research Council, *Completed Research in Health, Physical Education and Recreation.* Washington. V.1, 1959-date.

2. Ref 371.732 A512a3 — American Alliance for Health, Physical Education, Recreation and Dance. *Abstracts of Research Papers,* 1973-

3. Education Office R371.73 H434 — *Health, Physical Education, and Recreation Microcard Bulletin.* Eugene, Oregon, University of Oregon, School of Health, Physical Education and Recreaion, Microcard Publication, V.1. 1965-date.

4. R371.732016 p543i — Phi Epsilon Kappa. *Index and Abstracts of Foreign Physical Education Literature.* Indianapolis. V.1., 1955- V.20, 1975.

5. Index Table 790.05 P578 — *Physical Education Index,* V.1, 1978-date.

6. R378.242016 T674 — *A Topical List of Theses and Dissertations in Health Education.* Washington, Association for the Advancement of Health Education. American Alliance for Health, Physical Education, and Recreation, V.1, 1970- V.3, 1978.

7. qR371.732   University of Illinois at Urbana - Champaign. *Dic-*
    I29d   *tionary Catalog of the Applied Life Studies Library* (for-
                          merly Physical Education Library). 4 vols. (and
                          Supplements) Boston, G.K. Hill, 1977.

PSYCHOLOGY

1. 150.72   Reed, Jeffrey G. and Baxter, Pam M. *Library Use: a*
    R3241   *Handbook for Psychology.* Washington, D.C., Ameri-
                          can Psychological Association, 1983.

2. Ref.   *How to Do a Literature Search in Psychology,* by Donald B.
    150.285   Weaver and others. Dallas, Texas, Resource Press,
    H847   1982.

SPECIAL EDUCATION

1. Index Table   *Developmental Disabilities Abstracts.* Washington, G.P.O.,
    R132.2016   V.12, 1977-date. (Formerly *Mental Retardation Ab-*
    M549   *stracts,* 1964-1976).

2. Periodical   *Exceptional Child Education Resources.* Washington,
    Index Table   Council for Exceptional Children, V.9, 1977-78 to
                          date. (Formerly *Exceptional Child Education Abstracts,*
                          1969-1977.

3. Education   *Research Relating to Children, Bulletin.* Washington,
    Index Table   G.P.O. No. 2, 1952- No. 42, 1979.
    R301.431407
    R432

BIBLIOGRAPHY OF
PHYSICAL EDUCATION AND RECREATION
MATERIALS

Compiled by M. Kathy Cook

Southern Illinois University
at Carbondale
Education/Psychology Library
January 1981

I. GENERAL AIDS

1. qR025.49   United States, Library of Congress. *Library of Congress Subject Headings*. 2v.9th ed. Washington: Library of Congress, 1980.
2.   Southern Illinois University, Carbondale. Library. *Morris Library Periodicals List*. 1978.

II. BIBLIOGRAPHIES AND INDEXES

1. Index Table   *Current Index to Journals in Education*. New York, Oryx
    R370.5   Press. V.1- . 1969.   . (Monthly)
    C976
2. Index Table   *Education Index*. New York, H.W. Wilson Co., V.1-
    R370.5   1929-   . (Monthly except July and August. An-
    E24   ual cumulations)
3. Index Table   *Physical Education/Sports Index*. New York, Marathon
    R796.016   Press. v.1 . 1978-   (Quarterly)
    P578
4. R050   *Reader's Guide to Periodical Literature*. New York, H.W.
    R286   Wilson Co., V.1- . 1900-   . (Monthly Annual cumulations)
5. Index Table   U.S. Office of Education. *Resources in Education*.
    R370.78016   Washington, DC, 1975-date. (Published 12 times a
    R432   year. Semi-annual cumulative indexes). Formerly *Research in Education* Nov. 1966-Dec. 1974.
6. R025.49   *Thesaurus of ERIC Descriptors*, 8th ed. Phoenix, Ar-
    E24t   zona, Oryx Press, 1980.
    ed.8

III. ENCYCLOPEDIAS, DICTIONARIES, ALMANACS

1. qR370.3
   E565
   The Encyclopedia of Education; ed. by Lee C. Deighton. New York, Macmillan & The Free Press, 1971, 10 v.

2. qR796
   N567
   New York Times Encyclopedia of Sports; ed. by Gene Brown. New York, Arno Press, 1979, 14 v.

3. R796.03
   F932s
   Frommer, Harvey, *Sports Lingo; A Dictionary of the Language of Sports.* New York, Atheneum, 1979.

4. R370.3
   G646d
   1973
   Good, C.V., *Dictionary of Education.* 3rd ed., NY, McGraw-Hill, 1973.

5. R796.03
   W385
   Webster's Sports Dictionary. Springfield, Mass, G & C. Merriam Co., 1976.

6. Education
   R317.3
   W927
   World Almanac and Book of Facts. New York, Newspaper Enterprise Association. (Annual)

IV. DIRECTORIES, GUIDES

1. R371.74
   B65
   Blue Book of College Athletics. Akron, Ohio, Rohrich Corp., 1980. (Annual)

2. R371.74058
   B658
   Blue Book of Junior College Athletics. Cleveland, Ohio, Rohrich Corp., 1980. (Annual)

3. R796.05873
   N277
   National Directory of College Athletics. ed. by Ray Franks. Armarillo, Texas, Ray Franks Publishing Ranch, 1980. (Annual)

4. qR790.1
   R311
   Recreation and Outdoor Life Directory; ed. by Paul Wasserman. Detroit, Gale, 1979.

5. R796.5405
   P228
   Parents' Guide to Accredited Camps: Midwest. Martinsville, IN American Camping Association. (Annual)

6. R796.5405
   P2281
   Parents' Guide to Accredited Camps: Northeast. Martinsville, IN. American Camping Association. (Annual)

7. R796.5405
   P2282
   Parents' Guide to Accredited Camps: South. Martinsville, IN. American Camping Association. (Annual)

8. R796.5405
   P2283
   Parents' Guide to Accredited Camps: West. Martinsville, IN. American Camping Association. (Annual)

V. SCHOOL LAW

1. R371.1330973
   W842r
   Woellner, Elizabeth H. *Requirements for Certification. Teachers, Counselors, Librarians, Administrators for Elementary Schools, Secondary Schools, Junior Colleges.* Chi-

cago, University of Chicago Press, 1st- . 1935-
. (Annual)

2. R379.14773   Illinois. Law, Statutes, etc. *The School Code of Illinois.*
    I29s   Springfield, 19 - . (Bi-annual)

VI. SCHOOL DIRECTORIES

1. R373.025   *Education Directory: Local Education Agencies.* Washington,
    E24A2   GPO (Annual)
2. R370.6   Illinois. Dept. of Public Instruction. *Directory of Illinois*
    I29i   *Schools.* Springfield, 1916- . (Annual)
3. qR370.973   *Patterson's American Education.* North Chicago, IL, Edu-
    P318   cational Directories, 1904- . (Annual)

VII. WRITING MANUALS

1. R378.242   Turabian, Kate L. *A Manual for Writers of Term Papers,*
    T929m   *Theses, and Dissertations.* 4th ed. Chicago and Lon-
    1973   don, The University of Chicago Press, 1973.
2. R150.149   American Psychological Association. *Publication Man-*
    A512p   *ual.* 1974 rev. Washington, 1974.
    1974

VIII. OFFICIAL RULES

1. R796.323   *Official National Collegiate Athletic Association Basketball*
    0132   *Rules and Interpretations.* Shawnee Mission, KA,
                NCAA 1974- (Annual)
2. R796.332   *Official National Collegiate Athletic Association Football Rules*
    0132   *and Interpretations.* Shawnee Mission, KA, NCAA
                1974- (Annual)
3. R796.334   *Official National Collegiate Athletic Association Soccer Guide.*
    0132   40th Annual Guide. Shawnee Mission, KA,
                NCAA 1980. (Annual)
4. R796.812   *Official National Collegiate Athletic Association Wrestling*
    0132   *Guide.* 53rd Annual Guide. Shawnee Mission, KA,
                NCAA 1979. (Annual)
5. R796.32   National Association for Girls & Women in Sport.
    A512b   *NAGWS Guide: Basketball.* Reston, VA. AAHPERD,
                (Annual)
6. 796.352   National Association for Girls & Women in Sport.
    N277n   *NAGWS Guide: Bowling-Golf.* Washington, D.C.
                AAHPER, (Biennial)

7. R797.2
   N277n

National Association for Girls & Women in Sport. *NAGWS Guide: Competitive Swimming and Diving.* Reston, VA. . AAHPERD, (Annual)

8. 796.355
   N277n

National Association for Girls & Women in Sport. *NAGWS Guide: Field Hockey.* Washington, D.C. AAHPER, (Biennial)

9. R796.3320202
   N277n

National Association for Girls & Women in Sport. *NAGWS Guide: Flag Football, Speedball.* Washington, D.C. AAHPER, (Biennial)

10. R796.4102
    G997A2

National Association for Girls & Women in Sport. *NAGWS Guide: Gymnastics.* Reston, VA, AAHPERD, (Biennial)

11. 796.347
    N277n

National Association for Girls & Women in Sport. *NAGWS Guide: Lacrosse.* Washington, D.C. AAHPER, (Biennial)

12. 796.9305
    N277n

National Association for Girls & Women in Sport. *NAGWS Rules: SKiing.* Washington, D.C. AAHPER, (Biennial)

13. R796.33402
    N277n

National Association for Girls & Women in Sport. *NAGWS Guide: Soccer.* Reston, VA, AAHPERD, (Annual)

14. R796.3578
    S791

National Association for Girls & Women in Sport. *NAGWS Guide: Softball.* Washington, D.C. AAHPER, (Biennial)

15. R797.2
    N277ns

National Association for Girls & Women in Sport. *NAGWS Guide: Synchronized Swimming.* Washington, D.C. AAHPERD, (Annual)

16. 796.345
    032

National Association for Girls & Women in Sport. *NAGWS Guide: Tennis, Badminton, Squash.* Washington, D.C. AAHPER, (Biennial)

17. 796.325
    V923

National Association for Girls & Women in Sport. *NAGWS Guide: Volleyball.* Reston, VA, AAHPERD, (Annual)

IX. CLASSIFIED PERIODICALS

1. qR790.068
   P235

Design. Washington, National Park Service, 1957- (Quarterly)

2. qR790.068
   P2351A2

Grist. Washington, National Park Service, v.15- 1971- (Bimonthly)

3. 796.058
   I61

International Review of Sport Sociology. Warsaw, Polish Scientific Publishers, v.1- 1966- (Quarterly)

4. 796.01
   J86

Journal of the Philosophy of Sport. Minneapolis, Philosophic Society for the Study of Sport. v.1- 1974- (Annual)

5. 371.7305   *Quest*. Champaign, Illinois, National Association for
   Q5   Physical Education in Higher Education. v.1-
                                  1963-   (Biennial)

6. 796.05   *Review of Sport and Leisure*. Park Forest South, Illinois,
   R454   Governors State University, v.1- 1976-   (Bien-
                                    nial)

7. qR790.068   *Trends*. Washington, National Park Service. v.1-
   P2353   1964-   (Quarterly)

APPENDIX D
VISUAL AIDS USED WITH RATING SCALES

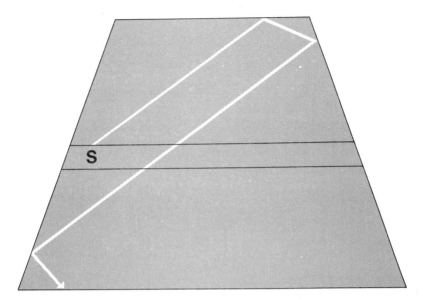

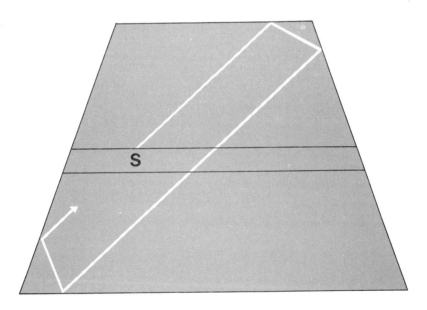

Figure 5-1. Serves in Racquetball

Section I--Arm Stroke

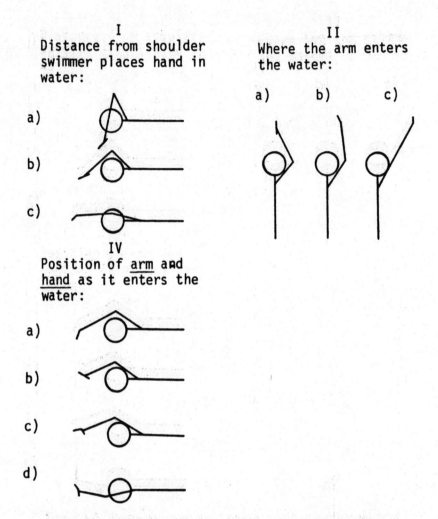

I
Distance from shoulder
swimmer places hand in
water:

a)

b)

c)

II
Where the arm enters
the water:

a)   b)   c)

IV
Position of arm and
hand as it enters the
water:

a)

b)

c)

d)

Figure 5-2. Diagnostic score sheet for errors in beginning swimming.

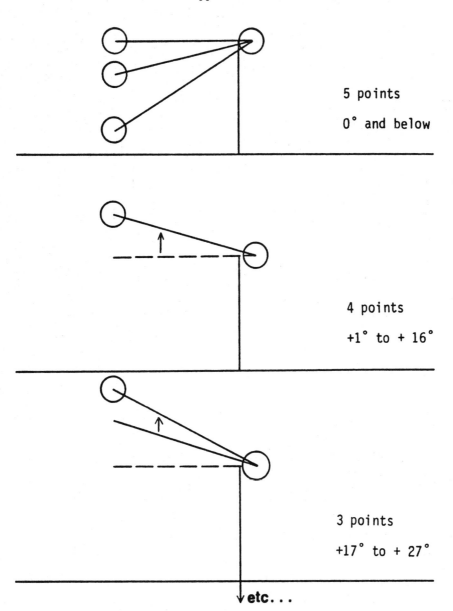

5 points

0° and below

4 points

+1° to + 16°

3 points

+17° to + 27°

↓etc. . .

Figure 5-3. Assessment of angle of projection of the volleyball spike.

APPENDIX E

MEDFORD SCALE AND
WALTERS QUESTIONNAIRE

MEDFORD COACH-PLAYER INTERACTION INVENTORY
PLAYER'S FORM

NOTE: Strict Confidentiality is Assured

Test Number: _____

Sport: _____

 On the following page, you will be shown a large number of characteristics. I am asking you to use those characteristics in order to describe *your coach,* that is, I would like you to indicate, on a scale from 1 to 7, how true of *your coach* these characteristics are. Please do not leave any characteristics unmarked.

Example: Prompt

 Mark a 1 if it is *Never or Almost Never True* that your coach is prompt.

 Mark 2 if it is *Usually Not True* that your coach is prompt.

 Mark 3 if it is *Sometimes But Infrequently True* that your coach is prompt.

 Mark 4 if it is *Occasionally True* that your coach is prompt.

 Mark 5 if it is *Often True* that your coach is prompt.

 Mark 6 if it is *Usually True* that your coach is prompt.

 Mark 7 if it is *Always or Almost Always True* that your coach is prompt.

 Thus, if you feel the characteristics of *Sometimes but Infrequently True* that your coach is "prompt," *Never or Almost Never True* that your coach is "healthy" then you should mark these characteristics as follows:

Prompt	3
Healthy	1
Etc.	

 The only difference between the player's form and the coaches' form is the phrase "coaches' form" replaces the phrase "player's form."

MEDFORD COACH-PLAYER INTERACTION INVENTORY
(Continued)

	1	2	3	4	5	6	7
	Never or Almost Never True	Usually Not True	Sometimes but Infrequently True	Occasionally True	Often True	Usually True	Always or Almost Always True

Clear	
Confident	
Conscientious	
Consistent	
Constructive	
Perceptive*	
Energetic	
Exemplary	
Fair	
Firm	
Friendly	
Good Sport	

Honest	
Resourceful**	
Intelligent	
Leader	
Mature	
Motivating	
Open	
Sincere	
Thorough	
Understanding	
Versatile	

*Perceptive is the adjective replacing "discerning" in the original version.

**Resourceful is the adjective replacing "imaginative" in the original version.

WALTERS QUESTIONNAIRE ON PAST EXPERIENCE

Name _____ Age _____

College Attending _____

Circle the answer that best describes your *high school* experience in basketball.

1. I played on an interscholastic high school basketball team for:
   - (A) 4 years   (5pts)*
   - (B) 3 years   (4 pts)
   - (C) 2 years   (3 pts)
   - (D) 1 year   (2 pts)
   - (E) Never played in high school   (1 pt)

2. My high school was:
   - (A) larger than 3,000 students
   - (B) between 1,000 and 2,000 students
   - (C) between 500 and 1,000 students
   - (D) between 100 and 500 students
   - (E) under 100 students

3. An average season in my high school program was:
   - (A) 25 or more games
   - (B) 20-24 games
   - (C) 15-19 games
   - (D) 10-14 games
   - (E) under 10 games

4. During the summers while in high school, I have:
   - (A) participated for 4 years in a basketball camp
   - (B) participated for 3 years in a basketball camp
   - (C) participated for 2 years in a basketball camp
   - (D) participated for 1 year in a basketball camp
   - (E) never participated in a basketball camp

5. While in high school, I played basketball for other organizations (such as the Y.W.C.A. or A.A.U.):
   - (A) for 4 years
   - (B) for 3 years
   - (C) for 2 years
   - (D) for 1 year
   - (E) never

---

*The scoring system was not on the questionnaire given to the subjects.

6. In each of the high school games, I;
   (A) always played in the varsity games
   (B) usually played in the varsity games
   (C) sometimes played in the varsity games
   (D) seldom played in the varsity games
   (E) never played in the varsity games
7. During high school I played under a very knowledgeable coach.
   (A) yes
   (B) no
8. During high school I played under an experienced coach.
   (A) yes
   (B) no
9. If you received any honor(s) while playing basketball in high school, please list them in the column on the left. In the column on the right, please tell how you were selected for that specific honor.

HONOR(S)   METHOD OF SELECTION

_____   _____
_____   _____
_____   _____
_____   _____
_____   _____

Circle the answer that best describes your *collegiate* experience in basketball.

1. I played on an intercollegiate basketball team for:
   (A) 4 or more years
   (B) 3 years
2. During the summers while in college, I have:
   (A) participated for 4 or more years in a basketball camp
   (B) participated for 3 years in a basketball camp
   (C) participated for 2 years in a basketball camp
   (D) participated for 1 year in a basketball camp
   (E) never participated in a basketball camp
3. While in college, I played basketball for other organizations (such as A.A.U.):
   (A) for 4 or more years
   (B) for 3 years
   (C) for 2 years
   (D) for 1 year

(E) never

4. In collegiate basketball, I have been a varsity player:
   (A) for 4 or more years
   (B) for 3 years
   (C) for 2 years
   (D) for 1 year
   (E) never

5. In collegiate basketball, I have been a starter on the varsity squad:
   (A) for 4 or more years
   (B) for 3 years
   (C) for 2 years
   (D) for 1 year
   (E) never

6. In each of the collegiate games, I:
   (A) played approximately 90% of the time
   (B) played approximately 75% of the time
   (C) played approximately 50% of the time
   (D) played approximately 25% of the time
   (E) played under 25% of the time

7. In collegiate basketball, I have been a junior varsity player:
   (A) for 4 or more years
   (B) for 3 years
   (C) for 2 years
   (D) for 1 year
   (E) never

8. During my college career, I have played under a very knowledgeable coach.
   (A) yes
   (B) no

9. During my college career, I have played under an experienced coach.
   (A) yes
   (B) no

10. If you have received any honor(s) while playing basketball in college, please list them in the column on the left. In the column on the right, please tell how you were selected for that specific honor.

HONOR(S)   METHOD OF SELECTION

_____   _____
_____   _____
_____   _____
_____   _____
_____   _____
_____   _____

APPENDIX F
EVALUATIVE SCALES FOR
RESEARCH REPORTS

I. Title of article or report
   A. Precise identification of problem area, often including specification of independent and dependent variables and identification of target population
   B. Sufficient clarity and conciseness for indexing of title
   C. Effective arrangement of words in title

II. The problem
   A. Description and statement of problem
      1. Statement of basic (felt) difficulty or problem situation — significance and importance of the problem area in either basic or applied research.
      2. Careful analysis of known and suspected facts and explanation of existing information and knowledge that may have some bearing on problem — the spelling out of specific factors giving rise to the basic difficulty, of their interrelationships, and of their relevance to the problem area.
      3. Soundness of the logic underlying selection of variables or factors to be studied and expression of their relationship to the problem area.
      4. Systematic and orderly presentation of the interrelationships of relevant facts and concepts underlying the problem.
      5. Clear identification of the problem statement through use of an appropriate heading or paragraph caption (the same requirement holding for other major categories of the research).
      6. Succinct, precise, and unambiguous statement of the research problem (including the delineation of independent, dependent, and classificatory variables), of the major questions to be resolved, or of the objectives to be investigated.
      7. Distinction (if required) between problems or questions that are either factually oriented or value oriented.
      8. Distinction in the instance of theoretically oriented research or of basic research between the purpose, which is often goal-oriented or instrumental in relation to certain pragmatic objectives, and the research problem which is primarily directed toward the finding of relationships, the making of comparisons, or the noting of changes (possible cause and effect relationships) relative to operationally formulated research hypotheses.

---

¹Isaac and Michael, pp. 223-225.

FORM FOR THE EVALUATION OF AN ARTICLE[2]

Characteristic	Completely Incompetent (1)	Poor (2)	Mediocre (3)	Good (4)	Excellent (5)
1. Problem is clearly stated					
2. Hypotheses are clearly stated					
3. Problem is significant					
4. Assumptions are clearly stated					
5. Limitations of the study are stated					
6. Important terms are defined					
7. Relationship of the problem to previous research is made clear					
8. Research design is described fully					
9. Research design is appropriate for the solution of the problem					
10. Research design is free of specific weaknesses					
11. Population and samples are described					
12. Method of sampling is appropriate					
13. Data-gathering methods or procedures are described					
14. Data-gathering methods or proceducres are appropriate to the solution of the problem					
15. Data-gathering methods or procedures are utilized correctly					
16. Validity and reliability of the evidence gathered are established					

[2]Isaac and Michael, p. 220.

Characteristic	Completely Incompetent (1)	Poor (2)	Mediocre (3)	Good (4)	Excellent (5)
17. Appropriate methods are selected to analyze the data					
18. Methods utilized in analyzing the data are applied correctly					
19. Results of the analysis are presented clearly					
20. Conclusions are clearly stated					
21. Conclusions are substantiated by the evidence presented					
22. Generalizations are confined to the population from which the sample was drawn					
23. Report is clearly written					
24. Report is logically organized					
25. Tone of the report displays an unbiased, impartial scientific attitude					

RESEARCH REPORT EVALUATION FORM[3]

Name _____ Date _____ Grade _____

+ adequate   −inadequate

TITLE

clear and concise _____

PROBLEM

clearly stated _____
specific questions raised _____
clear statement of hypothesis _____
testable hypothesis _____
significance recognized _____
properly delimited _____
assumptions stated _____
important terms defined_____

DATA ANALYSIS

perceptive recognition of data
  relationships _____
effective use of tables _____
effective use of figures _____
concise report of findings _____
appropriate statistical treatment _____
logical analysis _____

SUMMARY

problem restated _____
questions/hypothesis restated _____
procedures described _____
concisely reported _____
supporting data included _____
conclusions based on data
  analysis _____

REVIEW OF RELATED LITERATURE

adequately covered _____
well-organized _____
important findings noted _____
studies critically noted _____
effectively summarized _____

PROCEDURES

described in detail _____
adequate sample _____
appropriate design _____
variables controlled _____
effective data-gathering instruments or
  procedures _____

FORM AND STYLE

typing _____
spacing _____
margins _____
balance _____
table of contents _____
list of tables _____
list of figures _____
headings _____
pagination _____
citations/quotations _____
footnotes _____
tables _____
figures _____
bibliography _____
appendix _____
spelling _____
punctuationg _____
sentence structure _____
proofreading _____
clear and concise style _____

---

[1]Best, p. 414.

EVALUATION OR THESIS BRIEF[4]

Rated From 0-4

Choice of Topic	
Delineation of Problem	
Introduction	
Need for Study	
Statement of Problem	
Purposes	
Definition of Terms	
Delimitations	
Limitations	
Thoroughness of Related Literature	
Appropriateness of Procedures	
Expected Results	
Style of Writing	
Use of Documentation	
Mechanics — Spelling, Headings, Summaries, Etc.	
Bibliography	
Overall Impression	
TOTAL	GRADE

[4]Thorpe for P.E. 500

APPENDIX G

THE USE OF COMPUTERS IN RESEARCH

THE USE OF COMPUTERS IN RESEARCH

The author is indebted to Ron Hickman[1] for this section of the Appendixes.

The purpose of this appendix is to provide a model for input, output, and interpretation for the SAS, SPSSX, and BMDP programs as they may be useful in the studies which are typical in the research of physical education.

The data base is described on the following pages. The computer printouts are presented after that.

---

[1] Ron Hickman was for many years a major contributor in programming and advising in Academic Computing at Southern Illinois University, Carbondale. He is now the Manager of the Information Center at the University of South Florida. Tampa. His unusual skills enabled the completion of enumerable master's and doctoral theses and faculty research.

TITLE: Three Methods of Releasing the Ball in Bowling
3 classes (coed) n's = 20, 20, 20
3 methods = Hook 1, Hook 2, Straight
Games recorded:　　　1, 2, 3, 4 = Pretest
　(Average & Print)　13, 14, 15, 16 = Posttest
　　　　　　　　　　9, 10, 11, 12

	Sex	Class I	Class II	Class III
X^2	Males	11	12	11
	Females	9	8	9
		n = 20	n = 20	n = 20

	Experience	Class I	Class II	Class III
X^2	0-10 Very Little = 1	4	8	7
	11-39 Some = 2	12	7	6
	40-50 Considerable = 3	4	5	7

	Preference for Approach	Class I	Class II	Class III
X^2	None = 1	5	4	3
	3-step = 2	3	4	5
	4-step = 3	8	8	7
	5-step = 4	4	4	5
		n = 20	n = 20	n = 20

Knowledge Test Results: Percentage Correct — 0 to 100%

χ^2 *Attitude Toward Physical Activity (ATPA)* Range of Scores = 6-42
　(6 Factors 1-7 for each)
　Factors are: Social, Fitness, Thrill, Beauty, Release, Work
　　　　　　　(S)　　(F)　　(T)　　(B)　　(R)　　(W)

Regression Analysis — Step-wise
　Posttest Average = Experience + Knowledge + ATPA
　Bowling Score　　　　(P_1)　　　　(P_2)　　　　(P_3)

COMPUTATIONS REQUESTED

1. ANOVA for three methods — change score = dependent variable
2. t_1 Males vs. Females on Pre and Posttests
3. t_c Pre to Posttest Change

4. X^2 Sex, Experience, Approach Preference, ATPA
5. Duncan's Multiple Range Test for #1 (ANOVA)
6. Repeated measures ANOVA for pretest and posttest reliability
   > Day 1, Game 1, Day 1, Game 1
   > Day 1, Game 1, Day 2, Game 2
7. Pearson's *r* Intercorrelation of all variables recorded
8. Regression — Step-wise Posttest Average as criterion Experience,
   > Knowledge test, ATPA Score as predictors

SAS Data Step:

```
PROC FORMAT;
    VALUE METHOD 1='HOOK AT 9:00'
                 2='HOOK AT 11:00'
                 3=STRAIGHT;
    VALUE $SEX   'F'=FEMALE
                 'M'=MALE;
    VALUE PREFER 1=NONE
                 2='3-STEP'
                 3='4-STEP'
                 4='5-STEP';
    VALUE EXPER  1=VERY LITTLE
                 2=SOME
                 3=CONSIDERABLE;
DATA BOWLING;
    INPUT (SUBNO D1-D6 G1-G12)
          (2. 1. 2. 1. $1. 2. 13*3.);
      IF  0<D2<11 THEN D7=1;
      IF 10<D2<40 THEN D7=2;
      IF 39<D2    THEN D7=3;
      G_PRE=MEAN(OF G1-G4);
      G_POST=MEAN(OF G5-G8);
      G_TEST=MEAN(OF G9-G12);
      G_DIFF=G_POST-G_PRE;
      G_DIF2=G_TEST-G_PRE;
LABEL D1=METHOD
      D2=EXPERIENCE SCORE
      D3=APPROACH PREFERENCE
      D4=SEX
      D5=ATPA SCORE
      D6=KNOWLEDGE SCORE
      D7=EXPERIENCE CATEGORY
      G1=GAME 1 SCORE
      G2=GAME 2 SCORE
      G3=GAME 3 SCORE
      G4=GAME 4 SCORE
      G5=GAME 13 SCORE
      G6=GAME 14 SCORE
      G7=GAME 15 SCORE
      G8=GAME 16 SCORE
      G9=GAME 9 SCORE
     G10=GAME 10 SCORE
     G11=GAME 11 SCORE
     G12=GAME 12 SCORE
   G_PRE=AVERAGE SCORE GAME 1 TO 4
  G_POST=AVERAGE SCORE GAME 13 TO 16
  G_TEST=AVERAGE SCORE GAME 9 TO 12
  G_DIFF=DIFFERENCE G_POST MINUS G_PRE
  G_DIF2=DIFFERENCE G_TEST MINUS G_PRE;
CARDS;
```

Research Question: Does method (D1) account for variability in the difference between the average score on the pretest games (1 thru 4) and the average score on the posttest games (13 thru 16)?

SAS Model:
```
PROC GLM;
CLASS D1;
MODEL G_DIFF=D1;
MEANS D1/DUNCAN;
```

GENERAL LINEAR MODELS PROCEDURE

CLASS LEVEL INFORMATION

CLASS	LEVELS	VALUES
D1	3	HOOK AT 11:00 HOOK AT 9:00 STRAIGHT

NUMBER OF OBSERVATIONS IN DATA SET = 60

GENERAL LINEAR MODELS PROCEDURE

DEPENDENT VARIABLE: G_DIFF   DIFFERENCE G_POST MINUS G_PRE

SOURCE	DF	SUM OF SQUARES	MEAN SQUARE	F VALUE	PR > F	R-SQUARE	C.V.
MODEL	2	845.43958333	422.71979167	1.10	0.3406	0.037083	260.6533
ERROR	57	21953.07187500	385.14161184			ROOT MSE	G_DIFF MEAN
CORRECTED TOTAL	59	22798.51145833				19.62502514	7.52916667

SOURCE	DF	TYPE I SS	F VALUE	PR > F		TYPE III SS	F VALUE	PR > F
D1	2	845.43958333	1.10	0.3406		845.43958333	1.10	0.3406

Explanation: The F-ratio for the above model has yielded an F-value with an associated probability of occurrence of .3406 and given an alpha level of .05 is considered nonsignificant (accept the null hypothesis of no difference between the methods). The amount of variance between the pretest and posttest averages accounted for by method is only 3.7% of the total variance in the bowling difference scores. Knowledge of the method of delivery with this group of subjects does not help to account for the variability in the difference scores obtained.

GENERAL LINEAR MODELS PROCEDURE

DUNCAN'S MULTIPLE RANGE TEST FOR VARIABLE: G_DIFF
NOTE: THIS TEST CONTROLS THE TYPE I COMPARISONWISE ERROR RATE,
NOT THE EXPERIMENTWISE ERROR RATE.

ALPHA=0.05   DF=57   MSE=385.142

MEANS WITH THE SAME LETTER ARE NOT SIGNIFICANTLY DIFFERENT.

DUNCAN	GROUPING	MEAN	N	D1
A		11.462	20	HOOK AT 11:00
A				
A		8.650	20	HOOK AT 9:00
A				
A		2.475	20	STRAIGHT

Explanation: The Duncan's Multiple Range test would not be performed for
the above statistical model since the null hypothesis could
not be rejected. It is performed here merely to illustrate
the SAS output that would be produced and to provide an
explanation of that output.

Each pair of method means is compared statistically and any
pair of means connected by the same GROUPING letter are not
statistically different from each other. Since all of the
means in the above Duncan's test are connected by the same
GROUPING letter none of them are statistically different
from each other in this sample data.

SAS output for an analysis with significantly different
means might look like the following:

DUNCAN	GROUPING		MEAN	N	AGEGP
A			20.504	92	UNDER 21
A					
A	B		13.743	67	21 TO 55
	B				
	B		6.842	83	56 AND OVER

In this example the means for groups 1 (UNDER 21) and 2 (21
TO 55) have the same GROUPING letter "A" so they are not
statistically different from each other. Groups 2 (21 TO 55)
and 3 (56 AND OVER) have the same GROUPING letter "B" so
they are not statistically different from each other. But,
groups 1 (UNDER 21) and 3 (56 AND OVER) do not have the same
GROUPING letter so they would be considered statistically
different from each other at the .05 alpha level.

Research Question: Does method (D1) account for variability in the difference between the average score on the pretest games (1 thru 4) and the average score on the test games (9 thru 12)?

SAS Model:
```
PROC GLM;
CLASS D1;
MODEL G_DIF2=D1;
```

GENERAL LINEAR MODELS PROCEDURE

CLASS LEVEL INFORMATION

CLASS	LEVELS	VALUES
D1	3	HOOK AT 11:00 HOOK AT 9:00 STRAIGHT

NUMBER OF OBSERVATIONS IN DATA SET = 60

GENERAL LINEAR MODELS PROCEDURE

DEPENDENT VARIABLE: G_DIF2   DIFFERENCE G_TEST MINUS G_PRE

SOURCE	DF	SUM OF SQUARES	MEAN SQUARE	F VALUE	PR > F	R-SQUARE	C.V.
MODEL	2	1003.25833333	501.62916667	0.97	0.3835	0.033073	269.7873
ERROR	57	29331.73750000	514.59188596			ROOT MSE	G_DIF2 MEAN
CORRECTED TOTAL	59	30334.99583333				22.68461783	8.40833333

SOURCE	DF	TYPE I SS	F VALUE	PR > F
D1	2	1003.25833333	0.97	0.3835

SOURCE	DF	TYPE III SS	F VALUE	PR > F
D1	2	1003.25833333	0.97	0.3835

Explanation: The F-ratio for the above model has yielded an F-value with an associated probability of occurrence of .3835 and given an alpha level of .05 is considered nonsignificant (accept the null hypothesis of no difference between the methods). The amount of variance between the pretest and test averages accounted for by method is only 3.3% of the total variance in the bowling difference scores. Knowledge of the method of delivery with this group of subjects does not account for variability in the difference scores obtained.

Research Question: Does sex account for variability in the average score on the pretest games (1 thru 4)?

SAS Model: PROC TTEST; CLASS D4; VAR G_PRE;

TTEST PROCEDURE

VARIABLE: G_PRE   AVERAGE SCORE GAME 1 TO 4

D4	N	MEAN	STD DEV	STD ERROR	MINIMUM	MAXIMUM	VARIANCES	T	DF	PROB > |T|
FEMALE	26	101.93269231	20.27246380	3.97575725	67.50000000	143.00000000	UNEQUAL	-4.9266	57.9	0.0001
MALE	34	130.96323529	25.36059132	4.34930553	81.25000000	227.25000000	EQUAL	-4.7816	58.0	0.0001

FOR H0: VARIANCES ARE EQUAL, F' = 1.56 WITH 33 AND 25 DF   PROB > F' = 0.2501

Explanation: Since the independent variable D4 (sex) has only two levels a t-test for independent samples is appropriate.

The test for the homogeneity of the sample variances is not significant at the alpha equal .05 level, therefore, the T for EQUAL sample variances is used to test the hypothesis that the means for each sex group are equal. In this case, male bowlers had significantly higher average pretest scores at a probability level of .0001 with a T value of -4.7816 and 58.0 degrees of freedom.

Research Question: Does sex account for variability in the average score on the posttest games (13 thru 16)?

SAS Model: PROC TTEST; CLASS D4; VAR G_POST;

TTEST PROCEDURE

VARIABLE: G_POST   AVERAGE SCORE GAME 13 TO 16

D4	N	MEAN	STD DEV	STD ERROR	MINIMUM	MAXIMUM	VARIANCES	T	DF	PROB > |T|
FEMALE	26	116.25961538	18.14049073	3.55764293	69.75000000	155.50000000	UNEQUAL	-3.1823	58.0	0.0023
MALE	34	133.29411765	23.32124719	3.99956090	78.75000000	179.25000000	EQUAL	-3.0779	58.0	0.0032

FOR H0: VARIANCES ARE EQUAL, F' = 1.65 WITH 33 AND 25 DF   PROB > F' = 0.1972

Explanation: The test for the homogeneity of the sample variances is not significant at the alpha equal .05 level, therefore, the T for EQUAL sample variances is used to test the hypothesis that the means for each sex group are equal. Male bowlers had significantly higher average posttest scores at a probability level of .0032 with a T value of -3.0779 and 58.0 degrees of freedom.

Research Question: Does sex account for variability in the average score on the test games (9 thru 12)?

SAS Model: PROC TTEST; CLASS D4; VAR G_TEST;

TTEST PROCEDURE

VARIABLE: G_TEST   AVERAGE SCORE GAME 9 TO 12

D4	N	MEAN	STD DEV	STD ERROR	MINIMUM	MAXIMUM
FEMALE	26	119.18269231	17.87268274	3.50512146	89.75000000	159.00000000
MALE	34	132.61029412	19.60192778	3.36170288	89.75000000	179.25000000

FOR H0: VARIANCES ARE EQUAL, F' = 1.20 WITH 33 AND 25 DF   PROB > F' = 0.6393

VARIANCES	T	DF	PROB > |T|
UNEQUAL	-2.7648	56.2	0.0077
EQUAL	-2.7305	58.0	0.0084

Explanation: The test for the homogeneity of the sample variances is not significant at the alpha equal .05 level, therefore, the T for EQUAL sample variances is used to test the hypothesis that the means for each sex group are equal. Male bowlers had significantly higher average test scores at a probability level of .0084 with a T value of -2.8305 and 58.0 degrees of freedom.

Research Question: Does sex account for variability in the difference scores obtained by subtracting the average pretest score from the average posttest score?

SAS Model: PROC TTEST; CLASS D4; VAR G_DIFF;

TTEST PROCEDURE

VARIABLE: G_DIFF   DIFFERENCE G_POST MINUS G_PRE

D4	N	MEAN	STD DEV	STD ERROR	MINIMUM	MAXIMUM
FEMALE	26	14.32692308	17.51153466	3.43429450	-13.25000000	47.75000000
MALE	34	2.33088235	19.85703835	3.40545398	-48.00000000	44.75000000

VARIANCES	T	DF	PROB > |T|
UNEQUAL	2.4803	56.8	0.0161
EQUAL	2.4386	58.0	0.0178

FOR HO: VARIANCES ARE EQUAL, F'= 1.29 WITH 33 AND 25 DF   PROB > F' = 0.5204

Explanation: The test for the homogeneity of the sample variances is not significant at the alpha equal .05 level, therefore, the T for EQUAL sample variances is used to test the hypothesis that the means for each sex group are equal. Female bowlers had significantly higher average difference scores at a probability level of .0178 with a T value of 2.4386 and 58.0 degrees of freedom.

Research Question: Does sex account for variability in the difference scores obtained by subtracting the average pretest score from the average test score?

SAS Model: PROC TTEST; CLASS D4; VAR G_DIF2;

TTEST PROCEDURE

VARIABLE: G_DIF2   DIFFERENCE G_TEST MINUS G_PRE

D4	N	MEAN	STD DEV	STD ERROR	MINIMUM	MAXIMUM
FEMALE	26	17.25000000	17.26195238	3.38534739	-11.00000000	54.25000000
MALE	34	1.64705882	24.18286690	4.14732746	-91.75000000	42.50000000

VARIANCES	T	DF	PROB > |T|
UNEQUAL	2.9145	57.8	0.0051
EQUAL	2.7888	58.0	0.0071

FOR HO: VARIANCES ARE EQUAL, F'= 1.96 WITH 33 AND 25 DF   PROB > F' = 0.0849

Explanation: The test for the homogeneity of the sample variances is not significant at the alpha equal .05 level, therefore, the T for EQUAL sample variances is used to test the hypothesis that the means for each sex group are equal. Female bowlers had significantly higher average difference scores at a probability level of .0071 with a T value of 2.7888 and 58.0 degrees of freedom.

Research Question: Are the average pretest score (games 1 thru 4) and the average posttest score (games 13 thru 16) the same?

Research Question: Are the average pretest score (games 1 thru 4) and the average test score (games 9 thru 12) the same?

SAS Model:
```
PROC CORR NOSIMPLE;
VAR G_PRE G_POST G_TEST D2;
PROC MEANS N MEAN STD STDERR T PRT;
VAR G_PRE G_POST G_TEST G_DIFF G_DIF2;
```

CORRELATION COEFFICIENTS / PROB > |R| UNDER H0:RHO=0 / N = 60

	G_PRE	G_POST	G_TEST	D2
G_PRE AVERAGE SCORE GAME 1 TO 4	1.00000 0.0000	0.70508 0.0001	0.57655 0.0001	0.70014 0.0001
G_POST AVERAGE SCORE GAME 13 TO 16	0.70508 0.0001	1.00000 0.0000	0.64981 0.0001	0.49210 0.0001
G_TEST AVERAGE SCORE GAME 9 TO 12	0.57655 0.0001	0.64981 0.0001	1.00000 0.0000	0.41654 0.0009
D2 EXPERIENCE SCORE	0.70014 0.0001	0.49210 0.0001	0.41654 0.0009	1.00000 0.0000

VARIABLE	LABEL	N	MEAN	STANDARD DEVIATION	STD ERROR OF MEAN	T	PR>|T|
G_PRE	AVERAGE SCORE GAME 1 TO 4	60	118.38333333	27.28240053	3.52214276	33.61	0.0001
G_POST	AVERAGE SCORE GAME 13 TO 16	60	125.91250000	22.71795681	2.93287561	42.93	0.0001
G_TEST	AVERAGE SCORE GAME 9 TO 12	60	126.79166667	19.88186331	2.56673752	49.40	0.0001
G_DIFF	DIFFERENCE G_POST MINUS G_PRE	60	7.52916667	19.65745275	2.53776624	2.97	0.0043
G_DIF2	DIFFERENCE G_TEST MINUS G_PRE	60	8.40833333	22.67493047	2.92732094	2.87	0.0057

Explanation: As can be noted in the correlation matrix above there is a strong relationship between the pretest and posttest, test scores for this group of subjects. The difference score averages for both G_DIFF and G_DIF2 are positive and are statistically significant changes with T values of 2.97 and 2.87 and probabilities of occurrence of .0043 and .0057.

Research Question: Are method (D1) and approach preference (D3) independently distributed?

SAS Model:
```
PROC FREQ;
  TABLES D1*D3/CHISQ;
  FORMAT D1 METHOD. D3 PREFER.;
```

TABLE OF D1 BY D3

D1   METHOD   D3   APPROACH PREFERENCE

FREQUENCY PERCENT ROW PCT COL PCT	NONE	3-STEP	4-STEP	5-STEP	TOTAL
HOOK AT 9:00	5 8.33 25.00 41.67	3 5.00 15.00 25.00	8 13.33 40.00 34.78	4 6.67 20.00 30.77	20 33.33
HOOK AT 11:00	4 6.67 20.00 33.33	4 6.67 20.00 33.33	8 13.33 40.00 34.78	4 6.67 20.00 30.77	20 33.33
STRAIGHT	3 5.00 15.00 25.00	5 8.33 25.00 41.67	7 11.67 35.00 30.43	5 8.33 25.00 38.46	20 33.33
TOTAL	12 20.00	12 20.00	23 38.33	13 21.67	60 100.00

STATISTICS FOR 2-WAY TABLES

WARNING: OVER 20% OF THE CELLS HAVE EXPECTED COUNTS LESS THAN 5. TABLE IS SO SPARSE THAT CHI-SQUARE MAY NOT BE A VALID TEST.

CHI-SQUARE	1.241	DF= 6	PROB=0.9748
PHI	0.144		
CONTINGENCY COEFFICIENT	0.142		
CRAMER'S V	0.102		
LIKELIHOOD RATIO CHISQUARE	1.249	DF= 6	PROB=0.9744

Explanation: Since the chi-square calculated for the joint frequency distribution of method by approach preference is not significant at the alpha=.05 level the relationship between the two variables can be considered statistically independent. Further, no systematic relationship exists between the distributions.

Research Question: Are method (D1) and sex of bowler (D4) independently distributed?

SAS Model:
```
PROC FREQ;
TABLES D1*D4/CHISQ;
FORMAT D1 METHOD. D4 SEX.;
```

TABLE OF D1 BY D4

D1   METHOD   D4   SEX

FREQUENCY PERCENT ROW PCT COL PCT	FEMALE	MALE	TOTAL
HOOK AT 9:00	9 15.00 45.00 34.62	11 18.33 55.00 32.35	20 33.33
HOOK AT 11:00	8 13.33 40.00 30.77	12 20.00 60.00 35.29	20 33.33
STRAIGHT	9 15.00 45.00 34.62	11 18.33 55.00 32.35	20 33.33
TOTAL	26 43.33	34 56.67	60 100.00

STATISTICS FOR 2-WAY TABLES

CHI-SQUARE	0.136	DF= 2	PROB=0.9344
PHI	0.048		
CONTINGENCY COEFFICIENT	0.048		
CRAMER'S V	0.048		
LIKELIHOOD RATIO CHISQUARE	0.136	DF= 2	PROB=0.9341

Explanation: Same as for the TABLE OF D1 BY D3.

Research Question: Are method (D1) and level of experience (D7) independently distributed?

SAS Model:
```
PROC FREQ;
 TABLES D1*D7/CHISQ;
 FORMAT D1 METHOD. D7 EXPER.;
```

TABLE OF D1 BY D7

D1   METHOD   D7   EXPERIENCE CATEGORY

FREQUENCY PERCENT ROW PCT COL PCT	VERY LITTLE	SOME	CONSIDERABLE	TOTAL
HOOK AT 9:00	4 6.67 20.00 23.53	11 18.33 55.00 42.31	5 8.33 25.00 29.41	20 33.33
HOOK AT 11:00	6 10.00 30.00 35.29	9 15.00 45.00 34.62	5 8.33 25.00 29.41	20 33.33
STRAIGHT	7 11.67 35.00 41.18	6 10.00 30.00 23.08	7 11.67 35.00 41.18	20 33.33
TOTAL	17 28.33	26 43.33	17 28.33	60 100.00

STATISTICS FOR 2-WAY TABLES

CHI-SQUARE	2.756	DF= 4	PROB=0.5995
PHI	0.214		
CONTINGENCY COEFFICIENT	0.210		
CRAMER'S V	0.152		
LIKELIHOOD RATIO CHISQUARE	2.825	DF= 4	PROB=0.5876

Explanation: Same as for the TABLE OF D1 BY D3.

Research Question: Are approach preference (D3) and sex of bowler (D4)
                      independently distributed?

SAS Model: PROC FREQ;
              TABLES D3*D4/CHISQ;
              FORMAT D3 PREFER. D4 SEX.;

TABLE OF D3 BY D4

D3   APPROACH PREFERENCE   D4   SEX

FREQUENCY PERCENT ROW PCT COL PCT	FEMALE	MALE	TOTAL
NONE	7 11.67 58.33 26.92	5 8.33 41.67 14.71	12 20.00
3-STEP	7 11.67 58.33 26.92	5 8.33 41.67 14.71	12 20.00
4-STEP	9 15.00 39.13 34.62	14 23.33 60.87 41.18	23 38.33
5-STEP	3 5.00 23.08 11.54	10 16.67 76.92 29.41	13 21.67
TOTAL	26 43.33	34 56.67	60 100.00

STATISTICS FOR 2-WAY TABLES

CHI-SQUARE	4.537	DF= 3	PROB=0.2090
PHI	0.275		
CONTINGENCY COEFFICIENT	0.265		
CRAMER'S V	0.275		
LIKELIHOOD RATIO CHISQUARE	4.672	DF= 3	PROB=0.1974

Explanation: Same as for the TABLE OF D1 BY D3.

Research Question: Are approach preference (D3) and level of experience (D7) independently distributed?

SAS Model: PROC FREQ;
            TABLES D3*D7/CHISQ;
            FORMAT D3 PREFER. D7 EXPER.;

TABLE OF D3 BY D7

D3   APPROACH PREFERENCE   D7   EXPERIENCE CATEGORY

FREQUENCY PERCENT ROW PCT COL PCT	VERY LITTLE	SOME	CONSIDERABLE	TOTAL
NONE	4 6.67 33.33 23.53	6 10.00 50.00 23.08	2 3.33 16.67 11.76	12 20.00
3-STEP	3 5.00 25.00 17.65	3 5.00 25.00 11.54	6 10.00 50.00 35.29	12 20.00
4-STEP	7 11.67 30.43 41.18	11 18.33 47.83 42.31	5 8.33 21.74 29.41	23 38.33
5-STEP	3 5.00 23.08 17.65	6 10.00 46.15 23.08	4 6.67 30.77 23.53	13 21.67
TOTAL	17 28.33	26 43.33	17 28.33	60 100.00

STATISTICS FOR 2-WAY TABLES

CHI-SQUARE	4.445	DF= 6	PROB=0.6166
PHI	0.272		
CONTINGENCY COEFFICIENT	0.263		
CRAMER'S V	0.192		
LIKELIHOOD RATIO CHISQUARE	4.367	DF= 6	PROB=0.6271

WARNING: OVER 20% OF THE CELLS HAVE EXPECTED COUNTS LESS THAN 5. TABLE IS SO SPARSE THAT CHI-SQUARE MAY NOT BE A VALID TEST.

Explanation: Same as for the TABLE OF D1 BY D3.

Research Question: Are sex of bowler (D4) and level of experience (D7) independently distributed?

SAS Model:
```
PROC FREQ;
TABLES D4*D7/CHISQ;
FORMAT D4 SEX. D7 EXPER.;
```

TABLE OF D4 BY D7

SEX   D7   EXPERIENCE CATEGORY

D4	VERY LITTLE	SOME	CONSIDERABLE	TOTAL
FREQUENCY PERCENT ROW PCT COL PCT				
FEMALE	13 21.67 50.00 76.47	9 15.00 34.62 34.62	4 6.67 15.38 23.53	26 43.33
MALE	4 6.67 11.76 23.53	17 28.33 50.00 65.38	13 21.67 38.24 76.47	34 56.67
TOTAL	17 28.33	26 43.33	17 28.33	60 100.00

STATISTICS FOR 2-WAY TABLES

CHI-SQUARE	11.122	DF= 2	PROB=0.0038
PHI	0.431		
CONTINGENCY COEFFICIENT	0.395		
CRAMER'S V	0.431		
LIKELIHOOD RATIO CHISQUARE	11.466	DF= 2	PROB=0.0032

Explanation: Since the chi-square calculated for the joint frequency distribution of sex of bowler by level of experience is sigificant at the alpha=.0038 level the relationship between the two variables can not be considered statistically independent. A systematic relationship appears to be occurring in that level of experience is distributed very nearly with a reverse frequency distribution for each of the sexes. That reversal accounts for the magnitude of the resultant chi-square of 11.122.

Research Question: Do experience (D2), attitude toward physical activity (D5), and knowledge (D6) account for variability in the average score on the posttest games (13 thru 16)?

SAS Model: PROC REG;
             MODEL G_POST=D2 D5 D6;

DEP VARIABLE: G_POST   AVERAGE SCORE GAME 13 TO 16

SOURCE	DF	SUM OF SQUARES	MEAN SQUARE	F VALUE	PROB>F
MODEL	3	7996.188	2665.396	6.647	0.0007
ERROR	56	22454.040	400.965		
C TOTAL	59	30450.228			

ROOT MSE	20.024111	R-SQUARE	0.2626
DEP MEAN	125.912	ADJ R-SQ	0.2231
C.V.	15.9032		

VARIABLE	DF	PARAMETER ESTIMATE	STANDARD ERROR	T FOR H0: PARAMETER=0	PROB > |T|	VARIABLE LABEL
INTERCEP	1	80.021281	23.982667	3.337	0.0015	INTERCEPT
D2	1	0.696713	0.168621	4.132	0.0001	EXPERIENCE SCORE
D5	1	-0.524582	0.474939	-1.105	0.2741	ATPA SCORE
D6	1	0.530801	0.426964	1.243	0.2190	KNOWLEDGE SCORE

Explanation: The full model is significant with an F of 6.647 and a probability of .0007. Further inspection of the model reveals that the experience score (D2) accounts for a statistically significant portion of the variability in the average posttest score, as evidenced by the T value of 4.132 with associated probability of .0001. Neither of the other predictor variables accounts for a significant portion of the variability in the average posttest score.

Research Question: Do experience (D2), attitude toward physical activity (D5), and knowledge (D6), account for variability in the difference between the average score on the pretest games (1 thru 4) and the average score on the posttest games (13 thru 16)?

SAS Model: PROC REG;
MODEL G_DIFF=D2 D5 D6;

DEP VARIABLE: G_DIFF   DIFFERENCE G_POST MINUS G_PRE

SOURCE	DF	SUM OF SQUARES	MEAN SQUARE	F VALUE	PROB>F
MODEL	3	3938.307	1312.769	3.898	0.0134
ERROR	56	18860.205	336.789		
C TOTAL	59	22798.511			

ROOT MSE	18.351822	R-SQUARE	0.1727
DEP MEAN	7.529167	ADJ R-SQ	0.1284
C.V.	243.7431		

VARIABLE	DF	PARAMETER ESTIMATE	STANDARD ERROR	T FOR H0: PARAMETER=0	PROB > |T|	VARIABLE LABEL
INTERCEP	1	18.130439	21.979784	0.825	0.4129	INTERCEPT
D2	1	-0.488374	0.154539	-3.160	0.0025	EXPERIENCE SCORE
D5	1	-0.273900	0.435275	-0.629	0.5317	ATPA SCORE
D6	1	0.099041	0.391307	0.253	0.8011	KNOWLEDGE SCORE

Explanation: The full model is significant with an F of 3.898 and a probability of .0134. Further inspection of the model reveals that the experience score (D2) accounts for a statistically significant portion of the variability in the average posttest score with a T of -3.160 and probability of .0025. Neither of the other predictor variables accounts for a significant portion of the variability in the average difference score.

```
SPSSX Data Step:


DATA LIST FIXED FILE=INLINE RECORDS=1
 / SUBNO 1-2 D1 3-3 D2 4-5 D3 6-6 D4 7-7 (A) D5 8-9 D6 10-12
   G1 TO G12 13-48
IF (D2 GT 0 AND D2 LT 11) D7=1
IF (D2 GT 10 AND D2 LT 40) D7=2
IF (D2 GT 39) D7=3
COMPUTE G.PRE=MEAN(G1 TO G4)
COMPUTE G.POST=MEAN(G5 TO G8)
COMPUTE G.TEST=MEAN(G9 TO G12)
COMPUTE G.DIFF=G.POST-G.PRE
COMPUTE G.DIF2=G.TEST-G.PRE
VARIABLE LABELS
        D1 'METHOD'
        D2 'EXPERIENCE SCORE'
        D3 'APPROACH PREFERENCE'
        D4 'SEX'
        D5 'ATPA SCORE'
        D6 'KNOWLEDGE SCORE'
        D7 'EXPERIENCE CATEGORY'
        G1 'GAME 1 SCORE'
        G2 'GAME 2 SCORE'
        G3 'GAME 3 SCORE'
        G4 'GAME 4 SCORE'
        G5 'GAME 13 SCORE'
        G6 'GAME 14 SCORE'
        G7 'GAME 15 SCORE'
        G8 'GAME 16 SCORE'
        G9 'GAME 9 SCORE'
       G10 'GAME 10 SCORE'
       G11 'GAME 11 SCORE'
       G12 'GAME 12 SCORE'
    G.PRE 'AVERAGE SCORE GAME 1 TO 4'
   G.POST 'AVERAGE SCORE GAME 13 TO 16'
   G.TEST 'AVERAGE SCORE GAME 9 TO 12'
   G.DIFF 'DIFFERENCE G.POST MINUS G.PRE'
   G.DIF2 'DIFFERENCE G.TEST MINUS G.PRE'
VALUE LABELS
   D1 1 'HOOK AT 9:00'
      2 'HOOK AT 11:00'
      3 'STRAIGHT'/
   D3 1 'NONE'
      2 '3-STEP'
      3 '4-STEP'
      4 '5-STEP'/
   D4 'F' 'FEMALE'
      'M' 'MALE'/
   D7 1 'VERY LITTLE'
      2 'SOME'
      3 'CONSIDERABLE'
BEGIN DATA
```

Research Question: Does method (D1) account for variability in the difference
between the average score on the pretest games (1 thru 4)
and the average score on the posttest games (13 thru 16)?

SPSSX Model: ONEWAY G.DIFF BY D1(1,3)/
RANGES=DUNCAN

- O N E W A Y -

VARIABLE   G.DIFF   DIFFERENCE G.POST MINUS G.PRE
BY VARIABLE D1   METHOD

ANALYSIS OF VARIANCE

SOURCE	D.F.	SUM OF SQUARES	MEAN SQUARES	F RATIO	F PROB.
BETWEEN GROUPS	2	845.4396	422.7198	1.098	0.3406
WITHIN GROUPS	57	21953.0719	385.1416		
TOTAL	59	22798.5115			

- O N E W A Y -

VARIABLE   G.DIFF   DIFFERENCE G.POST MINUS G.PRE
BY VARIABLE D1   METHOD

MULTIPLE RANGE TEST

DUNCAN PROCEDURE
RANGES FOR THE 0.050 LEVEL -

2.83   2.98

THE RANGES ABOVE ARE TABLE RANGES.   THE VALUE ACTUALLY COMPARED WITH MEAN(J)-MEAN(I) IS..
13.8770 * RANGE * DSQRT(1/N(I) + 1/N(J))

NO TWO GROUPS ARE SIGNIFICANTLY DIFFERENT AT THE 0.050 LEVEL

HOMOGENEOUS SUBSETS   (SUBSETS OF GROUPS, WHOSE HIGHEST AND LOWEST MEANS DO NOT DIFFER BY MORE THAN THE SHORTEST
SIGNIFICANT RANGE FOR A SUBSET OF THAT SIZE)

SUBSET   1

GROUP	GRP 3	GRP 1	GRP 2
MEAN	2.4750	8.6500	11.4625

Explanation: Same as for the corresponding SAS Model.

Research Question: Does method (D1) account for variability in the difference between the average score on the pretest games (1 thru 4) and the average score on the test games (9 thru 12)?

SPSSX Model: ONEWAY G.DIF2 BY D1(1,3)

```
- - - - - - - - - - - - - - O N E W A Y - - - - - - - - - - - - -
VARIABLE  G.DIF2    DIFFERENCE G.TEST MINUS G.PRE
BY VARIABLE  D1       METHOD
```

ANALYSIS OF VARIANCE

SOURCE	D.F.	SUM OF SQUARES	MEAN SQUARES	F RATIO	F PROB.
BETWEEN GROUPS	2	1003.2583	501.6292	0.975	0.3835
WITHIN GROUPS	57	29331.7375	514.5919		
TOTAL	59	30334.9958			

Explanation: Same as for the corresponding SAS Model.

Research Question: Does sex account for variability in the average score on the pretest games (1 thru 4)?

Research Question: Does sex account for variability in the average score on the posttest games (13 thru 16)?

Research Question: Does sex account for variability in the average score on the test games (9 thru 12)?

Research Question: Does sex account for variability in the difference scores between the posttest and pretest games?

Research Question: Does sex account for variability in the difference scores between the test and pretest games?

SPSSX Model: T-TEST GROUPS=D4('F','M')/
VARIABLES=G.PRE G.POST G.TEST G.DIFF G.DIF2

```
GROUP 1 - D4        EQ F
GROUP 2 - D4        EQ M
```

--- T-TEST ---

VARIABLE	NUMBER OF CASES	MEAN	STANDARD DEVIATION	STANDARD ERROR	F VALUE	2-TAIL PROB.	POOLED VARIANCE ESTIMATE T VALUE	DEGREES OF FREEDOM	2-TAIL PROB.	SEPARATE VARIANCE ESTIMATE T VALUE	DEGREES OF FREEDOM	2-TAIL PROB.
G.PRE AVERAGE SCORE GAME 1 TO 4												
GROUP 1	26	101.9327	20.272	3.976	1.56	0.250	-4.78	58	0.000	-4.93	57.86	0.000
GROUP 2	34	130.9632	25.361	4.349								
G.POST AVERAGE SCORE GAME 13 TO 16												
GROUP 1	26	116.2596	18.140	3.558	1.65	0.197	-3.08	58	0.003	-3.18	57.97	0.002
GROUP 2	34	133.2941	23.321	4.000								
G.TEST AVERAGE SCORE GAME 9 TO 12												
GROUP 1	26	119.1827	17.873	3.505	1.20	0.639	-2.73	58	0.008	-2.76	56.15	0.008
GROUP 2	34	132.6103	19.602	3.362								
G.DIFF DIFFERENCE G.POST MINUS G.PRE												
GROUP 1	26	14.3269	17.512	3.434	1.29	0.520	2.44	58	0.018	2.48	56.76	0.016
GROUP 2	34	2.3309	19.857	3.405								
G.DIF2 DIFFERENCE G.TEST MINUS G.PRE												
GROUP 1	26	17.2500	17.262	3.385	1.96	0.085	2.79	58	0.007	2.91	57.77	0.005
GROUP 2	34	1.6471	24.183	4.147								

Explanation: Same as for the corresponding SAS Models.

Research Question: Are the average pretest score (games 1 thru 4) and the average posttest score (games 13 thru 16) the same?

Research Question: Are the average pretest score (games 1 thru 4) and the average test score (games 9 thru 12) the same?

SPSSX Model: T-TEST PAIRS=G.PRE G.POST G.TEST

- - - - - - - - - - - - - T - T E S T - - - - - - - - - - - - -

VARIABLE	NUMBER OF CASES	MEAN	STANDARD DEVIATION	STANDARD ERROR	*(DIFFERENCE) MEAN	STANDARD DEVIATION	STANDARD ERROR	* CORR.	2-TAIL PROB. *	T VALUE	DEGREES OF FREEDOM	2-TAIL PROB.
G.PRE AVERAGE SCORE GAME 1 TO 4	60	118.3633	27.282	3.522	-7.5292	19.657	2.538	0.705	0.000	-2.97	59	0.004
G.POST AVERAGE SCORE GAME 13 TO 16		125.9125	22.718	2.933								
G.PRE AVERAGE SCORE GAME 1 TO 4	60	118.3633	27.282	3.522	-8.4083	22.675	2.927	0.577	0.000	-2.87	59	0.006
G.TEST AVERAGE SCORE GAME 9 TO 12		126.7917	19.882	2.567								

Explanation: Same as for the corresponding SAS Model.

Research Question: Are method (D1) and approach preference (D3) independently distributed?

SPSSx Model: CROSSTABS TABLES=D1 BY D3/
OPTIONS 3 4
STATISTICS 1

C R O S S T A B U L A T I O N   O F   APPROACH PREFERENCE - - - - - PAGE 1 OF 1

D1   METHOD   BY D3

COUNT ROW PCT COL PCT	D3 NONE	3-STEP	4-STEP	5-STEP	ROW TOTAL
D1	1	2	3	4	
HOOK AT 9:00 1	5 25.0 41.7	3 15.0 25.0	8 40.0 34.8	4 20.0 30.8	20 33.3
HOOK AT 11:00 2	4 20.0 33.3	4 20.0 33.3	8 40.0 34.8	4 20.0 30.8	20 33.3
STRAIGHT 3	3 15.0 25.0	5 25.0 41.7	7 35.0 30.4	5 25.0 38.5	20 33.3
COLUMN TOTAL	12 20.0	12 20.0	23 38.3	13 21.7	60 100.0

CHI-SQUARE	D.F.	SIGNIFICANCE	MIN E.F.	CELLS WITH E.F.< 5
1.24080	6	0.9748	4.000	9 OF 12 (75.0%)

NUMBER OF MISSING OBSERVATIONS = 0

Explanation: Same as for the corresponding SAS Model.

Research Question: Are method (D1) and sex of bowler (D4) independently
                      distributed?

SPSSX Model: CROSSTABS TABLES=D1 BY D4/
                OPTIONS 3 4
                STATISTICS 1

- - - - - - -   C R O S S T A B U L A T I O N   O F - - - - - - - - - - - - - -
   D1   METHOD   BY D4
                                        SEX   PAGE 1 OF 1

```
                  D4
        COUNT   |
        ROW PCT |FEMALE   MALE     ROW
        COL PCT |F        M        TOTAL
                |----------------+
D1              |                 |
HOOK AT 9:00  1 |   9       11     |    20
                |  45.0     55.0   |   33.3
                |  34.6     32.4   |
                |----------------+
HOOK AT 11:00 2 |   8       12     |    20
                |  40.0     60.0   |   33.3
                |  30.8     35.3   |
                |----------------+
STRAIGHT      3 |   9       11     |    20
                |  45.0     55.0   |   33.3
                |  34.6     32.4   |
                |----------------+
        COLUMN      26       34         60
        TOTAL      43.3     56.7      100.0
```

CHI-SQUARE	D.F.	SIGNIFICANCE	MIN E.F.	CELLS WITH E.F.< 5
0.13575	2	0.9344	8.667	NONE

NUMBER OF MISSING OBSERVATIONS = 0

Explanation: Same as for the corresponding SAS Model.

Research Question: Are method (D1) and level of experience (D7) independently distributed?

SPSSX Model: CROSSTABS TABLES=D1 BY D7/
                OPTIONS 3 4
                STATISTICS 1

- - - - - - - - - - C R O S S T A B U L A T I O N   O F - - - - - - - - - - - - -

   D1   METHOD   BY   D7   EXPERIENCE CATEGORY

- PAGE   1 OF   1

	D7				
COUNT		VERY LIT	SOME	CONSIDER	ROW
ROW PCT		TLE		ABLE	TOTAL
COL PCT		1.00	2.00	3.00	
D1					
HOOK AT 9:00	1	4 / 20.0 / 23.5	11 / 55.0 / 42.3	5 / 25.0 / 29.4	20 / 33.3
HOOK AT 11:00	2	6 / 30.0 / 35.3	9 / 45.0 / 34.6	5 / 25.0 / 29.4	20 / 33.3
STRAIGHT	3	7 / 35.0 / 41.2	6 / 30.0 / 23.1	7 / 35.0 / 41.2	20 / 33.3
COLUMN TOTAL		17 / 28.3	26 / 43.3	17 / 28.3	60 / 100.0

CHI-SQUARE	D.F.	SIGNIFICANCE	MIN E.F.	CELLS WITH E.F.< 5
2.75566	4	0.5995	5.667	NONE

NUMBER OF MISSING OBSERVATIONS =   0

Explanation: Same as for the corresponding SAS Model.

Research Question: Are approach preference (D3) and sex of bowler (D4)
                     independently distributed?

SPSSX Model: CROSSTABS TABLES=D3 BY D4/
               OPTIONS 3 4
               STATISTICS 1

- - - C R O S S T A B U L A T I O N   O F - - -

D3   APPROACH PREFERENCE   BY D4   SEX   PAGE 1 OF 1

	D4		
COUNT ROW PCT COL PCT	FEMALE F	MALE M	ROW TOTAL
D3			
NONE 1	7 58.3 26.9	5 41.7 14.7	12 20.0
3-STEP 2	7 58.3 26.9	5 41.7 14.7	12 20.0
4-STEP 3	9 39.1 34.6	14 60.9 41.2	23 38.3
5-STEP 4	3 23.1 11.5	10 76.9 29.4	13 21.7
COLUMN TOTAL	26 43.3	34 56.7	60 100.0

CHI-SQUARE	D.F.	SIGNIFICANCE	MIN E.F.	CELLS WITH E.F.< 5
4.53684	3	0.2090	5.200	NONE

NUMBER OF MISSING OBSERVATIONS =   0

Explanation: Same as for the corresponding SAS Model.

Research Question: Are approach preference (D3) and level of experience (D7) independently distributed?

SPSSX Model: CROSSTABS TABLES=D3 BY D7/
OPTIONS 3 4
STATISTICS 1

```
- - - - - - - - - - C R O S S T A B U L A T I O N   O F - - - - - - - - - -
    D3            APPROACH PREFERENCE              BY D7    EXPERIENCE CATEGORY
- - - - - - - - - - - - - - - - - - - - - - - - - - - - - - - - - -  PAGE  1 OF  1
```

D3	COUNT ROW PCT COL PCT	D7 VERY LITTLE 1.001	LIT SOME 2.001	CONSIDER ABLE 3.001	ROW TOTAL
NONE	1	4 33.3 23.5	6 50.0 23.1	2 16.7 11.8	12 20.0
3-STEP	2	3 25.0 17.6	3 25.0 11.5	6 50.0 35.3	12 20.0
4-STEP	3	7 30.4 41.2	11 47.8 42.3	5 21.7 29.4	23 38.3
5-STEP	4	3 23.1 17.6	6 46.2 23.1	4 30.8 23.5	13 21.7
COLUMN TOTAL		17 28.3	26 43.3	17 28.3	60 100.0

CHI-SQUARE	D.F.	SIGNIFICANCE	MIN E.F.	CELLS WITH E.F.< 5
4.44532	6	0.6166	3.400	6 OF 12 (50.0%)

NUMBER OF MISSING OBSERVATIONS =   0

Explanation: Same as for the corresponding SAS Model.

Research Question: Are sex of bowler (D4) and level of experience (D7)
                     independently distributed?

SPSSX Model: CROSSTABS TABLES=D4 BY D7/
               OPTIONS 3 4
               STATISTICS 1

- - - - - - - - - - - C R O S S T A B U L A T I O N   O F - - - - - - - - - - -
    D4   SEX   BY D7   EXPERIENCE CATEGORY   PAGE 1 OF 1

| | D7 | | | |
COUNT ROW PCT COL PCT	VERY LIT TLE 1.00	SOME 2.00	CONSIDER ABLE 3.00	ROW TOTAL
D4				
FEMALE F	13 50.0 76.5	9 34.6 34.6	4 15.4 23.5	26 43.3
MALE M	4 11.8 23.5	17 50.0 65.4	13 38.2 76.5	34 56.7
COLUMN TOTAL	17 28.3	26 43.3	17 28.3	60 100.0

CHI-SQUARE	D.F.	SIGNIFICANCE	MIN E.F.	CELLS WITH E.F.< 5
11.12201	2	0.0038	7.367	NONE

NUMBER OF MISSING OBSERVATIONS =   0

Explanation: Same as for the corresponding SAS Model.

Research Question: Do experience (D2), attitude toward physical activity (D5), and knowledge (D6) account for variability in the average score on the posttest games (13 thru 16)?

SPSSX Model: REGRESSION VARIABLES=G.POST,D2,D5,D6/
                        DEPENDENT=G.POST/
                        ENTER D2 TO D6

**** MULTIPLE REGRESSION ****

VARIABLE LIST NUMBER 1   LISTWISE DELETION OF MISSING DATA
EQUATION NUMBER 1   DEPENDENT VARIABLE..   G.POST   AVERAGE SCORE GAME 13 TO 16

BEGINNING BLOCK NUMBER 1.   METHOD: ENTER   D2   D5   D6

VARIABLE(S) ENTERED ON STEP NUMBER
1..   D6   KNOWLEDGE SCORE
2..   D2   EXPERIENCE SCORE
3..   D5   ATPA SCORE

MULTIPLE R	.51244	
R SQUARE	.26260	
ADJUSTED R SQUARE	.22309	
STANDARD ERROR	20.02411	

ANALYSIS OF VARIANCE

	DF	SUM OF SQUARES	MEAN SQUARE
REGRESSION	3	7996.18795	2665.39598
RESIDUAL	56	22454.04017	400.96500

F = 6.64745   SIGNIF F = .0006

------------- VARIABLES IN THE EQUATION -------------

VARIABLE	B	SE B	BETA	T	SIG T
D6	.53080	.42696	.28005	1.243	.2190
D2	.69671	.16862	.48166	4.132	.0001
D5	-.52458	.47494	-.24799	-1.105	.2741
(CONSTANT)	80.02128	23.98267		3.337	.0015

FOR BLOCK NUMBER 1   ALL REQUESTED VARIABLES ENTERED.

Explanation: Same as for the corresponding SAS Model.

Research Question:　Do experience (D2), attitude toward physical activity (D5), and knowledge (D6), account for variability in the difference between the average score on the pretest games (1 thru 4) and the average score on the posttest games (13 thru 16)?

SPSSX Model:　REGRESSION VARIABLES=G.DIFF,D2,D5,D6/
　　　　　　　　DEPENDENT=G.DIFF/
　　　　　　　　ENTER D2 TO D6

**** M U L T I P L E   R E G R E S S I O N ****

VARIABLE LIST NUMBER 1　LISTWISE DELETION OF MISSING DATA
EQUATION NUMBER 1　DEPENDENT VARIABLE..　G.DIFF　DIFFERENCE G.POST MINUS G.PRE

BEGINNING BLOCK NUMBER 1.　METHOD:　ENTER　D2　D5　D6

VARIABLE(S) ENTERED ON STEP NUMBER
1...　D6　KNOWLEDGE SCORE
2...　D2　EXPERIENCE SCORE
3...　D5　ATPA SCORE

MULTIPLE R　　　　　.41562
R SQUARE　　　　　.17274
ADJUSTED R SQUARE　.12843
STANDARD ERROR　 18.35182

ANALYSIS OF VARIANCE

	DF	SUM OF SQUARES	MEAN SQUARE
REGRESSION	3	3938.30661	1312.76887
RESIDUAL	56	18860.20484	336.78937

F = 3.89789　　　SIGNIF F = .0134

----------- VARIABLES IN THE EQUATION -----------

VARIABLE	B	SE B	BETA	T	SIG T
D6	.09904	.39131	.06039	.253	.8011
D2	-.48837	.15454	-.39020	-3.160	.0025
D5	-.27390	.43527	-.14964	-.629	.5317
(CONSTANT)	18.13044	21.97978		.825	.4129

FOR BLOCK NUMBER 1　ALL REQUESTED VARIABLES ENTERED.

Explanation:　Same as for the corresponding SAS Model.

BMDP Data Step for the Pretest:


```
/PROB       TITLE='REPEATED MEASURES GAME WITHIN DAY - PRE'.
/INPUT      VARIABLES=4.
            FORMAT='(12X,4F3.)'.
            CASES=60.
/VARIABLE NAMES=DAY1G1, DAY1G2, DAY2G1, DAY2G2.
/DESIGN     FORM='2(2(Y))'.
            NAMES=DAY,GAME.
/END
```


BMDP Data Step for the Posttest:


```
/PROB       TITLE='REPEATED MEASURES GAME WITHIN DAY - POST'.
/INPUT      VARIABLES=4.
            FORMAT='(24X,4F3.)'.
            CASES=60.
/VARIABLE NAMES=DAY1G1, DAY1G2, DAY2G1, DAY2G2.
/DESIGN     FORM='2(2(Y))'.
            NAMES=DAY,GAME.
/END
```

Note: This repeated measures design of game within day and with both factors being treated as replicates is being performed to measure reliability in the bowling scores as recorded for this group of subjects. The bowling scores being assessed in this model are the pretest data.

BMDP2V - ANALYSIS OF VARIANCE AND COVARIANCE WITH REPEATED MEASURES.

REPEATED MEASURES GAME WITHIN DAY - PRE

I N P U T   V A R I A B L E S .

VARIABLE INDEX	NAME	RECORD NO.	COLUMNS BEGIN	END	FIELD WIDTH	TYPE
1	DAY1G1	1	13	15	3	F
2	DAY1G2	1	16	18	3	F

VARIABLE INDEX	NAME	RECORD NO.	COLUMNS BEGIN	END	FIELD WIDTH	TYPE
3	DAY2G1	1	19	21	3	F
4	DAY2G2	1	22	24	3	F

DESIGN SPECIFICATIONS

DEPEND = 1   2   3   4
LEVEL = 2   2

BASED ON INPUT FORMAT SUPPLIED   1 RECORDS READ PER CASE.

NUMBER OF CASES READ   60

REPEATED MEASURES GAME WITHIN DAY - PRE

CELL MEANS FOR   1-ST DEPENDENT VARIABLE

	DAY	GAME	MARGINAL
DAY1G1	1	1	113.63333	113.63333
DAY1G2	1	2	117.45000	117.45000
DAY2G1	2	1	120.06667	120.06667
DAY2G2	2	2	122.38333	122.38333
MARGINAL			118.38333	118.38333
COUNT			60	60

STANDARD DEVIATIONS FOR   1-ST DEPENDENT VARIABLE

	DAY	GAME	
DAY1G1	1	1	32.73207
DAY1G2	1	2	37.51448
DAY2G1	2	1	31.93843
DAY2G2	2	2	28.69541

REPEATED MEASURES GAME WITHIN DAY - PRE

ANALYSIS OF VARIANCE FOR 1-ST
DEPENDENT VARIABLE - DAY1G1   DAY1G2   DAY2G1   DAY2G2

	SOURCE	SUM OF SQUARES	DEGREES OF FREEDOM	MEAN SQUARE	F	TAIL PROB.
1	MEAN ERROR	3363507.26667 175661.73333	1 59	3363507.26667 2977.31751	1129.71	0.0000
2	DAY ERROR	1938.01667 32159.98333	1 59	1938.01667 545.08446	3.56	0.0643
3	GAME ERROR	564.26667 23705.73333	1 59	564.26667 401.79209	1.40	0.2407
4	DG ERROR	33.75000 23483.25000	1 59	33.75000 398.02119	0.08	0.7719

Explanation: No statistically significant differences are present in the above
summary table for the game within day repeated measures analysis.
In sum, the mean scores do not differ significantly within days
or games and there is no interaction between days and games.
However, an inspection of the cell means does reveal that average
scores on day 2 are approximately 6 pins higher than the average
scores on day 1 and coupled with the large standard deviations
for each of the cells indicates a fair amount of fluctuation in
bowling performance.

290   *Methods of Research in Physical Education*

Note: This repeated measures design of game within day and with both factors being treated as replicates is being performed to measure reliability in the bowling scores as recorded for this group of subjects. The bowling scores being assessed in this model are the posttest data.

BMDP2V - ANALYSIS OF VARIANCE AND COVARIANCE WITH REPEATED MEASURES.

REPEATED MEASURES GAME WITHIN DAY - POST

I N P U T   V A R I A B L E S

VARIABLE INDEX	NAME	RECORD NO.	COLUMNS BEGIN	COLUMNS END	FIELD WIDTH	TYPE
1	DAY1G1	1	25	27	3	F
2	DAY1G2	1	28	30	3	F
3	DAY2G1	1	31	33	3	F
4	DAY2G2	1	34	36	3	F

DESIGN SPECIFICATIONS

```
DEPEND =  1  2  3  4
LEVEL  =  2  2
```

BASED ON INPUT FORMAT SUPPLIED   1 RECORDS READ PER CASE.

NUMBER OF CASES READ.   60

REPEATED MEASURES GAME WITHIN DAY - POST

CELL MEANS FOR 1-ST DEPENDENT VARIABLE

	DAY	GAME	MARGINAL	
DAY1G1	1	1	123.01667	123.01667
DAY1G2	1	2	122.68333	122.68333
DAY2G1	2	1	123.00000	123.00000
DAY2G2	2	2	134.95000	134.95000
MARGINAL			125.91250	125.91250
COUNT			60	60

STANDARD DEVIATIONS FOR 1-ST DEPENDENT VARIABLE

	DAY	GAME	
DAY1G1	1	1	25.30659
DAY1G2	1	2	26.25461
DAY2G1	2	1	26.70238
DAY2G2	2	2	31.23689

REPEATED MEASURES GAME WITHIN DAY - POST

ANALYSIS OF VARIANCE FOR 1-ST
DEPENDENT VARIABLE - DAY1G1 DAY1G2 DAY2G1 DAY2G2

	SOURCE	SUM OF SQUARES	DEGREES OF FREEDOM	MEAN SQUARE	F	TAIL PROB.
1	MEAN	3804949.83750	1	3804949.83750	1843.11	0.0000
	ERROR	121800.91250	59	2064.42225		
2	DAY	2250.93750	1	2250.93750	5.79	0.0193
	ERROR	22950.81250	59	388.99682		
3	GAME	2024.20417	1	2024.20417	5.59	0.0213
	ERROR	21345.54583	59	361.78891		
4	DG	2263.20417	1	2263.20417	11.13	0.0015
	ERROR	11993.54583	59	203.28044		

Explanation: The summary table above reveals a statistically significant
interaction between day and game. Inspection of the cell means
and a plot of those means reveals that game 1 on day 1 is just a
fraction of a pin larger than game 2 but the average difference is more than 12 pins
is true for game 2 but the average difference is more than 12 pins
which accounts for the presence of the significant interaction.
Since the interaction is significant the day and game effects,
though both statistically significant, can not be described as
main effects and additional statistical interpretation of those
terms as simple effects would be required and extends beyond the
scope of this analysis. Further, this analysis indicates that a
snapshot approach for estimating the average score of a bowler
is probably not a reliable technique in that you could easily
over or underestimate the true average score because of the large
day to day and game to game variability.

BMDP Data Step for the Pretest:


```
/PROB       TITLE='REPEATED MEASURES GAME WITHIN DAY - PRE'.
/INPUT      VARIABLES=4.
            FORMAT='(12X,4F3.)'.
            CASES=60.
/VARIABLE   NAMES=DAY1G1, DAY1G2, DAY2G1, DAY2G2.
/DESIGN     FORM='2(2(Y))'.
            NAMES=DAY,GAME.
/END
```


BMDP Data Step for the Posttest:


```
/PROB       TITLE='REPEATED MEASURES GAME WITHIN DAY - POST'.
/INPUT      VARIABLES=4.
            FORMAT='(24X,4F3.)'.
            CASES=60.
/VARIABLE   NAMES=DAY1G1, DAY1G2, DAY2G1, DAY2G2.
/DESIGN     FORM='2(2(Y))'.
            NAMES=DAY,GAME.
/END
```

Note: This repeated measures design of game within day and with both factors
being treated as replicates is being performed to measure reliability
in the bowling scores as recorded for this group of subjects. The
bowling scores being assessed in this model are the pretest data.

BMDP2V - ANALYSIS OF VARIANCE AND COVARIANCE WITH REPEATED MEASURES.

REPEATED MEASURES GAME WITHIN DAY - PRE

```
I N P U T   V A R I A B L E S .
  VARIABLE        RECORD      COLUMNS      FIELD   TYPE
INDEX   NAME       NO.     BEGIN   END     WIDTH
-----  ------     ------   -----  -----    -----   ----
  1    DAY1G1       1        13     15        3      F
  2    DAY1G2       1        16     18        3      F
```

```
                                                   RECORD      COLUMNS      FIELD   TYPE
  VARIABLE                                           NO.     BEGIN   END     WIDTH
INDEX   NAME                                       ------   -----  -----    -----   ----
  3    DAY2G1                                         1        19     21        3      F
  4    DAY2G2                                         1        22     24        3      F
```

DESIGN SPECIFICATIONS

```
     DEPEND =   1   2   3   4
     LEVEL  =   1   2
                2   2
```

BASED ON INPUT FORMAT SUPPLIED   1 RECORDS READ PER CASE.

NUMBER OF CASES READ.   60

REPEATED MEASURES GAME WITHIN DAY - PRE

CELL MEANS FOR 1-ST DEPENDENT VARIABLE

```
                                 MARGINAL

         DAY  GAME
DAY1G1    1    1      113.63333     113.63333
DAY1G2    1    2      117.45000     117.45000
DAY2G1    2    1      120.06667     120.06667
DAY2G2    2    2      122.38333     122.38333

         MARGINAL      118.38333     118.38333

          COUNT            60            60
```

STANDARD DEVIATIONS   FOR   1-ST DEPENDENT VARIABLE

```
         DAY  GAME
DAY1G1    1    1      32.73207
DAY1G2    1    2      37.51448
DAY2G1    2    1      31.93843
DAY2G2    2    2      28.69541
```

REPEATED MEASURES GAME WITHIN DAY - PRE

ANALYSIS OF VARIANCE FOR 1-ST
DEPENDENT VARIABLE - DAY1G1   DAY1G2   DAY2G1   DAY2G2

	SOURCE	SUM OF SQUARES	DEGREES OF FREEDOM	MEAN SQUARE	F	TAIL PROB.
1	MEAN	3363507.26667	1	3363507.26667	1129.71	0.0000
	ERROR	175661.73333	59	2977.31751		
2	DAY	1938.01667	1	1938.01667	3.56	0.0643
	ERROR	32159.98333	59	545.08446		
3	GAME	564.26667	1	564.26667	1.40	0.2407
	ERROR	23705.73333	59	401.79209		
4	DG	33.75000	1	33.75000	0.08	0.7719
	ERROR	23483.25000	59	398.02119		

Explanation: No statistically significant differences are present in the above
summary table for the game within day repeated measures analysis.
In sum, the mean scores do not differ significantly within days
or games and there is no interaction between days and games.
However, an inspection of the cell means does reveal that average
scores on day 2 are approximately 6 pins higher than the average
scores on day 1 and coupled with the large standard deviations
for each of the cells indicates a fair amount of fluctuation in
bowling performance.

Note: This repeated measures design of game within day and with both factors being treated as replicates is being performed to measure reliability in the bowling scores as recorded for this group of subjects. The bowling scores being assessed in this model are the posttest data.

BMDP2V - ANALYSIS OF VARIANCE AND COVARIANCE WITH REPEATED MEASURES.

REPEATED MEASURES GAME WITHIN DAY - POST

I N P U T   V A R I A B L E S

VARIABLE INDEX	NAME	RECORD NO.	COLUMNS BEGIN	END	FIELD WIDTH	TYPE
1	DAY1G1	1	25	27	3	F
2	DAY1G2	1	28	30	3	F
3	DAY2G1	1	31	33	3	F
4	DAY2G2	1	34	36	3	F

DESIGN SPECIFICATIONS

DEPEND = 1 2 3 4
LEVEL = 2 2

BASED ON INPUT FORMAT SUPPLIED   1 RECORDS READ PER CASE.

NUMBER OF CASES READ.   60

REPEATED MEASURES GAME WITHIN DAY - POST

CELL MEANS FOR   1-ST DEPENDENT VARIABLE

	DAY	GAME		MARGINAL
DAY1G1	1	1	123.01667	123.01667
DAY1G2	1	2	122.68333	122.68333
DAY2G1	2	1	123.00000	123.00000
DAY2G2	2	2	134.95000	134.95000
MARGINAL			125.91250	125.91250
COUNT			60	60

STANDARD DEVIATIONS FOR   1-ST DEPENDENT VARIABLE

	DAY	GAME	
DAY1G1	1	1	25.30659
DAY1G2	1	2	26.25461
DAY2G1	2	1	26.70238
DAY2G2	2	2	31.23689

REPEATED MEASURES GAME WITHIN DAY - POST

ANALYSIS OF VARIANCE FOR 1-ST
DEPENDENT VARIABLE - DAY1G1 DAY1G2 DAY2G1 DAY2G2

	SOURCE	SUM OF SQUARES	DEGREES OF FREEDOM	MEAN SQUARE	F	TAIL PROB.
1	MEAN	3804949.83750	1	3804949.83750	1843.11	0.0000
	ERROR	121800.91250	59	2064.42225		
2	DAY	2250.93750	1	2250.93750	5.79	0.0193
	ERROR	22950.81250	59	388.99682		
3	GAME	2024.20417	1	2024.20417	5.59	0.0213
	ERROR	21345.54583	59	361.78891		
4	DG	2263.20417	1	2263.20417	11.13	0.0015
	ERROR	11993.54583	59	203.28044		

Explanation: The summary table above reveals a statistically significant interaction between day and game. Inspection of the cell means and a plot of those means reveals that game 1 on day 1 is just a fraction of a pin larger than game 1 on day 2 and that the reverse is true for game 2 but the average difference is more than 12 pins which accounts for the presence of the significant interaction. Since the interaction is significant the day and game effects, though both statistically significant, can not be described as main effects and additional statistical interpretation of those terms as simple effects would be required and extends beyond the scope of this analysis. Further, this analysis indicates that a snapshot approach for estimating the average score of a bowler is probably not a reliable technique in that you could easily over or underestimate the true average score because of the large day to day and game to game variability.

REFERENCES

BOOKS

American Psychological Association. *Publication Manual,* 3rd edition. Washington, DC: American Psychological Association, 1983.

Baker, John A.W. and Collins, Mary S. *Research on Administration of Physical Education and Athletics 1971-1982: A Retrieval System.* Reseda, CA: Mojave Books, 1983.

Barr, A.J., Goodnight, J.H., and Helwig, J.T. *A User's Guide to S.A.S.* Raleigh, NC: S.A.S. Institute, N.C., 1982.

Barrow, Harold M. and McGee, Rosemary. *A Practical Approach to Measurement in Physical Education,* 3rd edition. Philadelphia, PA: Lea and Febiger, 1979.

Barzun, Jacques and Graff, Henry F. *The Modern Researcher,* 3rd edition. New York, NY: Harcourt, Brace, Jovanovick, Inc., 1977.

Baumgartner, T.A. and A.S. Jackson. *Measurement for Evaluation in Physical Education,* 2nd edition. Dubuque, IA: Wm. C. Brown Company, 1982.

Best, John W. *Research in Education,* 4th edition. Englewood Cliffs, NJ: Prentice-Hall, Inc., 1981.

Blalock, Jr., H.M. *Causal Inferences in Non-Experimental Research,* 1st edition. Chapel Hill, NC: The University of North Carolina Press, 1961.

Blalock, Jr., H.M. *Causal Models in the Social Sciences.* Chicago, IL: Aldine, 1971.

Bloom, Benjamin S. *Taxonomy of Educational Objectives.* New York, NY: David McKay Company, Inc., 1956.

Campbell, D. and Stanley, J. *Experimental and Quasi-Experimental Designs for Research.* Chicago, IL: Rand McNally, 1966.

Clarke, David H. and Clarke, H. Harrison. *Research Processes in Physical Education, Recreation and Health.* Englewood Cliffs, NJ: Prentice-Hall, Inc., 1970.

Cook, Thomas D. and Campbell, Donald T. *Quasi-Experimentation.* Boston, MA: Houghton Mifflin Company, 1979.

Cooper, John M., Adrian, Marlene, and Glassow, Ruth B. *Kinesiology,* 5th edition. St. Louis, MO: The C.V. Mosby Company, 1982.

Dampier, Sir William Cecil. *A History of Science and its Relations with Philosophy and Religion.* Cambridge University Press, 1929, 4th edition, 1948.

Department of Health, Education, and Welfare and National Institute of Education. *ERIC Manual.* Washington, DC: National Institute of Education.

Dollard, John. *Criteria for Life History.* New Haven, CT: Yale University Press, 1935. Reprinted in 1949 by Peter Smith.

Drew, Clifford J. *Introduction to Designing Research and Evaluation*. St. Louis, MO: The C.V. Mosby Company, 1976.

Duncan, O.D. *Introduction to Structural Equation Models*. New York, NY: Academic Press, 1975.

Eames, S. Morris. *Pragmatic Naturalism*. Carbondale and Edwardsville, IL: Southern Illinois University Press, 1977.

Edwards, Allen L. *Experimental Design in Psychological Research*. New York, NY: Holt, Rinehart, and Winston, 1963.

Edwards, Allen L. *Manual for the Edwards Personal Preference Schedule*. New York, NY: The Psychological Corporation, 1954.

Edwards, Allen L. *Techniques of Attitude Scale Construction*. New York, NY: Appleton-Century-Crofts, 1957.

Encyclopedia of Educational Research. New York, NY: American Educational Research Association, MacMillan Company, 1939 to date.

Ferguson, George A. *Statistical Analysis in Psychology and Education*. New York, NY: Mc-Graw Hill Book Company, 1966.

Foerster, Norman and Steadman, Jr., J.M. *Writing and Thinking*. Cambridge, MA: The Riverside Press, 1941.

Glass, Gene V. and Stanley, Julian C. *Statistical methods in Education and Psychology*. Englewood Cliffs, MJ: Prentice-Hall, Inc., 1970.

Goldberger, A.S. and Duncan, O.D. *Structural Equation Models in the Social Sciences*. New York, NY: Seminar Press, 1973.

Good, Carter V. *Essentials of Education Research*, 2nd edition. New York, NY: Meredith Corporation, 1972.

Grieve, D.W., et al. *Techniques for the Analysis of Human Movement*. London, England: Lepus Books, 1975.

Hay, J.G. *The Biomechanics of Sports Techniques*, 2nd edition. Englewood Cliffs, NJ: Prentice-Hall, Inc., 1978.

Heise, D.R. *Causal Analysis*. New York, NY: Wiley, 1975.

Isaac, Stephen and Michael, William B. *Handbook in Research and Evaluation*, 2nd edition. San Diego, CA: EdITS Publishers, 1981.

Johnson, Perry. AAHPER. "Oral Research Reports" in *Research Methods*, 1973.

Kelly, Francis J., Beggs, Donald L., and McNeil, Keith. *Research Design in the Behavioral Sciences Multiple Regression Approach*. Carbondale, IL: Southern Illinois University Press, 1969.

Kerlingers, Fred N. *Foundations of Behavioral Research*, 2nd edition. New York, NY: Holt, Rinehart and Winston, Inc., 1973.

Kidder, Louise H. *Research Methods in Social Relations*, 4th edition. New York, NY: Holt, Rinehart and Winston, Inc., 1981.

MacConaill, M.A. and Basmajian, J.V. *Muscles and Movement: A Basis for Kinesiology*. Huntington, NY: Robert E. Krieger Publishing Company, 1977.

Osgood, C.E., Suci, G.J., and Tannenbaum, P.H. *The Measurement of Meaning*. Urbana, IL: The University of Illinois Press, 1957.

Plagenhoef, S. *Patterns of Human Motion*. Englewood Cliffs, NJ: Prentice-Hall, Inc., 1971.

Roget's International Thesaurus, 3rd edition. New York, NY: Thomas Y. Crowell Company, 1962.

Rothney, John W. *Methods of Studying the Individual Child: The Psychological Case Study.* Waltham, MA: Blaisdell Publishing Company, 1968.

Russell, Bertrand. *A History of Western Philosophy.* New York, NY: Simon and Schuster, 1945.

Russell, Bertrand. *Introduction to Mathematical Philosophy.* London, England: Allen and Unwin, Ltd., 1919.

Ryle, Gilbert. "Ordinary Langauge" in *Collected Papers 1929-1968.* New York, NY: Barnes and Noble, 1971.

Safrit, Marjaret J. *Evaluation in Physical Education,* 2nd edition. Englewood Cliffs, NJ: Prentice-Hall, Inc., 1981.

Scott, M. Gladys and French, Ester. *Measurement and Evaluation in Physical Education.* Dubuque, IA: Wm. C. Brown Company, 1959.

Stewart, Charles J. and Cash, Jr., William B. *Interviewing,* 2nd edition. Dubuque, IA: Wm. C. Brown Company, 1974.

Tarski, Alfred. "Logical Empiricism" in *Readings in Philosophical Analysis.* New York, NY: Appleton-Century-Crofts, 1949.

Thilly, Frank and Wood, Ledger. *A History of Philosophy,* 3rd edition. London, England: Allen and Unwin, Ltd., 1919.

Travers, Robers M.W. *An Introduction to Educational Research,* 3rd edition. New York, NY: The MacMillan Company, 1969.

Turabian, Kate L. *A Manual for Writers,* 4th edition. Chicago, IL: The University of Illinois Press, 1973.

Van Dalen, D.B. *Understanding Educational Research.* New York, NY: McGraw-Hill Book Company, 1979.

Walker, Helen M. and Lev, Joseph. *Elementary Statistical Methods.* New York, NY: Holt, Rinehart and Winston, 1958.

Watkins, Floyd C. and Martin, Edwin T. *Practical English Handbook.* Boston, MA: Houghton Mifflin, 1961.

Winter, D.A. *Biomechanics of Human Movement.* New York, NY: John Wiley and Sons, 1979.

A Marriam-Webster. *Webster's New Collegiate Dictionary,* 9th edition. Springfield, MA: G and C Merriam Company, 1983.

Zeigler, Earle F. and Spaeth, Marcia J. *Administrative Theory and Practice in Physical Education and Athletics.* Englewood Cliffs, NJ: Prentice-Hall, Inc., 1975.

UNPUBLISHED MATERIALS

Acero, Jose. "Relationship Between Ball Velocity and Effectiveness of the Serve in Volleyball." M.S. thesis, Southern Illinois University at Carbondale, 1983.

Anthony, Robert P. "Running Death." Paper prepared for PE 530, Southern Illinois University at Carbondale, Spring, 1982.

Bandy, Nancy, "A Conceptual Analysis of Play, Game, Sport, and Athletics." Unpublished paper, PE 530, Southern Illinois University at Carbondale, Spring 1980.

Barnard, Leesa Jan. "Demographic Characteristics of Successful Student Teachers in Physical Education." M.S. thesis, Southern Illinois University at Carbondale, 1981.

Bauner, Ruth, compiler. "A Selected Bibliography of Research Aids in Education." Education/Psychology Division of the Morris Library, Southern Illinois University at Carbondale, June 1984.

Conn, James. "Response of Physical Education Majors and Non-Physical Education Majors to Sport Jargon." Unpublished paper for PE 530, Southern Illinois University at Carbondale, Spring 1979.

Cook, Cathy, compiler. "Bibliography of Physical Education and Recreation Materials." Education/Psychology Division of the Morris Library, Southern Illinois University at Carbondale, January, 1981.

Dameron, Mary Jane. "Augmented Knowledge of Results as an Aid to the Development of Velocity in the Overhand Softball Throw." M.S. thesis, Southern Illinois University at Carbondale, 1971.

Derouin, Barbara. "Administrative Structure of Athletic Departments and the Impact of Title IX." M.S. thesis, Southern Illinois University at Carbondale, 1981.

Eames, Elizabeth R. "Philosophical Methods." Unpublished section within Chapter VII (when submitted), Southern Illinois University at Carbondale, 1985.

Ermler, Kathy L. "The History of intercollegiate Athletics for Women at Southern Illinois University from 1921-1977." M.S. thesis, Southern Illinois University at Carbondale, 1978.

Ferrer, Jose R. "Errors Which Terminate Play in Women's Competitive Volleyball." M.S. thesis, Southern Illinois University at Carbondale, 1981.

Kenyon, G.S. "Values Held for Physical Activity by Selected Urban Secondary Students in Canada, Australia, England, and the United States." Washington, D.C.: United States Office of Education, 1978.

Kildea, Alice E. "Meaningfulness in Life, Locus of Control, and Sex-Role Orientation of Selected Female Athletes and Non-Athletes." Ph.D. dissertation, Southern Illinois University at Carbondale, 1979.

Kovalchik, Michael J. "Grades Received by Males and Females in General Activity Classes of Physical Education." Ph.D. dissertation, Southern Illinois University at Carbondale, 1981.

Martin, Robert G. "The Football Helmet: A Historical Perspective From 1860 Through 1979." M.S. thesis, Southern Illinois University at Carbondale, 1980.

McDonald, Suzan Kinn. "The Frequency of Occurrence and Effectiveness of Serves in Racquetball." M.S. thesis, Southern Illinois University at Carbondale, 1979.

Medford, Pamela R. "The Construction of an Inventory for Measuring Player-Coach Interaction." M.S. thesis, Southern Illinois University at Carbondale, 1980.

Mize, Monica. "Attitude Toward Physical Activity As a Function of Sex-role Orientation." Ph.D. dissertation, Southern Illinois University at Carbondale, 1979.

O'Hare, Deborah L. "Batting Performance With a Standard and an Angular Bat." M.S. thesis, Southern Illinois University at Carbondale, 1982.

Rogers, Virginia. "Three Methods of Assessing Velocity and Angle of Projection of the Volleyball Spike." M.S. thesis, Southern Illinois University at Carbondale, 1969.

Sampson, Barbara. "Description and Comparison of Performances for the Straight Drive in Field Hockey." M.S. thesis, Southern Illinois University at Carbondale, 1972.

Schultze, Jacquelyn. "A Case Study of a Remedial Swimmer." M.S. thesis, Southern Illinois University at Carbondale, 1969.

Sherrill, Claudine. "The Case Method Approach to the Professional Preparation of College Teachers in the General Education Program of Physical Education." Ph.D. dissertation, Teacher's College, Columbia University, 1961.

Suellentrop, Jeanne Marie. "A Variation of Russian Downhill Sprint Training for Selected College Students." M.S. thesis, Southern Illinois University at Carbondale, 1979.

Thorpe, Jo Anne L. "Rating Scale for Evaluating Thesis Briefs." Unpublished material for PE 500, Southern Illinois University at Carbondale, Illinois, 1985.

Walters, Betty L. "Response Accuracy of Female Collegiate Basketball Players in Complex Situations." M.S. thesis, Southern Illinois University at Carbondale, 1978.

West, Charlotte. "Estimates of Reliability and Interrelationships Among Components of Selected Projectile Skills." Ph.D. dissertation, University of Wisconsin, Madison, 1969.

Wood, Beth A. "Job Satisfaction in the Departments of Physical Education, Art, Health Education, and Zoology." M.S. thesis, Southern Illinois University at Carbondale, 1983.

Wyman, Dee. "Two Methods of Evaluating the Front Crawl in Swimming." M.S. thesis, Southern Illinois University at Carbondale, 1970.

PERIODICALS

American Alliance for Health, Physical Education, Recreation, and Dance. "Fiftieth Anniversary Issue." *Research Quarterly for Exercise and Sport* 51 (March, 1980).

American Alliance for Health, Physical Education, and Recreation. *Research Quarterly* (Reston, VA: AAHPERD, 1930 to date).

Cureton, T.K. "Elementary Principles and Techniques of Cinematographic Analysis as Aids in Athletic Research." *Research Quarterly* 10 (May, 1939):3-24.

Dotson, Charles O. "Logic of Questionable Density." *Research Quarterly* 51 (March, 1980):23-36.

Kenyon, Gerald S. "Values Held for Physical Activity by Selected Urban Secondary Students in Canada, Australia, England, and the United States." Washington, DC: The United States Office of Education, 1968.

Kildea, Alice E. "Meaningfulness in Life, Locus of Control, and Sex-Role Orientation of Selected Female Athletes and Non-Athletes." *Dissertation Abstracts International* 40 (February, 1980):4519-A and 4520-A.

Miller, D.I. and Petak, K.L. "Three-Dimensional Cinematography." *Kinesiology 1973* (Washington, DC: AAHPER).

Nixon, John E. "The Mechanics of Questionnaire Construction." *Journal of Educational Research* 67 (March, 1954):481-487.

Research Council of AAHPER. "Skill Learning and Performance." *Research Quarterly* 43 (October, 1972).

Research Council of AAHPER. "The Contributions of Physical Activity to Human Well-Being." *Research Quarterly* 31 (May, 1960).

Review of Educational Research (Washington, DC: American Educational Research Association, 1931).

Rogers, Virginia A. "Three Methods of Assessing Velocity and Angle of Projection of the Volleyball Spike." *Research Completed in HPER* 12 (1970): 215.

Sage, G. and Loudermilk, S. "The Female Athlete and Role Conflict," *RQES* 50 (March, 1979): 88-96.

Thorpe, J. and West, C. "A Test of Game Sense in Badminton." *Perceptual and Motor Skills* 28 (1969):159-169.

Thorpe, J. and West, C. "Game Sense and Intelligence." *Perceputal and Motor Skills* 29 (1969):326.

Thorpe, J. and West, C. "Estimation of Validity for a Test of Game Sense." *Perceptual and Motor Skills* 31 (1970):933-934.

Thorpe, J. and West, C. "Reliability of a Test of Game Sense." *Perceptual and Motor Skills* 31 (1970):582.

AUTHOR INDEX

A

Acero, Jose, 38, 195
Adrian, Marlene, 124
American Alliance for Health, Physical Education, Recreation, and Dance, 32
American Educational Research Association, 32
American Psychological Association, 17, 18
Anthony, Robert P., 28

B

Baker, John A. W., 9
Bandy, Nancy, 160
Barnard, Leesa Jan, 38
Barr, A. J., 84
Barrow, Harold M., 68, 114, 115, 123, 191, 193
Barzun, Jacques, 152, 169
Basmajian, J. V., 124
Baumgartner, T. A., 123
Bauner, Ruth, 103
Beggs, Donald L., 82, 90
Best, John, 21, 101, 103, 104, 117, 118, 131, 135, 137, 144, 147, 148, 150, 151, 152, 169
Blalock, Jr., H. M., 137
Bloom, Benjamin S., 122

C

Campbell, Donald T., 131, 135, 137, 139, 140, 146, 147
Cash, Jr., William B., 110
Clark, H. Harrison, 21
Clarke, David H., 21
Collins, Mary S., 9
Conn, James, 158
Cook, Cathy, 103
Cook, Thomas D., 131, 135, 137, 139, 140, 146, 147
Cooper, John M., 124
Cureton, T. K., 124

D

Dameron, Mary Jane, 206
Dampier, Sir William Cecil, 156, 157
Department of Health, Education, and Welfare and National Institute of Education, 33
Derouin, Barbara, 48, 106, 191
Dollard, John, 153
Dotson, Charles O., 9, 10, 169
Drew, Clifford J., 8
Duncan, O. D., 137

E

Eames, Elizabeth Ramsden, 155
Eames, S. Morris, 159
Edwards, Allen L., 84, 121, 140
Ermler, Kathy L., 150

F

Ferguson, Georgia, 58, 60, 108
Ferrer, Jose R., 27, 40, 48, 199
Foerster, Norman, 17
French, Ester, 123

G

Glass, Gene V., 55, 56
Glassow, Ruth, 124
Goldberger, A. S., 137
Good, Carter V., 21, 124, 135, 153, 161
Goodnight, J. H., 84
Graff, Henry F., 152, 169
Grieve, D. W., 124

H

Hay, J. G., 124
Heise, D. R., 137
Helwig, J. T., 84
Hickman, Ron, 257

SUBJECT INDEX